Interpreting the *Amistad* Trials

Literatures, Cultures, Translation

Literatures, Cultures, Translation presents books that engage central issues in translation studies such as history, politics, and gender in and of literary translation, as well as books that open new avenues for study. Volumes in the series follow two main strands of inquiry: one strand brings a wider context to translation through an interdisciplinary interrogation, while the other hones in on the history and politics of the translation of seminal works in literary and intellectual history.

Volumes in the Series

Translation and the Making of Modern Russian Literature
Brian James Baer

Interpreting in Nazi Concentration Camps
Edited by Michaela Wolf

Exorcising Translation: Towards an Intercivilizational Turn
Douglas Robinson

Literary Translation and the Making of Originals
Karen Emmerich

The Translator on Stage
Geraldine Brodie

Transgender, Translation, Translingual Address
Douglas Robinson

Western Theory in East Asian Contexts: Translation and Translingual Writing
Leo Tak-hung Chan

The Translator's Visibility: Scenes from Contemporary Latin American Fiction
Heather Cleary

The Relocation of Culture: Translations, Migrations, Borders
Simona Bertacco and Nicoletta Vallorani

The Art of Translation in Light of Bakhtin's Re-accentuation
Edited by Slav Gratchev and Margarita Marinova

Migration and Mutation: New Perspectives on the Sonnet in Translation
Edited by Carole Birkan-Berz, Oriane Monthéard, and Erin Cunningham

This Is a Classic: Translators on Making Writers Global
Edited by Regina Galasso

Language Smugglers: Postlingual Literatures and Translation within the Canadian Context
Arianne Des Rochers

Translating Warhol
Edited by Reva Wolf

Cold War Women: Female Translators of Russian and Soviet Literature in the Twentieth Century
Cathy McAteer

Interpreting the Amistad *Trials: How Interpreters and Translators Make and Shape History*
Jeanette Zaragoza-De León

Interpreting the *Amistad* Trials

How Interpreters and Translators Make and Shape History

Jeanette Zaragoza-De León

BLOOMSBURY ACADEMIC
NEW YORK • LONDON • OXFORD • NEW DELHI • SYDNEY

BLOOMSBURY ACADEMIC
Bloomsbury Publishing Inc
1359 Broadway, New York, NY 10018, USA
50 Bedford Square, London, WC1B 3DP, UK
29 Earlsfort Terrace, Dublin 2, Ireland

BLOOMSBURY, BLOOMSBURY ACADEMIC and the Diana logo are trademarks of Bloomsbury Publishing Plc

First published in the United States of America 2025

Cover design by Daniel Benneworth-Gray and Eleanor Rose

Cover image: Composite image © Jaime Vargas Jurado; Profile of John Quincy Adams, Collection of the Massachusetts Historical Society; Portrait of James Covey courtesy of Connecticut Museum of Culture and History; Map of America & Africa and the Atlantic Ocean courtesy of David Rumsey Map Center, Stanford University Libraries

Library of Congress Cataloging-in-Publication Data available

ISBN: HB: 9781-5013-9460-7
ePDF: 9781-5013-9462-1
eBook: 9781-5013-9461-4

Typeset by Deanta Global Publishing Services, Chennai, India

A mami.
Daisy De León Martínez

¡Se oyen los barriles allá en la central
Hay un baile e' bomba, y yo voy pa' llá!

Norberto Sánchez Rivera (1960–2020)
Género musical: Bomba Puertorriqueña[1]
Ritmo de Gracimá

[1] Trans. Spanish to English: "From the Sugar Mill, you can hear the drums; they are playing Bomba, there I gotta go." Call-and-response of a contemporary *Bomba* song in the *Gracimá* rhythm. *Bomba* is a Puerto Rican musical genre that combines Afro Caribbean rhythms and Native instruments. The space created among the drummers, the singers, and the dancer is called the *batey. El batey* became the seed of liberation conspiracies among both the enslaved and free communities (Jesús y Dimas Sánchez Cepeda, *Ritmos Afro Puertorriqueños* [Fundación Rafael Cepeda. 2022], 19). Racialized laws prohibiting the enslaved from playing the *barriles,* the *Bomba* drums, abounded in the Caribbean racializing music. In other parts of the Caribbean, enslaved communities organized riots when their agreements to play the drums between them and the plantation owners were not honored (Gloria García Rodríguez, *Conspiraciones y Revueltas: La actividad política de los negros en Cuba (1790–1845)* [Santiago de Cuba: Editorial Oriente, 2003], 32–3). Reproduced with permission.

Contents

Definitions

Abolitionist

Someone committed to the elimination of direct or indirect ramifications of systemic structures of dehumanization through their actions or activities. In this nineteenth-century story, the Africans, their allies, many of the interpreters, and some translators were abolitionists. They organized and provided services to end the institution of slavery in that century. Today, slavery continues in the form of human trafficking and colonization and through the proliferation of the prison complex. Work remains to be done.

Interpreter

Someone who derives and mediates meaning through auditive, signed, cultural, social, corporal, and political contextual cues from one oral or Sign Language into another language. Interpretation refers to spoken or Sign Language converted into another spoken or Sign Language. Interpreting occurs when a speech delivered in one language is interpreted into another language by an interpreter.

Translator

Someone who derives and mediates meaning through cultural, social, and political contextual cues from one written language to another one. Translation occurs when a text in one language is transformed into a text in another language by a translator.

Figures

The *Amistad* Interpreters and Translators

(in order of appearance)

The *Amistad* Interpreters

Antonio Ferrer
Thomas Meade
John Ferry
Bowle
Grabbeau
George Day
James Covey
Charles Pratt
Thomas Gallaudet
John Jay Hyde
Mr. Ribeiro
Mr. Desa
Theodore Sedgwick, III
Kinna
Kale

The *Amistad* Translators

William Jay
John Quincy Adams
Robert Greenhow
William Hodgson

Foreword

In August and September 1828, nine Ho-Chunk men were tried for murder in a special US circuit court held in Prairie du Chien on the Upper Mississippi River. Half of the jurors spoke French only; the other half spoke only English. The defendants and most of the witnesses gave their testimony in Ho-Chunk. The territorial judge, James Duane Doty, appointed an interpreter for the Ho-Chunk defendants, but quickly realized on examination that the man could only interpret into French. Doty needed someone fluent in English, French, and Ho-Chunk, so he examined several more interpreters but found them all "incompetent." Finally, Doty appointed John Shaw from St. Louis, Missouri, who had been retained by the War Department to interpret for the prosecuting US attorney. Shaw travelled 500 miles upriver to attend the trial and interpreted "everything that passed either from the court, the lawyers, witnesses, or jurors."[1]

According to both the US attorney, John Scott, and the court-appointed defense attorney, Charles S. Hempstead, Shaw "performed the duty well." But we might raise several questions about the role of an interpreter and this murder trial in the Territory of Michigan. Did Shaw faithfully interpret the meaning and intentions of the Ho-Chunk defendants and witnesses? If he was initially retained by the War Department for the prosecution, did he introduce biases against the defense? Two Ho-Chunk men were convicted and sentenced to execution by hanging on December 26, 1828. When the territorial governor of Michigan learned that the local sheriff in Prairie du Chien was disqualified from serving in office and no one could be appointed to carry out the death sentence, he stayed the execution and referred the entire matter to the president of the USA, John Quincy Adams.[2]

1 *John Shaw v. United States*, 1 Court of Claims 17 (1856); reported in House Reports, 34th Congress, 1st Session, Report C. C. No. 1.

2 Samuel G. Drake, *Biography and History of the Indians of North America* (Boston: Benjamin B. Mussey & Co.): 639. On the verdict and pardon, see *United States v. Chichongsic and Waniga*, typescript, p. 10, Iowa and Crawford Counties, Clerk of the Circuit Court, Criminal Case Files, 1824–36, Iowa Series 20, University of Wisconsin Platteville. On the role of the Crawford County sheriff and President Adams's pardon, see James Witherell to Lewis Cass, November 4, 1828, in "James Witherell's Reminiscences," *Wisconsin Historical Collections*, Vol. III (1857), 333–8. For the most recent, scholarly account of the Ho-Chunk trials, see Stephen Kantrowitz, *Citizens in a Stolen Land: A Ho-Chunk History of the Nineteenth-Century United States* (Chapel Hill: University of North Carolina Press, 2023).

We do not know whether Adams reviewed the record of the trial, or if he had doubts about the role of the interpreter, John Shaw, but on November 3, 1828, Adams pardoned the Ho-Chunks and ordered their immediate release from the prison at Fort Crawford in Prairie du Chien. Twelve years later, when John Quincy Adams stepped in to defend the Africans accused of murder on the *Amistad*, he knew from both diplomatic and presidential experience the decisive and potentially prejudicial role that interpreters played in courts organized for a colonizing and slaveholding power.

Until recently, the role of interpreters and translators in US legal history was little studied. Historians and legal scholars took for granted that Anglophone courts from the colonies of British North America through the twentieth century conducted their proceedings in English. Yet, any examination of the archival records of American territorial and state courts reveals a plethora of documents in Spanish, Portuguese, French, Japanese, Chinese, Indigenous, and African languages, as well as German, Dutch, and Russian. Non-English speakers abounded in eighteenth- and nineteenth-century legal proceedings across North America.[3]

Unlike today, in this period, neither state nor federal law required interpreters, and no courts recognized a constitutional or common law right to a court-appointed interpreter. Instead, judges appointed interpreters and translators for cases where their services were deemed especially warranted. American courts, however, often went to great lengths to obtain witness testimony, sending or appointing commissioners to London, Spain, Paris, Mexico, Canada, Cuba, and to Indigenous nations within the lands claimed by the USA. Nearly all depositions and other records collected by court-appointed commissioners required translation. With the Louisiana Purchase in 1803 and the acquisition of Florida in 1821, the USA absorbed territories with French, Spanish, and Indigenous legal traditions, as well as deeds, titles, wills, and other instruments recorded in parish and county courts. In some cases, American judges paid little attention to translation and barrelled ahead with proceedings in English. In other cases, the multiplicity of languages or the seriousness of the litigation forced judges to secure competent interpreters.

Few courts were more in need of interpreters and translators than federal courts of admiralty, where maritime law applied. Cases in these courts involved acts committed on the high seas and navigable waters, including prize cases, crimes, and cases involving maritime contracts, transactions,

[3] For one of the only historical analysis of interpreters and translators, see John Alcalde, "Babel Fish: Court Interpreters in America (1790–1921)," PhD dissertation, Northern Illinois University, 2022.

and shipping. Historian Lauren Benton has described the high seas and navigable waters as corridors and enclaves where imperial powers attempted to establish sovereignty. "The high seas were not a lawless zone," she observes, "but a legal space constructed by interimperial tensions." In the prize or admiralty courts held in port cities around the Atlantic rim, the imperial powers, including the USA, asserted legal authority to enforce laws against piracy, the slave trade, and smuggling. These trials in admiralty, she argues, more than the influence of abstract ideas like the law of nations, shaped the construction of the international legal order in the Atlantic World. Similarly, historian and legal scholar Maggie Blackhawk (Fond du Lac Band of Lake Superior Ojibwe) has stressed the vitality and fluidity of the borderlands, like the high seas, in the development of American law and constitutionalism. "Paradoxically, borderlands are spaces of both subordination and empowerment," Blackhawk has written, "They are areas where 'universal' rules of liberal constitutionalism apply selectively or not at all to 'savages.' But they are also spaces of legal and constitutional pluralism that allow colonized peoples some powers to govern and innovate."[4]

Perhaps no case in US federal courts raised the role of interpreters and translators more forcefully than *U.S. v. The Amistad*. In 1839, fifty-three Africans were captured, taken to Lomboko, incarcerated in a slave factory in what is today Sierra Leone, sold to Portuguese slave traders, and bound for Havana, Cuba. All the European powers and the USA had outlawed the slave trade, but Spain and other powers did little to enforce the law on the high seas and turned a blind eye on the trade that continued in the colonies. The ban on the international slave trade increased demand in Cuba and other Spanish colonies, a demand that illicit slave traffickers were more than willing to meet. Once in Havana, local Spanish authorities fraudulently licensed the Africans as "*Ladinos*," a term for those fluent in Spanish and assimilated or born in the Spanish colonies, not brought from Africa in contravention of Dutch, British, French, Spanish, Portuguese, and US laws against the international slave trade. When two Spanish enslavers, José Ruiz and Pedro Montes, purchased the fifty-three Africans in Havana and brought them aboard a coastal cargo schooner named *Amistad*, they possessed official *licencias* (passports) attesting that the Africans were "*Ladinos*." On the voyage to another region of Cuba, the Africans, led by Sengbe Pieh (or "Cinque"), revolted, killed the crew, and took command of the vessel, forcing

[4] Lauren Benton, *A Search for Sovereignty: Law and Geography in European Empires, 1400–1900* (Cambridge: Cambridge University Press, 2010): 1–39; Maggie Blackhawk, "The Constitution of American Colonialism," *Harvard Law Review* Vol. 137, No. 1 (November 2023): 1–152.

Ruiz and Montes to sail for Africa. The Amistad ran aground on Long Island in New York and there, captured by US officers who towed the Amistad to New London, Connecticut, where they filed a claim in federal admiralty court for salvage. Under the law of salvage, the US officers expected to receive an award for the value of the sale of the ship and its cargo, including the forty-three surviving Africans classified in the ship's papers as "*Ladinos*," meaning those who were enslaved legally in a Spanish colony. The Spanish government, as well as Ruiz and Montes, pressured the USA to prosecute Sengbe Pieh for murder. Both took the position that all the Africans on board were enslaved under Spanish law and should be returned to their possession.[5]

At issue in *U.S. v. The Amistad* was whether the Spanish documents claiming the Africans were "*Ladinos*" were fraudulent and whether the US Custom Office's translation of *Ladinos* as "sound negroes" was an intentional obfuscation meant to bolster the Spanish claim. If the Africans were instead "*Bozales*"—people who were kidnapped in Africa, had never resided in a Spanish colony, and were being transported in the illicit slave trade—then the Spanish had violated international treaties, and the Africans had a legitimate claim to freedom. The term "*Ladinos*" implied that the Africans on the *Amistad* were long-held slaves in Cuba being transported to another part of the island legally. How would the Spanish *licencias* be translated? And who would interpret the many languages spoken by the Africans on the *Amistad* to find out not only where they had come from but also if they were, in fact, the individuals listed by name on the ship's *licencias.*

When the US naval officers claimed salvage rights in the Federal District Court in New London, the initial hearing was so hastily assembled that it took place on board the *Amistad.* One of the officers, Lieutenant Richard Meade, served as the interpreter for the Spanish enslavers Ruiz and Montes and for several of the other Spanish witnesses. Meade may have spoken the language "elegantly and fluently," but if the forty-three surviving Africans on board were lawfully enslaved "*Ladinos*," he personally stood to reap a small fortune.

No one at this initial hearing interpreted the proceedings for Sengbe and the other Africans accused of murdering the *Amistad*'s captain and cook.

Historian Jeanette Zaragoza-De León offers the first comprehensive assessment of the role of the interpreters and translators in the landmark

[5] The standard citation is *United States v. The Amistad*, 40 U.S. 518 (1841). See especially Marcus Rediker, *The Amistad Rebellion: An Atlantic Odyssey of Slavery and Freedom* (London, Viking Penguin, 2012) and Howard Jones, *The Mutiny on the Amistad: The Saga of a Slave Revolt and Its Impact on American Abolition, Law, and Diplomacy* (Oxford: Oxford University Press, 1987).

Amistad case. Piecing together the story from newspapers, court documents, diaries, and correspondence, Zaragoza-De León recovers a hidden history of the fifteen interpreters and four translators who worked on the case. James Covey, an eighteen-year-old African-born former slave working with the British navy to interdict traffickers, is the most well-known of the interpreters, but Zaragoza-De León tracks down others who have not been as fully recognized, including John Ferry, the first African-born interpreter on the case; and Thomas Gallaudet, a sign language interpreter. Among Zaragoza-De León's many contributions in this impressive study are to draw our attention to translation and interpreting as cultural power in a legal order decidedly against marginalized peoples like the Africans on the *Amistad*. For decades, much of the US government, including the US Supreme Court, protected slavery, considered enslaved people to be property, and consistently upheld the rights of slaveholders.

But when the Africans on the *Amistad* seized the ship on the high seas, they did so in a geographic space where US sovereignty depended, at least in part, on enforcing Congressional acts that outlawed the Atlantic slave trade and on upholding international treaties the USA signed that banned the slave trade. The US circuit court ruled right away that it did not have jurisdiction over crimes committed on the high seas that did not involve US citizens. There would be no trial for murder or mutiny. Instead, the circuit court directed the lower District Court to determine whether the Africans on the *Amistad* were "property" or not. Because the law of salvage was at issue, the court heard evidence that might not have been introduced or allowed in other civil or criminal cases involving enslaved people. To take advantage of this possibility, of the improvisational interplay of US sovereignty and admiralty law, the Africans on the *Amistad* needed reliable and trustworthy interpreters.[6]

On January 13, 1840, US District Court Judge Andrew T. Judson ruled that the *Amistad* captives were "born free" and had been kidnapped in violation of international law. They could not be considered property in a US court of law. The revolt on the *Amistad*, however bloody, was justified by the "love of liberty natural to all men, and by the desire of returning to their families and

[6] For the legal arguments and proceedings in the US circuit court, see *The African Captives: Trial of the Prisoners of the Amistad on the Writ of Habeas Corpus, before the Circuit Court of the United States for the District of Connecticut, at Hartford; Judges Thompson and Judson, September Term, 1839* (New York: 1839).

kindred."[7] To appease US slaveholders and placate the Spanish government, the Van Buren administration appealed the decision to the US Supreme Court. Abolitionist supporters appealed to former president John Quincy Adams to argue the case for the Africans, a dramatic scene made famous by Steven Spielberg's 1997 film *Amistad.* From his long service in the State Department, his presidency, and his own role in the *Amistad* case, Adams knew that the interpreters and translators had made the crucial difference in what he called "the cause of justice."[8]

Who were the *Amistad* interpreters and translators? We are indebted to Jeanette Zaragoza-De León for telling their inspiring, instructive, and important story in *Interpreting the* Amistad *Trials: How Interpreters and Translators Make and Shape History.*

William G. Thomas III
June 20, 2024

[7] For a detailed account of the District Court case, including a transcription of Judge Andrew Judson's decree, see Douglas O. Linder, "Trial History of the Amistad Case," in *Famous Trials* (UMKC School of Law), https://famous-trials.com/amistad/1233-ami-tri (accessed May 15, 2024). Judson's decree is also available in *Thomas R. Gedney v. Schooner Amistad, U.S. District Court for the District of Connecticut, 1789–*, Final Records Book, Vol. 10, pp. 105–143, RG 21, National Archives and Records Administration at: https://artsandculture.google.com/story/trial-of-a-century-la-amistad-u-s-national-archives/hAWh-QFK4k8HIQ?hl=en (accessed May 15, 2024), p. 136; Jones, *The Mutiny on the Amistad,* 129.

[8] *Argument of John Quincy Adams, Before the Supreme Court of the United States: in the Case of the United States, Appellants, vs. Cinque, and Others, Africans, Captured in the Schooner Amistad, by Lieut. Gedney* (New York: S. W. Benedict, 1841): 135.

Preface

Sometimes research chooses you. This is what happened in my case. In 2011, while working as a court interpreter at the Superior Court in New Jersey, USA, I began translating a brief article on the *Amistad* story. In that activity, I came across the name of James Covey, described as the court interpreter for the Mende Africans; I paused. This was not the first time I had heard about the *Amistad* story; in fact, many years before I had attended a reception for the opening of the *Amistad* opera. But this time around, my locus was different. As a professional in the court interpreting field, I knew the challenges and opportunities one faced as an interpreter, as well as the positive impact that linguistically mediated services could provide in the courts. I became curious.

My initial search revealed ample scholarship on this key historical event. But little was found on Covey and his role as an interpreter for the incarcerated Africans, or much on the translation issues. Back then, I consulted Howard Jones,[1] the late Amistad historian, who corroborated the missing role of the interpreting and translation issues. This is how the story of this book began.

I perused microfilms, newspapers, and secondary sources, quilting together the fragmented story of the interpreting and translation matters in the *Amistad* case. Uplifted by the promise of an edifying and meaningful journey, I applied to an MA in research in the field of Interpreting and Translation Studies (ITS)[2] followed by a PhD program in the same field. My whole body said, "yes." The doctoral thesis defended toward the completion of this degree became the basis for this book.

My personal background pulled me into the plot of this story. Sharing my proclivities constitutes a duty, because "when we take up a work of history, our first concern should be not with the facts which it contains but with the historian who wrote it."[3] What we are drawn to as researchers, our preferential selection for archival materials, our interpretations of them, and conclusions, follow a trail. They reveal who we are, our ways of learning, and making

[1] Personal communication, *c.* March 2012.

[2] The term "translation" has been privileged over the term "interpreting," even when speaking about academic matters pertaining to the interpreting field. The term "Interpreting and Translation Field" in this work underlines the emphasis on the interpreting scholarly contributions.

[3] Edward Hallett Carr, *What is History?* 1961, 24.

sense of the truth.[4] The *Amistad* story provided fertile ground where my background and interests converged. I am a Puerto Rican cisgender–middle-class woman who grew up on the island, and who has lived an equal amount of time in the USA. I identify as an Afro-descendant *Boricua*, a Spanish and English bilingual person, and somewhat bicultural. In 1993, I joined the United Church of Christ (UCC), a historical Protestant denomination that claims the legacy of Christian abolitionists in the *Amistad* story. Caribbean born and raised, I am cognizant of the 500 years of colonial history under Spanish and US rule, also part of my heritage, daily impacting my personal and communal history. In response to this reality, I have dedicated time to support various struggles, especially those aiming at decolonization, excarceration of US political prisoners, and eliminating racism.

The importance of this research topic speaks to my desire to dig into the impact of slavery, racialized trauma, US and Spanish colonialism and imperialism, and, particularly, the development of the interpreting profession and its history. The *Amistad* offers a vehicle to voice the above while bringing to the forefront the transatlantic journey of this story woven by the enslaving and liberation threads of Portugal, Spain, Africa, la Gran Colombia (Venezuela), Puerto Rico, Cuba, and the USA.

In addition, for over fifteen years, I have worked as a certified judicial and medical interpreter and freelance translator. These combined personal and professional backgrounds provide their own methodological filters. I sympathize with the Mende Africans and the *Amistad* interpreters. I am inspired by the abolitionist-Christian minority committed to securing the judicial and human rights of those imprisoned against the colonial-enslaving system. Simultaneously, I remain critical of the colonizing-Christian ways of the same abolitionists, as will be seen in the following pages. Today, people who profess their faith individually or through a church would benefit from the teachings and inspiration of the *Amistad*–abolitionist movement, joining in their efforts to eliminate systemic racism and the colonial injustices of the times, while committing not to repeat the same mistakes of the past.

With all of this in mind, I entered the *Amistad* archival records, more specifically from the field of interpreting and translation (IT) studies. Each professional field records its history—its beginning, development, and impact through the centuries. I entered through this perspective and exited

4 Gabriela Saldanha and Sharon O'Brien, *Research Methodologies in Translation Studies* (London: Routledge, 2014), 10. And as stated by Saldanha and O'Brien, those proclivities in selecting a research topic are as important as other rigorous methodological issues: "It is far too easy to delve into a research project without first questioning one's own view of the world, and, especially, of knowledge acquisition and truth."

via the door of interdisciplinarity, a natural occurrence in the *Amistad* thread of events. At first glance, language mediates the day-to-day of all medullar human activities. As such, interpreting and translation exercises abound amid human interactions. The interpreting issues in the Amistad story intersected with human events and activities that are the subject of other academic interests: the Atlantic World, ethnicity, enslavement, racialization, gender, class, imperialism, theology, slave narratives, Latin America and the Caribbean, and stories of resistance. They all influenced the fabric of the *Amistad* interpreting and translation events, and interpreting and translation shaped their tales. As a recent adept IT historian, I had the desire to highlight it all—a daunting task. Though I may fall short of this goal, I hope you see how they create a historical collage. I hope you also see the past and the present in a new light, and yourself in this narrative in a future of justice-driven possibilities.

Acknowledgements

The completion of this book project was indeed made possible by the support of many.

To start, I would like to thank Bloomsbury Publishing, Inc. for accepting my book proposal as part of their Translation and Interpretation in Literary Studies division. A project of this kind requires constant email communication and flexibility in the decision-making process, for which I thank Haaris Naqvi, editorial director, and Hali Han, editorial assistant. For his initial urge to submit the book proposal, I thank Brian Baer, co-editor of the Literatures, Cultures, Translation series, alongside Michelle Woods, both enthusiasts about this research project from its inception. Thanks also to Sophia Groff for her meticulous proofreading and for key edits to the final manuscript.

For financial support, I am grateful to the Louisville Institute, Project Grant for Researchers; the National Endowment for the Humanities, Summer Stipend program; and the Leonard Tucker Alumni Fellow at the Massachusetts Historical Society. It is with their support that this book project was able to come to fruition, and I will always be grateful to all of you for supporting the various writing stages of this research.

I am grateful for my time as a Yale University Visiting Fellow at the Yale Divinity School, which provided me the privilege of accessing a number of vital resources—the Baldwin Family Papers as well as other abolitionist's writings at the Manuscript and Archives's repository; relevant secondary sources through Sterling Memorial Library and the Manuscript division of the Lillian Goldman Law Library, as well as the Widener Library at Harvard University. During my fellowship, I am also grateful for the significant research guidance of Tisa Wenger, scholar in American Religious History, and to our "Garden Fellowship" that harvested an enduring friendship. The encouragement and feedback of Willie Jennings, historian and theologian at the Yale Divinity School, helped to map my research findings.

I am grateful to the University of Puerto Rico, Río Piedras Campus (UPR RP) for their support during the last editing stages of this manuscript, particularly, to Aurora Sotográs Saldaña, my immediate supervisor and the executive director of the Department of Continuous Education and Professional Studies (DECEP), as well as Aurora Lauzardo Ugarte, former coordinator of the Graduate Translation Program at the UPR RP. Thanks, also, to Isabel Ballester Rojas for her assistance making possible the completion of the book index.

My research period at El Archivo Nacional de la República de Cuba in La Habana remains a key time in my analysis of the *Amistad* story. For facilitating access to the archival materials at the "Archivo," I am particularly grateful to Niurdis Ferrer Prada, Archival Service Specialist, and Yolanda Díaz Martínez, Senior Researcher. Similarly, I am thankful to Lisa C. Moore, head of Research Services, at the *Amistad* Research Center, in New Orleans, Louisiana—her keen eyes and gracious hospitality allowed the expansion of this research. The Connecticut Museum of Culture and History, in Hartford, CT, through Sierra Dixon, manager of the Research Center, provided the image of James Covey, the main court interpreter of the *Amistad* trials featured in the book cover. The Adams Family Papers and the Sedgwick Family Papers at the Massachusetts Historical Society (MHS) unearthed critical interpreting and translation matters in the *Amistad* story. In addition, the MHS provided the profile of John Quincy Adams incorporated in the design of this book cover. To Kid Wongsrichanalai, Director of Research and the MHS staff, I am grateful for their time and support during and after my MHS research period. I am grateful to Joseph Keefe from the National Archives in Waltham, MA, for his support during my research from the beginning of this quest.

To my dear friends and colleagues who read various versions of my manuscript providing valuable feedback, I remain grateful: Mariluz Franco Ortiz, Evelyne Laurent Perrault, Agustina Luvis Núñez, Randi Walker, Jimmy Seale Collazo, Anaida Pascual Morán, and Kathy Calzone. To Judge Miguel A. de la Carrera who encouraged me from the beginning to follow this research venture and who contributed important perspectives on key judicial matters of the *Amistad* story. I am also grateful for the insight provided by William G. Thomas, III, and for his well-framed Foreword. I also thank Khalil Anthony Johnson, Jr. for the brainstorming session that conjured the latest version of the book title. While not all are named in this important process, I want to express my deepest appreciation for all of you who gifted me with your time, patience, love, and encouragement.

I am profoundly grateful: to my mom, Daisy De Léon Martínez, for all her sacrifices, love, and commitments to see this book project through; to Ginger Basher-Cunningham and family, for providing a home away from home, spaces for writing, inspiring walks, and warm-hearty meals by Chef Milton Basher-Cunningham; to Reinaldo Basilio Austin, for his unconditional support and the multiple readings of the many versions of this manuscript, even in the early morning hours; to my adopted niece, Ileana María López Jiménez, for believing in this project; and to Imna Arroyo, for her spiritual accompaniment.

To all of you, *¡Gracias!*

As I reminisce on those who journeyed with me, I think of two people who have flown to the *Amistad* heavens—*Amistad* historian Howard Jones, who swayed me into further investigating the lack of research connecting the interpreting and translation matters to the *Amistad* narrative. I also remember Captain Bill Pickney, first captain of the *Amistad* schooner replica, who gifted me with an autographed picture of the new *Amistad* vessel that watched over me as I pieced together this story. I learned of their untimely passing as I was completing this manuscript, which I hope made them proud.

Finally, and most importantly, this work was only possible because of the courage of the *Amistad* Africans who rebelled, the moral and racialized fortitude of the abolitionists who allied with them, and the care and foresight of those who, through their nineteenth-century letter writing, newspaper publishing, and archival preservation, ensured the aliveness of the *Amistad* story to this date. For this inspiring story that transformed me, I give thanks.

Introduction

Not all stories of the *Amistad* case have been told, particularly, those of the fifteen *Amistad* interpreters and four translators.

In June of 1839, enslaved Africans were sequestered as they were taken via the Middle Passage to Cuba. Shortly thereafter, fifty-three of them were forced into a second vessel—the *Amistad* schooner, a racialized ship composed of the enslaved, the enslavers, and those in between. Afraid of their impending death and taking advantage of deafening storm-related sounds, one of the men, named Cinque Pieh, led a revolt and took control of the vessel. Some Africans, along with Captain Ferrer and Celestino, the cook, lost their lives. Wanting to return to Africa, the Africans strategically kept their slave traders, José Ruiz and Pedro Montes, alive and gave them specific instructions to sail east. However, they did not respect their wishes. Instead, they maneuvered the vessel along the US[1] coastline, aided by the North Atlantic Current,[2] until they were discovered by the US naval authorities on August 26, 1839, off Montauk, Long Island, in New York State (refer to Figure 0.1). When seized, the Spaniards told their version of their story via an interpreter, and hence were freed; the Africans did not enjoy this same right, and hence were incarcerated. The Cuban Spaniards were native Spanish speakers; the Africans were multilingual speakers of several African languages. Through eavesdropping and hearsay, Christian abolitionists sensed that the Africans were not *Ladinos*,[3] as registered in the visa-like documents known as *licencias* as claimed by the Spaniards. To corroborate the fact that this claim was an orchestrated lie became the mission of the *Amistad* abolitionists. But for this, they needed an interpreter.

1 This book uses interchangeably both acronyms "US" and "USA." US is mostly used when referring to the governmental agencies of the USA. USA is used when referring to the country, the United States of America.

2 The late Captain Bill Pickney, first captain of the replica of the twentieth-century version of the *Amistad* schooner, surmised that, given the poor conditions of the vessel, this oceanic current guided the Amistad northward journey. (personal communication, January 8, 2017.)

3 *Ladinas* or *Ladinos* defined both freed and enslaved Africans who had lived long enough in Latin America to adapt culturally and linguistically to the Spanish-colonial context. This definition differs, in part, to *Bozales* who recently were forced to migrate from Africa to the Americas. Both terms will be further expounded in subsequent chapters.

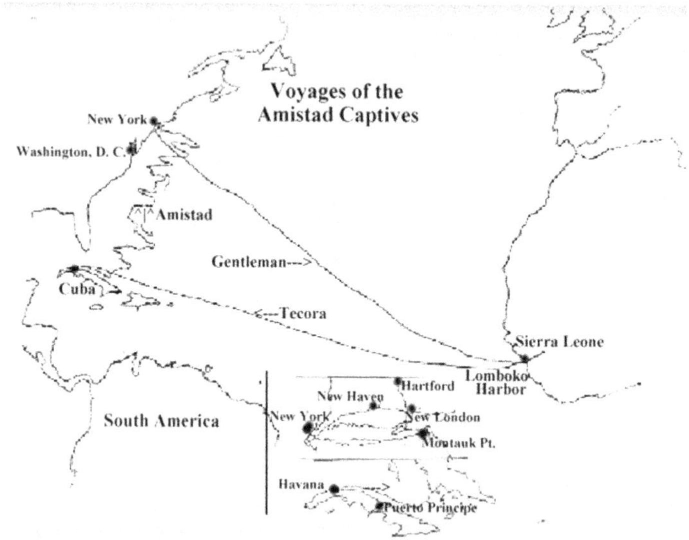

Figure 0.1 Voyages of the *Amistad* Captives (map). http://law2.umkc.edu/faculty/projects/ftrials/Amistad/AMISTD.HTM. Douglas O. Linder, "Map of the *Amistad* Case," Amistad Trials (1839–40), *Famous Trials*, https://famous-trials.com/amistad/1243-ami-map. This map depicts the long voyage of the Mende Africans from captivity to freedom. *Lomboko* Harbor in Sierra Leone to Cuba constituted the first leg of their trip. From Havana, Cuba, the *Amistad* zigzagged its way toward New York, the second portion of the trip. There they waited for two years until those who were still alive returned to West Africa.

Toward this goal, Christian abolitionists aligned all their resources and most of their social privileges to liberate the *Amistad* Africans. Proving that the Africans arrived in Cuba as a result of violations of international treaties and of illicit transatlantic slave trading became tantamount. Abolitionists believed in the African captives' human rights and right to freedom. To see this life-giving vision come true, a court interpreter[4] was required. Someone

[4] It bears repeating the meaning of the terms "interpreting" or "interpretation." These refer to either oral or signed renditions from one language to another oral or Sign Language; in contrast, "translation" or "translating" refer to a document conversion from one written language to another text form. Parallel definitions apply to the professional terms of "interpreter" and "translator." The former denotes one who mediates oral or signed locutions from one language to another, and the latter converts in writing one text to another. In the theological background section, "interpreting" refers to the hermeneutical process of deriving meaning from Scripture or religious events.

linguistically trained to speak English and an African language shared by most of the captives needed to be found. Without an interpreter to facilitate their testimony inside and outside the court, and with a highly probable anti-Black, racialized verdict against them, death in the gallows awaited them in Cuba, where the Spaniards falsely claimed that they had resided for two decades.

The US naval authorities who seized *la Goleta Amistad* (the *Amistad* schooner) towed the vessel to New London, Connecticut, where the *Amistad* legal battles began, rather than to New York City. There were reasons. By the time the Africans reached their next port, they were sick, desperate, angry, and afraid, conditions made all the worse by the linguistic and political obstacles they faced. As some historians have noted, "a [court] interpreter was just as badly needed as the doctor had been."[5] Thanks to the abolitionists' remarkable community-organizing strategies and the agency and stamina of the incarcerated Africans, the abolitionists found two British-Mende[6] sailors, James Covey and Charles Pratt, who were confirmed by the Africans to serve as their court interpreters.

However, not just anyone was fit for such a formidable task.

History mostly remembers the interpreters—Pratt and Covey, and John Ferry, who preceded them. In the end, the *Amistad* abolitionists preferred Covey for his linguistic competency over Pratt, who returned to sail back with his brig, leaving Covey as the primary interpreter for the Mende *Amistad* Africans. But they were not the only ones. Ten additional interpreters intervened in this story from when the Africans took control in July of 1839 to the January 1840 trial. And while Mende language-competent interpreters were scarce in New England at the time, the educational culture of the elite trained many translators as a language-learning technique at the service of the *Amistad* Africans. Additionally, the US Department of State (DOS) hired translators and dragomans to conduct their diplomatic relations and international policies. Two of each group intervened in the *Amistad* story, most notably John Quincy Adams. Yet, in the development of this case,

5 Helen Kromer, *Amistad: The Slave Uprising Aboard the Spanish Schooner* (Cleveland: The Pilgrim Press, 1997), 40.

6 Benjamin N. Lawrance, "*La Amistad's* 'Interpreter' Reinterpreted: James 'Kaweli' Covey's Distressed Atlantic Childhood and the Production of Knowledge about Nineteenth-Century Sierra Leone," in *Slavery Abolition and the Transition to Colonialism in Sierra Leone*, ed. Suzanne Schwarz and Paul Lovejoy (Trenton: Africa World Press, 2014), 36. Both spellings are accepted: "Mende"—a more modern spelling—and "Mendi"—the one commonly used in the enclosed analyzed data. The term "Mende" became known after finding Covey as interpreter. His expertise informed abolitionists and linguists that the Africans spoke Mende. The search was concentrated on finding an interlocutor able to speak the "Mandingo" language, presumably, from the same Mende area. Both spellings, Mende and Mendi, will be used interchangeably.

Covey marked a before-and-after. Regarding the essential role Covey played, legal historian Benjamin Lawrance recalls:

> Let us imagine for a moment what might have occurred without a Mende translator [*sic*]. Without a translator [*sic*], the story of Cinque and the others would have remained unknown, and their attorneys would have been unable to advance the argument that they were originally from Africa.[7]

Historians recognize the crucial role of interpreters as vehicles for the Africans to tell their stories, yet most *Amistad* scholars dedicate just a few paragraphs to the life, contribution, and background of James Covey.[8] Lawrance uncovered the untold life of Covey, from being kidnapped to docking at the New York City Port, events further discussed in Chapter 5, "The Transatlantic Interpreters in the *Amistad* Case." But overall, many court officers and members of the public hoped to see the interpreters' roles fade into the background.[9] Indeed, the interpreting and translation issues of the *Amistad* passengers faded gradually from the historical narrative. This trend combined with the lack of curiosity exercised by historians to expound on the contributions of interpreters and translators present in their archival sources increased the invisibility factor of researched materials and the historical corpus. The *Amistad* has been proven to be no exception. Despite the popularity of the *Amistad* plot, considerable gaps in recording the roles of the translation and interpreting have characterized most historical works about the case. The roles of interpreting and translation details of the *Amistad* story appear missing not only from the *Amistad* scholarship, but also, more broadly, from many other historical accounts, such as transatlantic, legal, and interpreting and translation histories.

During the nineteenth century, the *Amistad* storyline lingered in people's recollections, the arts, historical accounts, and US legislation. By the turn of the century, the story had dwindled, until the 1930s when the Talladega Murals, commissioned by Talladega College in Alabama, recaptured the story of the slaves' uprising and the trial to commemorate the 100-year anniversary of this iconic event. *Amistad* historians since then have returned to the archives, bringing this compelling nineteenth-century story back to light. Howard

7 Lawrance, "*La Amistad's* 'Interpreter' Reinterpreted," 219.

8 Lawrance, "*La Amistad's* 'Interpreter' Reinterpreted," 217.

9 Holly Mikkelson, "Evolving Views of the Court Interpreter´s Role: Between Scylla and Charybdis," in *Crossing Borders in Community Interpreting: Definitions and Dilemmas*, ed. A. Martin and C. Valero Garcés (Amsterdam: John Benjamins, 2008), 84.

Jones's[10] book and Spielberg's movie, especially, elicited a momentum that motivated the installation of the "*Amistad* Memorial" at New Haven's City Hall. This *Amistad* resurgence inspired Sengbe Pieh's descendants to further connect to Pieh's legacy, as narrated by Samuel Pieh, Sengbe Pieh's[11] great-grandson.[12] Spielberg's movie placed the storyline in the public consciousness and compelled historians to engage in further research, in part, to expose the inaccuracies in the film. In the still racialized and colonial context of the US twenty-first century, this successful battle against the racist institution of slavery has many relevant lessons to teach. Furthermore, the driving forces of the *Amistad* offer alternative theological models for religious action that are strikingly different from the ascendant conservative–evangelical positionings of today. Manisha Sinha, US abolitionist historian, notes the impact of the *Amistad* rebellion that "shipboard slave revolts in the age of abolition played out on a global political stage . . . the *Amistad* [1839] and the *Creole* 1841, respectively, helped revolutionize the abolition movement."[13] This book adds to the scholarship studying those revolutionizing and interlocking aspects of the *Amistad* story by critically analyzing the *Amistad*-abolitionist movement, the *Amistad* litigation strategies, and the contributing role of the *Amistad* interpreters and translators for today's struggles.

[10] Before and after Jones's book, *Mutiny on the Amistad* (New York: Oxford University Press, 1987), other *Amistad* researchers added to the *Amistad* historical corpus: Emma Gelders Sterne, *The Long Black Schooner: The Voyage of the* Amistad (New York: Aladdin Books, 1953); Mary Cable, *Black Odyssey: The Case of the Slave Ship Amistad* (New York: the Viking Press, 1971); Kromer, *Amistad: The Slave Uprising*; Karen Zeinert, *The Amistad Slave Revolt and American Abolition* (North Haven, CT: The Shoe String Press, 1997); Suzanne Jurmain, *Freedom's Sons: The True Story of the Amistad Mutiny* (New York: Lothrop, Lee & Shepard Books, 1998); Iyunolu Folayan Osagie, *The Amistad Revolt: Memory, Slavery, and the Politics of Identity in the United States and Sierra Leone* (Athens, GA: University of Georgia Press, 2000); Benjamin Lawrance, *Amistad's Orphans: An Atlantic Story of Children* (New Haven: Yale University Press, 2015); Lawrance, "*La Amistad's* 'Interpreter' Reinterpreted," 217–255; Marcus Rediker, *The Amistad Rebellion* (New York: Viking, Penguin Group, 2012); Marcus Rediker, *Outlaws of the Atlantic* (Boston, MA: Beacon Press, 2014); Michael Zeuske and Orlando García Martínez, "*La Amistad*: Ramón Ferrer in Cuba and the Transatlantic Dimensions of Slaving and Contraband Trade," in *Slavery and Antislavery in Spain's Atlantic Empire*, ed. J. M. Fradera and C. Schmidt-Nowara (New York: Berghahn Books, 2013), 200–228; and Michael Zeuske, *Amistad: A Hidden Network of Slavers and Merchants* (Princeton: Markus Wiener Publishers, 2015).

[11] Sengbe Pieh, aka Cinque Pieh aka Jingua, led the revolt on the *Amistad* schooner. Throughout this manuscript, all of his names will be used as their exact pronunciation and spelling seem to be just an approximation.

[12] Samuel Pieh, Zoom interview with author, February 8, 2023.

[13] Manisha Sinha, *The Slave's Cause: A History of Abolition* (New Haven, CT: Yale University Press, 2016), 406.

As I embark on this journey, remembering the distinctions between interpreting and translation will be necessary as described earlier. Although the terms "interpretation" and "translation" have been used interchangeably, both academically and in society at large, they refer to two different linguistic activities. Interpretation refers to spoken or signed language converted into another spoken or signed language. For instance, interpreting occurs when a speech delivered in one language is interpreted into another language. Translation occurs when a text in one language is transformed into another language via written form. Both of these skills and the professionals exercising them were showcased in the *Amistad* story: interpreters for the polyglot Africans and for others who did not speak the English language, and translators who converted documents from Spanish into English and from English into Spanish.

Additional definitions will help to contextualize this research. Most interpreting skills needed by the ideal linguist would be put to the test in the context of the courtroom, hence the recruitment efforts to find a "court interpreter." The term "court interpreting" pertains to any interpreting, whether through oral or Sign Language, performed within a legal or judicial setting, for example, within a courtroom or at attorney–client interviews. While court interpreting can be subdivided into quasi-judicial and judicial interpreting,[14] I prefer to use the categories "off-the-record" and "on-the-record" proceedings. As these terms suggest, on-the-record proceedings take place when a record is kept, as in a court of law or a deposition. Off-the-record proceedings include attorney–client meetings protected by confidentiality or informal meetings.

Finding a court interpreter in the *Amistad* case was an exigent challenge, since the United States of America (USA) lacked state and federal laws that mandated courts to furnish interpreters for non-English-speaking litigants. In the nineteenth-century judicial culture, the appointment of interpreters depended on the discretion of the presiding judge or upon the efforts of the party in need of this linguistic mediator, or on the advocacy of representing legal counsel. Other complications arose in the recruitment of court interpreters: for instance, the Mende Africans did not speak any of the European-hegemonic languages and neither did the *Amistad* abolitionists speak any of the African languages. To make matters worse, translation or interpreting organizations did not exist to assist in discerning the linguistic needs. Indeed, the search became so arduous that at one point the *Amistad*

[14] Roseann Dueñas González, Victoria F. Vásquez, and Holly Mikkelson, *Fundamentals of Court Interpretation: Theory, Policy and Practice*, 2nd ed. (Durham: Carolina Academic Press, 2012), 95.

legal team considered asking the court for a postponement in order to procure one from Africa, "if none can be found nearer home. In a case of life and death, surely, the court would allow time for this, as I think had been done in some former cases."[15]

Stories with interpreters and translators in legal settings are still missing from historical research accounts, but this does not mean that interpreting was completely absent from the judicial process in the nineteenth century. Between the Early Republic and the Progressive Era in the USA, the judiciaries did not pay much attention to placing interpreters as key protagonists in the court scene.[16] As in the *Amistad* case, until late in the twentieth century, most interpreters were ad hoc (untrained and uncertified) interpreters, people whose bilingual skills alone were considered sufficient qualification for the task at hand. One of the earliest cases involving interpreting services was the 1795 *United States v. Guinet* case heard in the Circuit Court of the Pennsylvania District involving the French language.[17] In 1809, the Supreme Court of Massachusetts heard the case of *Amory v. Fellowes*, which dealt with "a will of a former Bostonian resident in Cuba."[18] Other cases in 1814 and 1829 involved the need for interpreters to settle property affairs, one in Virginia and the other in New York, respectively.[19] The 1830 Connecticut Supreme Court heard a rape case that required the services of a Sign Language interpreter for the victim. And in 1834, the Circuit Court of the District of Massachusetts decided on a case that involved the swearing in, or not, of interpreters and the appointment of a Spanish interpreter because a Portuguese interpreter was incorrectly provided.[20] Moreover, legislation affecting the appointment and compensation of interpreters appeared as early as the middle of the nineteenth century (California Code of Civil Procedures §1884; New York Laws of 1869; Pennsylvania Act of March 27, 1865).[21]

And although legal historiography has barely scratched the surface on the interpreting history, this research project situates itself within a trajectory of judicial cases that record the story of the enslaved filing a suit against their enslavers, regardless of the pro-slavery laws or the anti-Black societal tendencies. It represented a defiant act, an empowering act, to uphold their

15 AMA Archives FI 4606. The *Amistad* Research Center, New Orleans, Louisiana, USA.
16 John Alcalde, "Babel Fish: Court interpreters in America (1790–1921)" (PhD diss., Northern Illinois University, Dekalb, 2022), 14.
17 Alcalde, "Babel Fish," 22.
18 Alcalde, "Babel Fish," 22.
19 Alcalde, "Babel Fish," 25.
20 Alcalde, "Babel Fish," 25. A similar situation presented itself in the *Amistad* case involving a Portuguese interpreter, which will be discussed later.
21 González et al., *Fundamentals of Court Interpretation*, 95.

undeniable humanity, expecting that the jurisprudence would affirm this reality. One of those is the 1849 Supreme Court of Georgia case in which a Black woman named Charity served as interpreter in an inheritance case.[22] This current *Amistad* perspective offers a unique opportunity to expand the history of Interpreting and Translation Studies (ITS) and to spark an interdisciplinary conversation between ITS, language matters, and other fields, such as Transatlantic, Slavery, African American, Africana, Americana, Afro-Caribbean and Latin American, (post) Colonial, Feminist, and Legal Studies. This project attempts to recover the role, impact, and challenges of the lives of the *Amistad* interpreters and translators, to demonstrate how meaning was created with them, and how they drew meaning of their experiences and circumstances, thus shaping and making history.

The *Amistad* interpreting and translation (IT) stories may offer the single most documented event of interpreting and translation in the early nineteenth century in the Americas in the context of a racialized and imperial conflict.[23] Malgorzata Tryuk, IT historian, observed that "the entire history of interpreting centers around wars, conquests, colonization, conversions, and the introduction of foreign rules, governments or administrations."[24] The *Amistad* was no exception. Without laws or mandates to secure interpretation for non-English speakers, courts became ethnic[25] and linguistic battlefields planted in the middle of political polarities along pro- and anti-slavery lines. Both Africans and the legal team of abolitionists faced life and death predicaments explained in greater detail in the chapter on the historical background of the case. Enslavement, imperial ideology, and contrasting legal practices—as in the *Amistad* case—influenced the roles and tasks of interpreters and translators. The interaction of power and domination through imperial politics played a significant role in the performance of interpretation and translation tasks, and vice versa. Conquerors of peoples and lands have relied on interpreters to make their violent ways inland through viable dialogues shaping language into weapon-like instruments. Conquerors traveling to the Americas brought interpreters

22 Alcalde, "Babel Fish," 61.

23 Since the turn of this century, additional scholars have turned their research interests in examining the historical role of interpreters and translators, their professional training, taxing contexts in situations of human conflicts, forced migration, violence, and war. (L. Ruiz Rosendo and C. Persaud, "Interpreting in Conflict Zones Throughout History," *Linguistica Antverpiensia*, New Series: Themes in Translation Studies 15 [2016]: 3).

24 Malgorzata Tryuk, *On Ethics and Interpreters* (Frankfurt am Main: Peter Lang, 2015), 15.

25 The working definition of the term "ethnic" in this research includes linguistic, religious, racial, geographic, and cultural elements that characterize groups of people not limited to a racialized definition.

as crew members in hopes that they may act as interlocutors. Not finding a linguistic match between the languages spoken by the interpreters and those of the native people, often children were kidnapped and taken back to a European metropolis and forced into cultural and linguistic immersion. This became one method used to develop interpreters who would provide better results for future expeditions. In other instances, Europeans who had been living with the native communities served as interpreters for newly arrived conquerors. Neither method reliably yielded the expected results. Some who accompanied the conquerors in their imperial expansions disappeared to return to the native communities and fight against the atrocities committed against the First Peoples. In contrast, the *Amistad* evidenced a different type of recruitment process designed to find someone from the inner "known" circles to be discussed in Chapter 4.

Leonel Antonio de la Cuesta described how Christopher Columbus was "less successful" than Hernán Cortés in his conquests of Latin America.[26] Cortés colonized with the assistance of interpreters who voiced his imperialistic strategies, while Columbus lacked the linguistic mediators to promote his intentions. When Cortés landed in what today is known as México, his first interpreters spoke Mayan and Náhuatl, two of the Aztec Empire's languages. However, eventually these interpreters became unfaithful to his intentions linguistically and politically and escaped to fight against Cortés for the cause of Indigenous rights to self-determination.[27] It was then that Cortés found *la Malinztin*, the daughter of a *cacique* in Veracruz, who was given the Spanish name of Doña Marina, also known as the *La Malinche*. Along with Jerónimo de Aguilar—who had lived among the Indigenous people for eight years—they used relay interpreting,[28] a skill that advanced the Spanish conquest that in time toppled the Aztec Empire. From the beginning, envoys of the Spanish Empire recognized the importance of interpreting and translation in their conquest and colonial exertions.

This book joins the scholarship of other interpreting and translation historians who have encountered similarly abundant archival materials

26 Leonel Antonio de la Cuesta, "Intérpretes y traductores en el descubrimiento y conquista del nuevo mundo," *Livius* 1 (1992): 25–34, https://buleria.unileon.es/bitstream/handle/10612/6323/Int%C3%A9rpretes%20y%20traductores%20en%20el%20descubrimiento.pdf?sequence=1 (accessed July 20, 2023).

27 de la Cuesta, "Intérpretes y traductores," 27.

28 Relay interpreting pertains to an interpreter rendering from language A to B, and another one interpreting from language B to C. In the *Amistad* story, relay interpreting occurred from Mende to Kissi and from Kissi to English.

generating monographs on a single historical event,[29] mostly in the twentieth century: Francesca Gaiba (1998), Malgorzata Tryuk (2015), Kayoko Takeda Tryuk (2015, 2021), Ting Guo (2016), and Jesús Baigorri-Jalón (2004, 2023). These IT historians share a common research theme centered before, during, and after the military activities of the Second World War. Gaiba's *The Origins of Simultaneous Interpretation: The Nuremberg Trial* compiles an administrative chronology of key interpretation details in the Nuremberg-European trials following the end of the Second World War in the twentieth century. Similarly, Baigorri-Jalón's *Interpreters at the United Nations: A History* explored an administrative history of interpreting in the United Nations born after the Second World War via research and employing the ethnographical tool of interviewing. The other works situate interpreters and translators in highly volatile contexts of war and egregious human rights violations. Baigorri-Jalón (2023) produced an extensive historiography on the role of the interpreters of both sides of the Spanish Civil War between 1936 and 1939. Malgorzata Tryuk, in her book *On Ethics and Interpreters*, traces the lives and roles of interpreters of all ages who willingly or by force served as linguistic mediators in Nazi concentration camps and at European war crime trials. Guo's *Surviving in Violent Conflicts: Chinese Interpreters in the Second Sino-Japanese War 1931–1945* explores the lives, roles, agency, and recruitment of these Chinese interpreters in the midst of a Chinese and Japanese war. Kayoko Takeda's *Interpreting the Tokyo War Crimes Tribunal: A Sociopolitical Analysis* looks at the interpreters who served during the parallel European Nuremberg Trials in Japan. In *Interpreters and War Crimes* (2021), she expounds on the trial of interpreters for war crimes during the Second World War, for which most of them were executed. She also applied an interdisciplinary approach to the archival material, analyzing the collected data through the lens of Critical Race Theory (CRT) to accentuate the racialized treatment and verdicts of the Japanese interpreters by the British tribunal. At the juncture of power, racialized issues and liberation, scholars approaching interpreting and translation issues from neighboring fields have found archival mines that visibilize the impact of these linguistic mediators, calling into question the apparent scarcity of primary sources involving interpreters and translators. *Muslim Interpreters in Colonial Senegal, 1850–1920: Mediations of Knowledge and Power in the Lower and Middle Senegal River Valley*, by Tamba M'bayo, delves into the multiple roles assumed by

[29] Additional ITS historians have contributed to the historical corpus with academic articles and editorial volumes: Mona Baker, Myriam Salama-Carr, María Carmen África Vidal Claramonte, Michael Cronin, Hilary Footitt, Moira Inghilleri, María Manuela Fernández, Gertrudis Payàs, and Michaela Wolf.

Muslim interpreters brokering power and culture through communication between the mid-nineteenth century and the early twentieth century during the period of French colonization. In *Beyond Babel: Translations of Blackness in Colonial Perú and New Granada*, Larissa Brewer-García explores the oral and written contributions of Black interpreters, namely, Andrés Sacabuche and Úrsula de Jesús in Spanish America during the sixteenth and seventeenth century. As with the *Amistad* interpreters and translators, the African-heritage linguistic mediators highlighted in these books challenged the balancing act of agency, identity, and survival within colonized and imperial systems. In another region of the Americas, in the early nineteenth century, *The Lost Translators of 1808 and the Birth of Civil Law in Louisiana* by Vernon Valentine Palmer explores the lives of two previously unnamed translators—Henry Paul Nugent and Auguste Davezac de Castera—and their translation strategies in the midst of geopolitical and judicial debates.

The *Amistad* IT services battled two distinct adversarial systems: the US court system and the national and international systems of colonial and enslaving laws. CRT explains the circumstances of the *Amistad* so well that it could have been born 185 years earlier with this case. Despite drastic postures in the USA banning the use of CRT in educational settings, CRT continues to be relevant in explaining the realities of US racialized communities inside and outside the legal system. CRT looks critically at the US judicial system from a racial and political point of view to expose how it has consistently underserved communities of African, Asian, Pacific Islanders, Native American, and/or Latin American descent: "Critical Race Theory not only dares to treat race as central to the law and policy of the United States, it dares to look beyond the popular belief that getting rid of racism means simply getting rid of ignorance, or encouraging everyone to just 'get along.'"[30] The *Amistad* case reveals how many US laws and their interpretations were biased against people of African descent.[31] The CRT movement, according to Delgado and Stefancic, involves redressing historical wrongs by applying particular strategies by the litigation team. In order to return to Africa, the *Amistad* captives, with the help of the Christian abolitionists, needed to

[30] Richard Delgado and Jean Stefancic, *Critical Race Theory: An Introduction* (New York: New York University Press, 2017), xviii.

[31] For instance, although the vessel was seized in Montauk, New York, it was towed to New London, Connecticut. US Navy officers stated that the vessel was not in optimal condition to withstand the longer trip to New York City. Connecticut slavery laws benefited the US Navy's claims for salvage, while the NY anti-slavery laws would have benefited the Africans. In court, these jurisdictional issues, which included a field visit, were argued based on Admiralty Laws and "high seas" definitions. In the end, the judged ruled that the *Amistad* schooner, though seized less than a mile from shore, was on the high seas.

challenge the systemic racism of the judicial system embodied in the laws and their main actors with multiple CRT strategies.

CRT looks at "the idea that each race has its own origins and ever-evolving history . . . no person has a single, easily stated, unitary identity."[32] They have the competence to speak about their ethnic experiences, including their experiences of race. The voice-of-color thesis encourages "black, American Indian, Asian, and Latino/a writers and thinkers . . . to communicate to their whiter counterparts matters that the whites are unlikely to know."[33] Other CRT concepts tangible in the *Amistad* stories comprise "legal storytelling, narratives, and counter-stories" coined by its theorists as court strategies to voice those unheard stories. Legal storytellers draw on inherent cultural practices of African, Native American, Asian and Pacific Islander, and Latin societies of telling their own stories—including slave narratives—as a form of historical preservation and cultural cohesion. Delgado and Stefancic assert that "legal storytelling and narrative analysis are clear-cut advances that the [CRT] movement can claim."[34] Via the assistance of interpreters, narratives "provide[d] a language to bridge the gaps in imagination and conception. . . . They reduce alienation for members of excluded groups, while offering opportunities for members of the majority group to meet them halfway."[35] In the *Amistad* story, IT matters bridged transatlantic–colonial and judicial gaps by facilitating the narratives of the *Amistad* Africans that prompted the US judicial system, via Christian abolitionists, to meet them halfway. In turn, the *Amistad* Africans became "CRT counter-storytellers," in order to deconstruct the social worlds of disadvantaged groups under constant attack within societies. Counter-stories reveal the humanity of its protagonists by challenging, and thus displacing, "pernicious narratives and beliefs."[36] The *Amistad* abolitionists' strategy required innovative legal tools, chief among them being the need for an interpreter. From Sign to Mende to the English language, the Africans told their story of enslavement and colonialism. And when the English translation of Spanish documents told a fraudulent story, they set out to uncover this aspect of their court adversaries' story. They wanted to tell a greater story: one that ended the institution of slavery. For them, slavery was a societal evil and a sin that needed to be eradicated, and the *Amistad* story came as a purposeful "blessing" toward this goal. As Gerrit Smith, a nineteenth-century abolitionist and social reformer, wrote about

[32] Delgado and Stefancic, *Critical Race Theory*, 9–10.
[33] Delgado and Stefancic, *Critical Race Theory*, 10.
[34] Delgado and Stefancic, *Critical Race Theory*, 46.
[35] Delgado and Stefancic, *Critical Race Theory*, 52.
[36] Delgado and Stefancic, *Critical Race Theory*, 50.

the African captives, "I cannot but look on these remarkable and exciting occurrences in a very cheering light. God has ordered them to hasten the overthrow of slavery."[37] Today, the *Amistad* stories in this book reflect a similar narrative pertinent to today's issues of racialization, colonialism, and the movements formed to abolish these inhumane realities. This book contributes to the overall counter-stories: judicial, the African-descendant, and the voices of European allies standing to build a different society within a compromised system that favors racism, internalized oppressions, imperial policies and narratives, toxic power, and domination.

The intersectionality between CRT and ITS contributes an analysis of another type of racism, namely linguistic racism, evident in the *Amistad* story, in the courtroom, and in the USA society at large. CRT joins ITS in critical analysis by focusing on how the linguistic and racialized ways of court procedures favored imperial powers, in one language, blocking due process for non-whites, in another language. Linguistic racism is not a new term.[38] It signals discrimination based on language or linguistic differences made by assumptions about people's wealth, intelligence, ethnicity, or social positioning that limit ample access, services, and treatment. This form of racism privileges "standard" expressions of English, characteristic of one hegemonic community in contrast to another. In the judicial context, linguistic racism impedes access to due process and justice when the courts fail to provide linguistic mediators who can interpret among defendants, claimants, and court officers, as occurred in the *Amistad* case, or when the courts make assumptions about those in need of an interpreter.

Linguistic racism manifests itself in other discriminatory ways when English-dominant individuals, groups, and institutions exert pressure on those native speakers of other languages to learn or adopt English and, at times, to discontinue usage of their vernacular. The *Amistad* abolitionists, mostly ministers and lawyers, understood that they were up against laws and a judicial system that favored slavery and racism by not mandating the appointment of linguistic mediators to litigants and witnesses. Therefore, they assumed the responsibility of furnishing their own African interpreter to tell a different *Amistad* legal story. Christian abolitionists were not exempt from fostering linguistic racism. They instituted English-language instruction and Christian education in the prison shortly after the arrival of the *Amistad* schooner "to civilize" the jailed Africans. Whether practiced by

[37] "Retracts from Correspondents," *The Emancipator*, September 29, 1839.

[38] See "Another Slice of Linguistic Racism," by Sarah Schulist. In https://anthropologyas.wordpress.com/2017/06/26/another-slice-of-linguistic-racism/.

imperial and/or religious institutions, these linguistic practices force ethnic groups to acquiesce to the melting pot concept by systematically imposing English dominance over native languages, causing ethnic groups to lose part of their ethnic identities. English proficiency and performance became interwoven as part of the national identity of the newly formed USA republic and its courts.[39] English, a *lingua franca*, then and today, serves as a vehicle to impart ideological assimilation as a way for non-English ethnic groups to surrender some of their power, in exchange for gaining partial acceptance in a linguistically and culturally hostile society. As Vicente L. Rafael has argued, "the hegemony of English is produced in and through the repression of other languages and their reorganisation into a linguistic hierarchy with significant social effects."[40] As a language of two empires—the USA and Britain—English carried an unavoidable burden and pressure as a colonizing language reinforced by the US court system.

This research steps away unapologetically from the "objective versus subjective" binary paradigm as a guiding tenet for the interpreter's code of ethics,[41] and, in fact, life in general. I propose instead that interpreters and translators assume that the cognitive nature as human beings affords them only the ability to be "subjective." This is good news. I propose that we step into our interpreting roles with all we are and have, instead of attempting the futile exercise of being neutral and objective. Affect, feelings, opinions, likes and dislikes, and other subjectivities are always present, making it virtually impossible to turn them off in the decision-making process. Instead, let's welcome them all as they too serve to inform and form our decisions and professional execution. In other words, instead of aiming at becoming "empty vessels," an impractical task, I suggest we embrace the fullness of our cognitive realities. From this stance, we will be able to achieve greater fairness and justice by assuming responsibilities for our actions and inactions, and claiming our agency.

Thanks to our subjective nature as interpreters, we analyze words, gestures, silences, cultural references, pauses, ourselves, others, and so on, in an exercise to derive meaning in milliseconds to transform significance in another language form. As subjective beings, we possess the ability to think, feel,

39 Alcalde, "Babel Fish," 8.

40 Vicente L. Rafael, "Linguistic Currencies: The Translative Power of English in Southeast Asia and the United States," *The Translator* 25, no. 2 (2019): 143. doi:10.1080/13556509.2019.1654061.

41 There is extensive scholarship at the crux of ethics and interpreting and translation issues. In addition to those already mentioned, see Kaisa Koskinen and Nike K. Pokorn, *The Routledge Handbook of Translation and Ethics* (New York: Routledge, 2021); Franz Pöchhacker, *Routledge Encyclopedia of Interpreting Studies* (New York: Routledge, 2015); Moira Inghilleri, *Interpreting Justice: Ethics, Politics and Language* (New York: Routledge, 2012).

analyze critically, be ethical and moral, weigh our options, and then choose. The question becomes then, not whether we are objective or subjective, but rather how are we being subjective or what are we being subjective about. Follow-up questions, such as how our feelings guide our actions; how what we know, how we know it, or how we don't know it informs our actions or inactions; what assumptions limit or expand our actions; what the impact of our actions or inactions is; how our silences or interventions make us complicit; how we feel about our choices; and who will not appreciate our choices, are inquiries that should inform our professional and academic choices. Erich Prunč has termed this exercise as "proactive transparency" defined as an "openness and clarity about the translator's [interpreter's] premises, strategies and choices."[42] Upholding objectivity as the ideal erroneously exonerates us from the impact of our inactions and social responsibilities. Somehow, we have been taught to believe that if we are "objective or neutral," fairness and equality will be attained. As the late Honorable Bishop Desmond Tutu illustrated: "if an elephant is stepping on a mouse's tail, and you remain neutral/objective, the mouse will not appreciate your neutrality/objectivity."[43]

Furthermore, this book invites researchers in other fields to scrutinize those archival crevices they come in contact with where IT matters hide in plain sight, by applying what I am calling an Interpreting and Translation Filter (ITF).[44] The theory or methodology of translation and interpreting has existed, primarily, to be consumed within the discipline.[45] In its development, ITS continues to adopt other theoretical models into the discipline, but not the other way around.[44] In order to expand the reach of ITS, an exportable methodological model for the non-ITS scholar is needed. The hope is that this will yield more scholarship in other fields that integrate IT queries, findings, and curiosities. Stories and histories need a comparable IT research tool that migrates to other disciplines for adoption and adaptation by academics in research. This model hopes to increase dialogue across fields, augment IT research results, and aid in deconstructing the apparent "invisibility" of interpretation and translation matters in primary sources. ITF invites scholars from other fields who often encounter interpreters and translators

42 Robin Setton and Erich Prunč. "Ethics," in *Routledge Encyclopedia of Interpreting Studies*, ed. Franz Pöchhacker (Abingdon, Oxon: Routledge, 2019), 144.

43 Desmond Tutu, https://citas.in/frases/680276-desmond-tutu-if-you-are-neutral-in-situations-of-injustice-you (accessed June 7, 2023).

44 Anthony Pym has been an exponent on historical translation methodology. See *Method in Translation History* (New York: Routledge, 2016) and Andrea Rizzi, Birgit Lang, and Anthony Pym, *What Is Translation History? A Trust-Based Approach* (Switzerland: Palgrave Macmillan, 2019).

45 Roberto Mayoral Asensio, "¿Existe la teoría de la traducción?," *Apuntes* 10, no. 4 (Otoño 2002): 12. Rizzi et al., *What Is Translation History?*, 6–7.

in their primary and secondary sources to deepen and to acknowledge the issues associated with these interlocutors. ITF brings to the surface the contributions of translators and interpreters in the shaping and making of history. This points to the ways in which they mediated access, power, and ethnicity through linguistic interlocutions and other interactions as they facilitated historical events and outcomes.

As an initial methodological step toward the application of ITF, I offer some guiding questions to scan primary and secondary sources at the intersection of IT and other fields. Did someone linguistically mediate a text or speech from one language to another? What are their names? Were they unnamed? Was there an interpreter, translator, or linguist mentioned, directly or indirectly? Should one have been mentioned but was not? What was the impact of providing interpreting and translation services, or the lack thereof? How, by whom, and/or why was this person recruited or trained? What were the requirements of the interpreter and translator? Did laws or institutions mandate their services? Were their roles explained or not? What ideology did interlocutors or recruiters profess, either explicitly or implicitly? What were their ethnic, racial, political, social, economic, cultural backgrounds, and gender identities? How did these influence or limit linguistic mediations? What were the micro and macro historical contexts? Were these adversarial, conflicting, or amicable contexts? Was their role a reflection of these or other contexts? How did privilege or discrimination play a role in their execution? How was power mediated through their interactions, services, silences, or inactions? Did their linguistic intervention affect the historical course of events? How did others perceive, facilitate, and/or prevent their tasks? Were their lives at risk or the lives of those they served? How did this reality impact their linguistic services? Who was favored or not in the process? How were their lives impacted? What were the consequences of the translation and interpreting tasks? How did they face the challenges? Did the interpreters, translators, recruiters, or those in the encounter align with the status quo or not? What ethical codes and professional standards reflect their performance and responsibilities? Tryuk's research questions further expand this list by highlighting ethical matters:

> [Who are those working] as interpreters in crisis or conflict situations during wars?; What conditions are put on their jobs?; Is their job safe, and what should interpreters do to protect themselves and their relatives?; and Does interpreting bring profits or gains to the interpreter or, by contrast, [does] it expose the interpreter and his or her relatives to danger?[46]

[46] Tryuk, *On Ethics and Interpreters*, 12.

Answers to these questions frame the *Amistad* legal interpreting and translation stories. The courts became an ethnic and linguistic battlefield planted in the broader transatlantic slave trade activities connected to the North versus South political polarities along pro- and anti-slavery lines in the USA. Set in the midst of this scenario, both Africans and the legal team of abolitionists faced life and death predicaments as they affirmed human and linguistic rights upholding freedom from an enslaving reality. Contexts of conflicts, slavery, and colonialism in the *Amistad* case influenced the roles and tasks of interpreters and translators. The specificities of the *Amistad* historical context demanded a special court interpreter recruitment process. The distinct strategies and requirements established by abolitionists revealed the prime intersection of ethnic, racialization, and power in this particular context.[47] Whereas demonstrating "how" the *Amistad* case served as a catalyst in various fronts and struggles does not constitute a novel hypothesis, the "critical" contribution of this research is to place the interpreters and translators, the search process, their roles, and their impact at the center of this judicial *Amistad* story.

This book frames the interpreting and translation services within an anti-slavery and pro-slavery continuum. Specifically, it addresses the question of how interpreting and translation issues in the *Amistad* case (1839) at times joined forces to eradicate slavery and at other times aided and abetted this systemic institution. At one end of the continuum, inspired by their theological beliefs, the abolitionists closed ranks to find an interpreter who would work to free the African captives, in the hopes of strengthening a feeble anti-slavery movement in the USA. And yet, despite their commendable *Amistad* search for a Mende interpreter, their actions also reflected racist practices supporting enslaving practices. At the opposite side of the continuum, fraudulent issuance of Spanish *licencias* in Cuba explicitly supported the colonial-enslaving systems. In this same ideological corner, the US government played a role. A Spanish to English translation of these documents publicly legitimized the institution of slavery, aligning themselves with the southern enslaving stronghold and the transatlantic slave trade. This manipulated translation, in effect, waved a white handkerchief to diplomatic relations between Spain and the US.

This book desires to problematize the intersection of language and racialization as an integral part of the *Amistad* narrative. Scholarship and people's lives have offered a multitude of definitions for the concept of race. For the *Amistad* abolitionists, race referred to the one "human race." Their

[47] Jeanette Zaragoza-De León, "The Search for a Mende-Court Interpreter in the *Amistad* Case in Order to Challenge the Institution of Slavery" (TFM, 2015).

political stance against the abolition of African descendants upheld their human rights and, therefore, their right to freedom as entitled members of the human race. At the same time, race took another meaning as a social construct to differentiate one group versus another according to phenotypical characteristics, such as skin color, hair texture, lips, eyes, and so forth.[48] This construct took on a shocking meaning when used to justify the corporal subjugation of Africans, Asians, and Native Peoples as colonized and enslaved communities from Africa to the Americas from the fifteenth century and onward. This intrinsic fusion between race and language acknowledges the ways and times in which the African captives and interpreters identified themselves or by others racially in connection to the linguistic matters in this story. As it has been observed by Joshua Martin Price, "the process of racialization went beyond skin color and extended to the *racialization of languages* themselves, as the racialization of knowledge and religion" [emphasis in original].[49] Through the development of the *Amistad* plot "racialization" wove the story. The term "racialization" describes:

> the effect or action of utilizing racial criteria to identify groups not previously represented in that way before. For instance, when ethnic groups from the African continent were classified as "black". . . . The term also applies to when the term "race" is used to explain, to represent, or to justify the behavior or situations of groups that should be explained in some other way.[50]

As this book will demonstrate, racialization permeated inside and outside the abolitionist movement. It percolated the selection of interpreting candidates, translation disputes, the way the African captives were addressed by the Spanish captors, and the USA pro-slavery movement, and, in some of the ways in which the *Amistad* Africans and the African interpreters were treated by the abolitionist movement or viewed in the public arena.

Interpreting the *Amistad* further contributes to the *Amistad* history from the ITS perspective, as well as to the wider corpus of interpreting and

48 Godreau, Isar, Mariluz Franco Ortiz, et al., *Arrancando Mitos de Raíz: guía para una enseñanza antirracista de la herencia Africana en Puerto Rico* (Colombia: nomos.com.co, 2013), 293.

49 J. Martin Price, *Translation and Epistemicide: Racialization of Languages in the Americas* (Crownhill: University of Arizona Press, 2023), 22.

50 Godreau, Isar, Mariluz Franco Ortiz, et al., *Arrancando Mitos de Raíz: guía para una enseñanza antirracista de la herencia Africana en Puerto Rico* (Colombia: nomos.com.co, 2013), 293.

translation histories during the nineteenth century. This contributes to the CRT movement centering the *Amistad* IT stories within the continuum of legal history, honing in on how linguistic racism hinders justice and suppresses the counter-stories that facilitate equality. This book belongs to the corpus of judicial cases from the late eighteenth to the late nineteenth century where Black litigants went to court demanding their rights to freedom.[51] The research joins other resources brought to live action, animation, and documentaries narrating the counter-stories of African-descent litigants in court, such as "Anna," and "The Bell Affair," co-produced by legal historian, William G. Thomas, III.[52] This research highlights the transnational aspects of the *Amistad* story, along with the racial and linguistic issues, focusing on the IT aspects of this narrative traveling from the African continent through the Caribbean and Latin American regions. This research adds to the corpus of slave narratives and stories of agency and linguistic empowerment at the height of the "second slavery" during the nineteenth century. It illustrates the blessings and contradictions of the transnational US abolitionist movement. IT methodology attempts to increase IT scholarship across disciplines, in hopes of widening the discussion regarding IT ethical codes and professional standards, by demonstrating instances in which attempting to be objective, in the midst of prevalent subjective factors, could prevent justice from prevailing. This book highlights the latent correlation between language and racialized matters through historical narratives, in contrast to divorcing these two important ethnic components. It calls for an awareness of the embedded power in language itself, as an imperial or colonizing language tool or as a means for resistance and survival. In the end, if you have lived in

[51] Scholarship in this field include: David A. Sklansky, *The Neglected Origins of the Hearsay Rule in American Slavery: Recovering Queen v. Hepburn* (September 12, 2022, 2022 Supreme Court Review), 416, Available at SSRN: https://ssrn.com/abstract=4207141 or http://dx.doi.org/10.2139/ssrn.4207141; Alejandro de la Fuente and Ariela Gross, *Becoming Free, Becoming Black: Race, Freedom, and Law in Cuba, Virginia, and Louisiana* (Cambridge: Cambridge University Press, 2020); Kelly M. Kennington, *In the Shadow of Dred Scott: St. Louis Freedom Suits and the Legal Culture of Slavery in Antebellum America.* (Athens: The University of Georgia Press, 2017); Loren Schweninger, *Appealing for Liberty: Freedom Suits in the South* (New York: Oxford University Press, 2018); Anne Twitty, *Before Dred Scott: Slavery and Legal Culture in the American Confluence, 1787–1857* (Cambridge: Cambridge University Press, 2016); Lea VanderVelde, *Redemption Songs: Suing for Freedom Before Dred Scott* (New York: Oxford University Press: 2014); Kimberly M. Welch, *Black Litigants in the Antebellum American South* (Durham: The University of North Carolina Press, 2018); and Gregory Ablavsky. "Making Indians 'White': the Judicial Abolition of Native Slavery in Revolutionary Virginia and Its Racial Legacy." (*University of Pennsylvania Law Review* 159, no. 5 (2011): 1457–1531. http://www.jstor.org/stable/41149900).

[52] https://history.unl.edu/william-thomas-iii; and http://annwilliamsfilm.com/.

an empire, after a few years the empire lives in you. This calls for a systemic practice to undo the imperial and colonizing ways learned consciously and unconsciously by living and taking part in the empire. US- and/or European-centered class, education, gender, cultural, racial and linguistic access, experiences, and positionings conjugate privilege. The *Amistad* invites us all to examine our privileges within these categories for the sake of everyone's humanity. This research hopes to inspire its readers through the unfolding IT stories of the *Amistad* saga.

To illustrate "how interpreters and translators make and shape history," the information in this book has been categorized under two main areas: the *Amistad* translation issues and the translators, followed by the *Amistad* interpreters and the interpreting aspects. Although both developed in tandem, most of the interpreting dilemmas occurred between August 1839 to January 1840, in contrast to the translation sequel which intensified after the January 1840 trial. Because translation issues supplement the historical background, their content precedes the copious archival materials on interpreting elements. This choice requires, at times, to go back and forth in history or repeat certain events to illustrate a different angle from either the interpreting or the translation standpoint.

More specifically, this book is organized into seven chapters. Following this Introduction, the first chapter expounds on the historical backdrop of the *Amistad* interpreters and translators. The background section explores the five main strands that offered specific challenges and opportunities to these professionals: the transatlantic slave trade; the political context of the US northern and southern divide; the abolitionist movement and their theological principles; the court interpreter's mandates in the US and the Spanish empires; and the international relations between the Spanish Empire and the newly formed US-imperial republic. The second chapter expounds on the crucial translation issues embedded in the evidentiary *licencias*, and the controversial terms of *Bozales* and *Ladinos* as racialized terms. This controversy sparked a mobilization effort by the highly educated *Amistad* abolitionists when the term *Ladino* was translated instead as "sound negroes" which incited an open public debate in newspapers between the pro- and anti-slavery sides. The third chapter introduces the two US DOS SPAN/ENG translators by name, Robert Greenhow and William B. Hodgson, along with two additional key *Amistad* translators, John Quincy Adams and William Jay, Esq. It follows the creation of a congressional subcommittee created by Adams to investigate who was behind the "fraudulent" translation of the *licencias.* Chapter 4 unwraps the distinct recruitment process for finding and identifying the ideal interpreter for the Mende Africans, elaborating on the requirements and qualifications that responded to the sociopolitical and racialized background faced by the Africans and their advocates. Surprisingly, the most important requirements were subjective in nature. This chapter also presents the interpreting candidates that travelled to New Haven hoping to breach the linguistic gap between the Africans and the rest of the world. Chapter 5 shows the fundamental change before and after finding James Kaweli Covey, the first interpreter who was able to converse "freely with all of them," capturing the iconic moment of this encounter when the imprisoned African community was overjoyed at having someone who could speak their own language(s). The most extensive section of this book names thirteen of the *Amistad* interpreters: Antonio Ferrer, Thomas Meade, John Ferry, Bowle, Grabbeau, George Day, James Covey, Charles Pratt, Thomas Gallaudet, John Jay Hyde, Mr. Ribeiro, Mr. Desa, and Theodore Sedgwick, all of whom interpreted on and off the record throughout the *Amistad* trials. It concentrates mostly on three of them: James Kaweli Covey, John Ferry, and Antonio Ferrer. Except for one of the *Amistad* interpreter candidates, John Shain—a "White" man[53]—and Sign Language interpreters Thomas Gallaudet and George Day, the rest of the *Amistad* interpreters were African born. By the time they arrived in New York, liberated from slavery in one way or another, their birthplace and their enslaved backgrounds bestowed them with a cultured tradition of African multilingualism and interpreting. The stories of the *Amistad* African interpreters merged with those of the African captives. This section reveals the six languages interpreted into or from throughout the duration of *Amistad* period: Mende, Kissi, Spanish, Sign Language, English, and Portuguese. In addition to court interpreters, the *Amistad* Africans needed medical, conference, and travel interpreters to ensure their rights and needs. Both consecutive and relay interpreting were utilized inside and outside the court as the Africans were finding ways to communicate between their world and stories and the outside world. Chapters 6 and 7 delve into the judicial hearings from the period when the *Amistad* Africans landed on Connecticut shores and before the January 1840 trial and how the interpreting and translation matters were discussed and resolved. Chapter 6 explores the public, racialized debate when Covey falls ill, apparently, causing the original November trial date to be postponed. And the last chapter traces the critical interpreting arguments in court that sought to discredit James Kaweli Covey to remove him to prevent the Africans from testifying in court, exploring how the opposing party and the trial judge neglected to find a Spanish interpreter for Antonio, ensuring that he would not testify against the US-Spanish pro-slavery side. *Amistad* attorney-of-

[53] Letters racialized Shain in this way. More about this will be explored in subsequent chapters.

record Theodore Sedgwick III stepped in offering his services as a Spanish interpreter, avoiding the appeal of the case on the basis for not having the appropriate language interpreter. Despite the historical hurdles, the interpreters and translators facilitated an ending that favored the liberation of the *Amistad* Africans and the cause of their allies.

These are the crucial *Amistad* translation and interpreting stories that need to be told.

1

Like Water for Chocolate

The Colonial and Enslaving Background of the *Amistad* Case

Transatlantic and Transnational Trade: The Backdrop of the *Amistad* Case

The late nineteenth century saw the demise of the transatlantic-African slave trade that, together with Catholic and Protestant Christianity, had so long enabled the building of the Spanish, French, and British global empires. During this century, Africans, Afro-descendants, and non-Africans had joined forces to tear down this systemic and inhumane institution. Their actions were marked by three major events: the Haitian Revolution (1804), the British abolition of the transatlantic slave trade (1807), and the Spanish and British treaty against the transatlantic slave trade (1817). These events should have led to further liberation efforts. Instead, those who had benefited from slavery expanded their reach. As Ada Ferrer points out, "the end of the slave trade, and then slavery in the British and parts of the French world actually encouraged and fuelled the expansion and intensification of slavery in emerging zones of commodity production, most notably in the US South (cotton), southern Brazil (coffee), and Cuba (sugar)."[1] Northern consumer demands characterized by capitalist avarice colluded with African financial interests influenced by internalized oppression to spawn a new era in the slavery continuum that Dale Tomich calls "the second slavery."[2] French planters from Haiti migrated to Cuba with their technology and slaves, Spaniards and others were granted permission to transport the enslaved, and

[1] Ada Ferrer, "Cuban Slavery and Atlantic Anti-Slavery," in *Slavery and Antislavery in Spain's Atlantic Empire*, ed. Josep M. Fradera and Christopher Schmidt-Nowara (New York: Berghahn, 2013), 136.

[2] Dale W. Tomich, *Through the Prism of Slavery: Labor, Capital, and World Economy* (New York: Rowman & Littlefield, 2004), 56.

the colonial Spanish elite knew how to take advantage of this momentum.[3] Though the number of ships arriving in Havana ports had initially dwindled after the triumphs of the abolitionist movements in Britain and Haiti, this inactivity only lasted for two years after 1807.[4]

According to Ada Ferrer, between 1807 and 1867 Cuba imported a staggering 86 percent of its total enslaved population. In addition, British and American companies continued human trafficking. In response to the 1817 treaty, the landing of slave ships and their illegal cargo in Cuba and other colonies skyrocketed. By the 1830s, the sugar industry had expanded its mobility and profits through the construction of a railway, which further boosted the slave trade by exploiting enslaved labor for construction, agriculture, and production purposes. As Ferrer explains, the slave trade "received a major impetus in the late 1830s, expressly to meet the needs of the sugar industry and enable rapid transport of sugar cane to mills . . . the slave trade to Cuba underwent another violent period of growth."[5]

Complicity between the colonial authorities and the slave traders only increased the illegal trade. Lax port regulations allowed *barcos esclavistas*, slave ships, to dock in Havana or off its coast at night, avoiding detection and prosecution by the British and Spanish Mixed Commission. Once the enslaved Africans landed, local officials aided and abetted slave traders in marching chained Africans to the open markets of the capital. The *Teçora*, a Portuguese vessel, was just such a *barco esclavista* that illegally transported Africans to Cuba, where they shortly afterward boarded the *Amistad* schooner.

The journey of the Mende-speaking Africans of the *Amistad*, however, began much earlier. Born and raised on the African continent, they were captured by Europeans with the assistance of African collaborators from their lands as a result of internal-ethnic disputes, unpaid debts, or collusion between European slave traders and African nationals. The institution of slavery had long existed on the African continent, but the later large-scale European involvement added a level of cruelty and brutality not previously seen. All throughout this period, some Africans continuously resisted, while some others colluded with the enslavers to facilitate the slave trade. As the

3 Ferrer, "Cuban Slavery and Atlantic Anti-Slavery," 141–7.
4 Ferrer, "Cuban Slavery and Atlantic Anti-Slavery," 148.
5 Ferrer, "Cuban Slavery and Atlantic Anti-Slavery," 151.

Europeans and the US Americans[6] mounted stronger pressure, the slave trade became much harder to combat. Iyunolu Folayan Osagie, a Sierra Leonean historian, describes this situation:

> The captive's stories narrated by the Africans were often similar. Many had been kidnapped, overpowered by several African slave catchers, while on a journey to their farms, on a trip to another village to buy goods, or while running some simple errand in the vicinity of home. . . . Throughout most of the 18th century, and increasingly in the early and mid-nineteenth century, both intertribal and intratribal wars in Africa were incited by the high demand for slavers in the West.[7]

Some countries abolished the transatlantic trade of humans in the early nineteenth century: England in 1807, the United States of America in 1808, Spain in 1811, and Portugal in 1815. Nevertheless, citizens of all these nations conducted covert slave trading activities even after it had been legally abolished in their countries, as exemplified by the many trips of the *Teçora*'s crew, which violated an international law that had been in effect for close to twenty years.

In April 1839, the Mende Africans began their Middle Passage from the *Jomboko*[8] Harbor on board the *Teçora*. Those who survived the brutal voyage to Cuba were forced into smaller vessels to shore and then led to the *barracón*, large warehouses built expressly to house and acclimatize

6 I have coined the term "US American" to refer to people born and raised in the United States of America or who identify as citizens of this country. Typically, "US Americans" self-identify, incorrectly, as "Americans." Active debates in Latin American and Caribbean circles argue in favor of the usage of the term "American" as a continental definition, encompassing anyone from the North, South, and Caribbean Americas, as it was commonly employed during the century in question. In a commitment to decolonize and to deimperialize language, this proposed term, "US Americans," subsumes USA global influence and power. I considered adopting the term "USians," however, its parallel to the term "Asian" deterred the author from employing it. Another term pondered was "USer," nonetheless, I opted for the terms of US American and US African American.

7 Osagie, *The Amistad Revolt*, 2.

8 Conversations between Sierra Leoneans and Marcus Rediker in "Ghosts of the *Amistad*" documented that the actual name was "*Jomboko*," not "*Lomboko*." The mistake was due to a misspelling of the word (Rediker 2013). Handwritten forms of the "J" and "L" may look similar depending on the writer. A missed transcription may have also contributed to this spelling mistake. Although it may be confusing since *Lomboko* prevails in the *Amistad* literature, I opted to incorporate *Jomboko* instead of the common term.

those recently arrived. At his deposition,[9] Dr. Richard Robert Madden testified that he had seen the Africans from the *Amistad* at the *misericordia barracón*, on the outskirts of Havana. Slaveholders held them there for a few weeks, attempting to restore their physical health after the treacherous Atlantic journey before parading them at the market. The Africans, soon to be known as the passengers of the *Amistad*, fifty-three in total, found themselves under new slaveholders. José Ruiz claimed forty-nine of the slaves, and Pedro Montes claimed three girls and a boy. All boarded a new vessel, *La Amistad*.

This was not the first time *La Amistad* had participated in covert trading activities. A total of six men composed the crew: Antonio—*el grumete*,[10] *"el negrito de cámara"*[11]—Ruiz; Montes; Captain Ramón Ferrer, aka Ramón Roselló, born in Ibiza, was approximately forty years old by 1838;[12] two sailors, Jacinto Verdagué, from Cataluña, and Manuel Padilla, from Santo Domingo; and the Puerto Rican cook, "*un mulato esclavo del capitán llamado Celestino*" (the captain's mulatto slave called Celestino).[13] José Ruiz, twenty-four, a bilingual Spanish–English speaker who studied in Connecticut, was from Rodezno, in Castilla la Vieja, Spain. Pedro Montes, aged fifty-eight, was from the city of Tortosa in Cataluña. Antonio Ferrer, Captain Ferrer's *grumete*, declared under oath during the third day of the *Amistad* trial that, "the schooner was accustomed to transport slaves. Ruiz had taken slaves in another vessel."[14] Captain Ferrer belonged to an extensive slave-trafficking network.[15] After 1820, control of the

9 Conversations with Judge Miguel A. de la Carrera concluded that during the *Amistad* period the terms "deposition" and "affidavit" were used interchangeably to mean an "affidavit" instead of the present distinctions between both terms (personal communication, April 21, 2024). A deposition alludes to an off-the-record testimony of a witness, most commonly, in response to an oral interrogation by a lawyer (Bryan A. Garner, ed., *Black's Law Dictionary*, 8th ed. [St. Paul, MN: Thomson West, 2004], 472). An affidavit, on the other hand, is a "voluntary declaration of facts written down and sworn to by the declarant before an officer authorized to administer oaths, such as a notary public" (Garner, *Black's Law Dictionary*, 62). Depositions by Charles Madden and of interpreters, John Ferry, Charles Pratt, and James Covey, resemble more the definition of an affidavit than a deposition.

10 Young person who learns the trade of being a sailor as an apprentice on a sailboat. (Definition adapted and translated from the one found at the *Real Academia Española*.) https://dle.rae.es/grumete (accessed April 10, 2024).

11 "*Viaje de la goleta Amistad*," *Noticioso de Ambos Mundos*, 28 de septiembre de 1839.

12 Michael Zeuske and Orlando García Martínez, "*La Amistad*: Ramón Ferrer in Cuba and the Transatlantic Dimensions of Slaving and Contraband Trade," in *Slavery and Antislavery in Spain's Atlantic Empire*, ed. Josep M. Fradera and Christopher Schmidt-Nowara (New York: Berghahn Books, 2013), 201–2.

13 "*Viaje de la goleta Amistad*," *Noticioso de Ambos Mundos*, 28 de septiembre de 1839.

14 "Third Day—Thursday," *The Emancipator*, January 16, 1840.

15 Zeuske and García Martínez, "*La Amistad*," 201–2.

Cuban slave trade lay in the hands of Catalans and merchants from Cadiz, France, and the USA.[16] Barcelona became a hub for slave traders originally from Catalan or other parts of Spain who amassed their fortunes in the Caribbean and Latin America, via the transatlantic human trade on behalf of the Spanish Empire.[17]

In preparation for the next voyage from Havana to Guanaja, also in Cuba, the *Amistad* crew was required to furnish travelling permits authorizing port transportation and paying the tariffs imposed by the Spanish Crown. These licenses or permits, known as *licencias,* named each traveller individually and specified the port of entry and exit as well as the physical characteristics of the passengers (refer to Figures 2.1 and 2.2). Their key relevance will be discussed in the chapter on translations. José Ruiz and Pedro Montes did obtain these "official" documents, but they did so illegally. Aided by local Spanish authorities complicit in human trafficking, Ruiz and Montes obtained these papers through bribery and corruption. Unbeknownst to the Mende Africans, these documents inaccurately identified them as *Ladinos*—those who have lived long enough in a Spanish-speaking territory to assimilate linguistically and culturally—instead of *Bozales*—those recently transplanted forcefully to Spain or its colonies. The cover-up involved the imposition of Spanish proper names for their African-given names, also unbeknownst to them. *Licencias* recorded their "Spanish" names as: "Antonio, Simon, Lucas, Pedro, Martin, Manuel, Andrés, Eduardo, Celedonio, Bartolo, Ramón, Augustín, Evanisto, Casimiro, Melchor, Gabriel, Santorion, Escalástico, Pascual, Estanilao, Desiderio, Nicholás, Esteban, Tomás, Cosme, Luis, Bartolo, Julián, Frederico, Salustiano, Ladislao, Celestino, Epifaneo, Tiburcio, Venducio, Felipe, Francis, Hipólito, Benito, Isodoro, Vicente, Dionisio, Apoloneo, Esequiel, León, Julio, Hipólito 2nd, and Zenon"[18]—instead of their actual African names, for instance: Cingue, Grabeau,[19] Kimbo, Konoma, Burna, Bartu, Gnakwoi,

[16] Zeuske and García Martínez, "*La Amistad*," 206.

[17] Martín Rodrigo y Alharilla, "Spanish Merchants and the Slave Trade: From Legality to Illegality, 1814–1870," in *Slavery and Antislavery in Spain's Atlantic Empire*, ed. Josep Fradera and Christopher Schmidt-Nowara, 176–199 (New York: Berghahn Books, 2013), 188. For instance, this was the case of Pedro Blanco Fernández de Trava from Malaga. Witnesses during the *Amistad* trial testified about the enslaving activities of Pedro Blanco in Jomboko who lived in both Cuba and Africa, eventually settling in Barcelona in 1842.

[18] John W. Barber, *A History of the Amistad Captives: Being a Circumstantial Account of the Capture of the Spanish Schooner Amistad, by the Africans on Board; Their Voyage, and Capture near Long Island, New York; with Biographical Sketches of Each of the Surviving Africans also, an Account of the Trials* (New Haven, CT: E. L. & J. W. Barber, 1840), 6.

[19] The written versions of their names were filtered through French, German, Spanish, or English phonetics and pronunciations. The following list represents the African names known, to date, of the living *Amistad* captives at the time of Barber´s chronicle.

Kwong, Fuliwa, Pie, Pungwuni, Sessi, Moru, Ndamma, Fuliwulu, Bau, Ba, Shule, Kale, Bagna, Sa, Kinna, Ngahoni, Fakinna, Faginna, Yaboi, Fabanna, Tsukama, Berri, Foni, Burna, Shuma, Kali, Teme, Kagne, and Margu, as later recorded in the court chronicle by Barber with the assistance of the court interpreter, James Covey.

Amistad scholar Howard Jones defined *Ladinos* as "slaves who had lived on the island long enough . . . to speak the Spanish language," while the term *Bozales* referred to those brought to the island after 1820 "for they have never been domiciled and were unable to speak Spanish."[20] Both terms were pejorative. *Bozal*, meaning muzzle, evokes the racialized inability of the enslaved to speak the colonial language instead of their native languages, established by the power of the Spanish-hegemonic language and all it represented. On the other hand, the term *Ladino* or *Ladina* covered the actions by the Spanish slaveowners and colonial authorities, as it was coined for those years in the process of inculturation. A variation of this term, *Ladino cristiano,* existed in Spain. Cynthia Giambruno, an ITS historian, elaborates on how the term referred to African residents of Spain who spoke Castilian and who had assimilated to Spanish customs and had converted to Catholicism in Spanish colonies.[21] On the one hand, the law protected the monetary transfer of Spanish-speaking *Ladinos* within the confines of Cuba. On the other hand, the same law deemed illegal the transfer of *Bozales.* In court, experts testified that this latter term better described the *Amistad* Africans. The polemic around the *licencias* and the debate about whether the Africans were *Ladinos* or *Bozales* became pivotal in winning the *Amistad* case in favor of the Africans. This is addressed in the chapter on translation.

With fraudulent *licencias* in hand, the non-Spanish-speaking Africans were forced into the *Amistad* vessel captained by Ferrer. Originally, this voyage was expected to last two to three days, but nature and resistance had a different plan. Strong winds and high waves extended the trip to more than a week, creating shortages in the food and water supply. In addition to treacherous weather, Captain Ferrer also ignored warnings he had been given. Ferrer had been cautioned "to keep a look out for the negroes, as they had attempted to rise and take the vessel in which they were brought from Africa."[22] As foretold, in June 1839, only a few days after leaving Havana and

[20] Jones, *Mutiny on the Amistad*, 21.

[21] Cynthia Giambruno, "The Role of the Interpreter in the Governance of Sixteenth- and Seventeenth-Century Spanish Colonies in the "New World"," in *Crossing Borders in Community Interpreting: Definitions and Dilemmas*, ed. Carmen Valero-Garcés and Anne Martin (Philadelphia: John Benjamins Publishing Company, 2008), 36.

[22] Zeuske and García Martínez, "*La Amistad*," 216.

Figure 1.1 The African captives: Retracts from correspondents. Death of Captain Ferrer, the captain of the *Amistad.* https://artgallery.yale.edu/collections/objects/26963.

off Cuban shores, forty-nine African slaves[23] rebelled and took control of the Schooner *Amistad.* The insurrection took lives on both sides, leading to the deaths of Africans and Spaniards. Facing the fear of death, coupled with other atrocities of the Middle Passage, sequestered Africans generated different forms of resistance aboard slave ships in the form of "creative resistance from those being transported, from hunger strikes to suicide to outright insurrection."[24] In the context of the *Amistad* rebellion, Osagie elaborates, "although the captive's bondage onboard *La Amistad* was, relatively speaking, less horrendous than their Middle Passage trip . . . the slaves reacted violently because Celestino [a slave from Puerto Rico] had taunted them."[25]

More lives were lost from among the Africans than the Spaniards, of whom two died, two escaped, and three others remained. Captain Ferrer and the *Amistad* cook lost their lives; for an artistic representation of the rebellious scene, refer to Figure 1.1. Ferrer mistreated the Africans, and Celestino threatened the Africans that they would be killed and served as a meal. Even if meant in jest, these remarks incited the Africans. According to the African retelling of the event, the mere thought of this prompted the rebellion. Geneviève Fabre, extrapolating from the autobiography of Olaudah Equiano,[26] concludes that in the eyes of the enslaved Africans

[23] The total of the enslaved were fifty-three, of whom three were girls.

[24] Marcus Rediker, *The Slave Ship: A Human History* (London: John Murray Publishers, 2007), 7.

[25] Osagie, *The Amistad Revolt*, 5.

[26] "The Interesting Narrative of the Life of Olaudah Equiano or Gustavus Vassa, the African," Beinecke Rare Book and Manuscript Library, Yale University, New Haven, CT.

"the white man's cannibalism explained his hunger for slaves and hence the slave trade."[27] Also, sailors and ship interpreters together instilled fear in the captives; rumors travelled from Senegambia to Angola that enslavers had an insatiable appetite for their human cargo.[28] This explains why Sengbe, one of the forty-nine Africans, took Celestino seriously when he used hand signs to communicate this threat of death to the African passengers. All his prior years as an enslaved person had trained Celestino, originally from Puerto Rico, to internalize the external racialized oppression of a well-orchestrated enslaving system against his kindred. Perhaps believing that he enjoyed a greater privilege than the recently arrived Africans and that the system would not turn against him as a mulatto cook, he assumed a position in the middle tier, between the enslaved Africans and the enslavers. Within the complex system of slavery, this middle tier was composed of cooks, interpreters, guards, sailors, and musicians. Their collaboration, even if they believed it was necessary for their survival, more often than not aided and abetted the enslavers in these vessels.[29]

Cinque debated between two alternatives sharing a common outcome: affirm his life and that of his compatriots, even if the end result leads to death, or surrender to a certain death foretold by Celestino. His resolve fuelled the successful insurrection, which the abolitionist movement later praised and which was one of the fundamental legal bases for winning the case: the right to bear arms to obtain freedom from enslavement. Cinque and the others became the first abolitionists in the *Amistad* story. Weeks after their arrival, the epigraph of one of the drawings painted of him read: "The brave Congolese chief, who prefers death to Slavery, and who now lives in Jail . . . awaiting trial for daring for freedom."[30] In the 1840s and the 1850s, respectively, Henry Highland Garnet and Frederick Douglass cited the *Amistad* rebellion as a leading example for why slaves needed to strike a blow in the face of horrific violence perpetrated by slaveowners.[31] Cinque and his companions, along with their interpreters and translators, engaged in abolitionist-like actions.

27 Geneviève Fabre, "The Slave Ship Dance," in *Black Imagination and the Middle Passage*, ed. Maria Diedrich, Henry Louis Gates, Jr., and Carl Pedersen (London: Oxford University Press, 1999), 38.

28 Fabre, "The Slave Ship Dance," 38.

29 Zeuske and García Martínez, "*La Amistad*," 216.

30 Connecticut Historical Society, "Extra Sun," Broadside 1839, C575J.

31 Benjamin Quarles, *Black Abolitionists* (New York: Oxford University Press, 1969), 226; David W. Blight, *Frederick Douglass: Prophet of Freedom* (New York: Simon & Schuster, 2018), 336, ProQuest Ebook Central.

Jacinto Verdagué and Manuel Padilla read the small print.[32] They managed to lower the small boat to be captured soon after by a whaling vessel and returned to Cuba. The Africans decided to keep the other three enslavers alive, which included Antonio Ferrer, José Ruiz, and Pedro Montes.[33] According to the historical compilation by John W. Barber in *The History of the Amistad Captives*, Antonio was *un Ladino*, a creole boy of African birth raised in Cuba, also an enslaved minor. Antonio would have been killed but proved helpful to the linguistic needs of the Mende Africans, since "he acted as interpreter between [them], as he understood both languages."[34] It is difficult to grasp what type of interpreting skills Antonio displayed. The Spanish narration of the events did not mention Antonio, *el negrito de cámara*, as an interpreter. Perhaps nonlinguistic communication took place between Antonio, the Africans, and the Spaniards. On the subject of how colonizers communicated during the Spanish conquest when an interpreter of the pair of languages was absent, Christopher Columbus documented in his diary, "*la comunicación con los naturales se hacía a través de lo que hoy llamamos la traducción intersemiótica o sea, por señas*" (communication with natives was done in what we now call intersemiotic translation, in other words, by signs).[35] Perhaps Antonio remembered some African words, but because interpreting was not a role solicited from Antonio during the *Amistad* proceedings, it is more likely that his communications on board the ship had been via hand and corporal signals.

The Africans spared the lives of José Ruiz and Pedro Montes solely so that they could steer the ship back to Africa, their eastward home. Early in the journey, the Africans identified Sengbe[36] as their leader, and he was the one who ordered Ruiz and Montes to sail in the direction of the "rising sun," back to Sierra Leone, West Africa. Ruiz and Montes, however, navigated in a completely different direction, praying they would land anywhere else but

[32] The Cuban archives, *Fondo Gobierno Superior Civil, Legajo* 1272, no. 49909, make reference to their "affidavit." They informed the authorities of the rebellion aboard the schooner. However, all attempts to find this document proved unsuccessful.

[33] The spelling of Pedro Montes's name varies in the historical literature, that is, Montes, Montez, and Monte. I adopted the spelling as printed in the newspaper *Noticioso de Ambos Mundos*, believing that it is the most accurate given its proximity to his cultural and linguistic heritage.

[34] Barber, *A History of the Amistad Captives*, 7. To date, this is the only primary source that cites Antonio as an interpreter. Antonio was not interviewed for this compilation. Either the interviewed Africans related this fact or James Covey did.

[35] De la Cuesta, "Intérpretes y traductores," 26.

[36] Different spellings of his name, Jingua, José, Cingue, Cinque, or Joseph Cinqué, abound throughout the primary sources and historical narratives.

on the African continent and hoping to be rescued by another vessel that would sympathize with their enslaving interests. Based on Montes's narration to the *Noticioso de Ambos Mundos*, he maneuvered the sails westward at night and eastward during the day "*siempre flameando las velas y no hacía mayor camino*" (always flapping the sails, halting speed).[37] While the Mende Africans hoped to get closer to home with each rising of the sun, Ruiz and Montes secretly aimed the schooner westward to make sure this did not happen. Aided by the North Atlantic Current, their zigzagging maneuvers lasted approximately two months, navigating northbound parallel to the US coast and toward New England (refer to Figure 1.1).

Not surprisingly, their supplies ran very low, and starvation claimed the lives of six Africans after they were forced to drink salt water.[38] In response to this crisis, Sengbe, along with his comrades, traded the vessel's bounty for water and food supplies, which required regular stops. Montes testified that they "anchored at least thirty times" along the US coast.[39] Unbeknownst to them, eyewitnesses along the coast generated newspaper articles reporting on a Black schooner commanded by "pirates" or "buccaneers," claiming that "the ship grew more and more sluggish, her sails rotting against the masts, her bottom heavy with barnacles and sea grass."[40]

On what would become their last supply-trading stop, on August 25, 1839, the Mende Africans believed that communications exchanged with Henry Green, aboard the US vessel, would open the way for their voyage back to Africa. Instead, the *Amistad* was captured and seized off Montauk, Long Island, New York, by the USS *Washington*, a US Navy ship. News of the "Black Schooner" had been reported on both sides of the Atlantic since July 1839 after it failed to arrive at its port of destination. The news catapulted others into action, like Lieutenant Richard W. Meade, who followed orders from Commander Gedney to intercept *La Amistad* off the coast of New York.

Lieut. Meade, a Spanish speaker, boarded *La Amistad* with his crew. No verbal communication transpired with the Africans, as they spoke neither English nor Spanish. Pro-slavery ears heard the version that Montes and Ruiz orchestrated and which was seconded by Antonio via this ad hoc Spanish interpreter. Meade conversed in Spanish with Montes and in English with Ruiz, a bilingual Spanish/English speaker who had at some point studied in Connecticut. Linguistic, class, and white privilege, coupled with anti-Black

[37] *Noticioso de Ambos Mundos*, 28 de setiembre de 1839.
[38] Kromer, *Amistad: The Slave Uprising*, 26.
[39] Barber, *A History of the Amistad Captives*, 7.
[40] Kromer, *Amistad: The Slave Uprising*, 26.

sentiments on both sides converged to result in their release. Meanwhile, linguistic racism and pro-slavery ideology led to the incarceration of the non-English and non-Spanish-speaking Africans.

The version of events recounted by Ruiz and Montes prevailed, making way for towing the *Amistad* to US soil. It was not, however, brought to a New York harbor as expected, but rather to New London, Connecticut. Meade and Gedney attributed their decision to the poor condition of the *Amistad*, which they felt would be unable to make the journey all the way to New York City. Certainly, the shorter distance between Montauk to New London in comparison to the longer travel journey to New York may have justified the port decision, but New London also offered a shorter route to enslavement and salvage.[41]

On August 26, 1839, the Spanish schooner anchored in New London. Gedney and Meade wasted no time in submitting their complaint to the District Court in order to claim their salvage. Judge Andrew T. Judson, who presided at the first *Amistad* hearing, was known for his strong pro-slavery ideology.[42] During a hurried hearing, which took place on board the schooner and the brig *Washington*, Lieut. Meade testified about his encounter with the *Amistad* and crew and also served as the court interpreter for the Spanish and Antonio. Barber recalled that Meade spoke "the Spanish language both elegantly and fluently, [and] acted as an interpreter between the Spaniards and the court."[43]

José Ruiz, Pedro Montes, and the cabin boy Antonio all testified in Spanish, assisted linguistically by Meade. Barber reports, "Antonio, the slave of the murdered Captain, was called before the court, and was addressed in Spanish, by Lieut. Meade, on the nature of an oath."[44] No verbal communication transpired with the Africans as they spoke neither English nor Spanish and no one spoke on their behalf. Moreover, no one demonstrated a willingness to listen or a desire to understand the body language and the signs they were trying to communicate with—freedom is warranted, fraud has been committed. Pro-slavery ears heard the version that Montes and Ruiz orchestrated, supported by Antonio via this biased ad hoc Spanish interpreter. The Mende Africans were not given equal judicial right to tell their side of the story through an able interpreter, after the Spaniards produced in court the falsified *licencias*. At the conclusion of this proceeding,

41 Kromer, *Amistad: The Slave Uprising*, 26. *Amistad* historian Jones explains: "perhaps because New York had abolished slavery, Gedney took his prize to New London."

42 Osagie, *The Amistad Revolt*, 7.

43 Barber, *A History of the Amistad Captives*, 6.

44 Barber, *A History of the Amistad Captives*, 7.

the Africans were accused of felony charges: "murder and piracy." *Amistad* historian Howard Johnson noted that, instead, they were charged with "murder and mutiny."[45]

Thus began a series of court proceedings and international correspondence between the USA and Spain. Early in the judicial process, the judge dismissed the criminal charges against the Africans based on lack of jurisdiction. Judge Thompson, the presiding judge in the civil trial of the *Amistad* case that took place in January 1840, ruled in favor of the Africans. However, the case was appealed by the prosecution, representing Spanish interests to the highest US court. A year after the trial, the Supreme Court of the United States upheld the initial decision, affirming the Africans' right to freedom and to fight for that freedom. After the Supreme Court decision, abolitionists redoubled their efforts on behalf of the *Amistad* Africans, this time to raise the necessary funds to return the Africans back to Sierra Leone. This was also the beginning of the Mende Mission and the American Missionary Association. The next section discusses in detail the involvement of the abolitionists with the *Amistad* Africans and their case.

The *Amistad* Christian Abolitionists: Some Friends in the Midst of an Unfriendly Environment

The *Amistad* Christian abolitionists were responsible for developing a comprehensive defense team on behalf of the captured Mende Africans. In contrast to most lawyers of Black litigants in the South who were not abolitionists, all lawyers representing the *Amistad* Africans, or supporting this cause identified as abolitionists.[46] Dwight P. Janes, an abolitionist of European descent based in Connecticut, authored the first two handwritten letters related to the *Amistad* case. Therein, he outlined how winning the *Amistad* case rested on finding an appropriate interpreter. The first letter was dated August 31, 1839, and urged Roger S. Baldwin, Esq., based in New Haven, to lead the legal representation of this case. The second letter was addressed to Rev. Joshua Leavitt, Esq. and apprised him of Janes's findings.[47]

[45] Clifton H. Johnson, "The *Amistad* Case and the Consequences in U.S. History," *Journal of the New Haven Colony Historical Society* 36, no. 2 (Spring 1990): 2.

[46] Welch, Kimberly M., *Black Litigants in the Antebellum American South*, 90. Project Muse. muse.jhu.edu/book/57346.

[47] American Missionary Association (AMA) Archives, FI 4593; 4594, respectively, *Amistad* Research Center at Tulane University, New Orleans, Louisiana, USA (hereafter cited as AMA Archives, FI 4593, The *Amistad* Research Center, New Orleans, Louisiana, USA).

From then on, Leavitt, a New York City abolitionist, consistently provided information on the events of the *Amistad* case as editor of *The Emancipator* newspaper. His documents became one of the major archival sources on the *Amistad* case and the abolitionist movement.

Janes's letters revealed his allyship establishing the core strategy of letting the captives tell their stories, which ran contrary to the pro-slavery narrative, via a skilled court interpreter. His letters also testified to his perceptions of the first public *Amistad* hearing aboard the US Navy Brig *Washington*. Reading the complicities and silences between the lines of the verbal and corporal languages, Janes felt perturbed by what he heard and saw. In his description of this court proceeding, he was the first to distinguish the nature of the captured Africans as *Bozales* versus *Ladinos* or *Mestizos*. Convinced of the positive impact of this "fortunate" occurrence in furthering the US anti-slavery cause within the context of the nineteenth century, these two letters spearheaded the genesis of the *Amistad* movement and provided hope for their liberation.

Both letters reveal insightful information about the origins of the Africans from an African-centered perspective. Janes ascertained that they spoke neither English nor Spanish, a sign that they had been only recently abducted from the African continent: they were not *Ladinos*. In the postscript to the letter from August 30, 1839, Janes exhorted Leavitt to pursue a possible material witness who could corroborate this fact. Proving it sustained the right of *Bozales* to bear arms in pursuit of their freedom, a stance upheld by many abolitionists of both African and European descent.[48] Janes's conclusions were confirmed not by a witness, however, but by the receipt of privileged information. Ruiz and Montes, assuming that Janes's light skin equalled sharing their pro-slavery views, confessed to him that the Africans had recently arrived from Africa. Janes knew that if this was proven it would reinforce the illegal nature of the capture of the Africans, provide justification for their revolt, and bring them closer to freedom. Antonio, Ferrer's enslaved sixteen-year-old, also seconded this truth:

> as near as I could understand, he said he was brot [*sic*] to Havanna when he was a very small boy. When asked how long the negroes had been there, he gave us [*sic*] to understand that they had just come. (refer to Figure 1.2)[49]

[48] Manisha Sinha, historian on abolitionism, argues that "abolitionists and even anti-slavery politicians found themselves defending the slaves' right to rebel" (Sinha, *The Slave's Cause*, 103).

[49] AMA Archives FI 4594, The *Amistad* Research Center, New Orleans, Louisiana, USA.

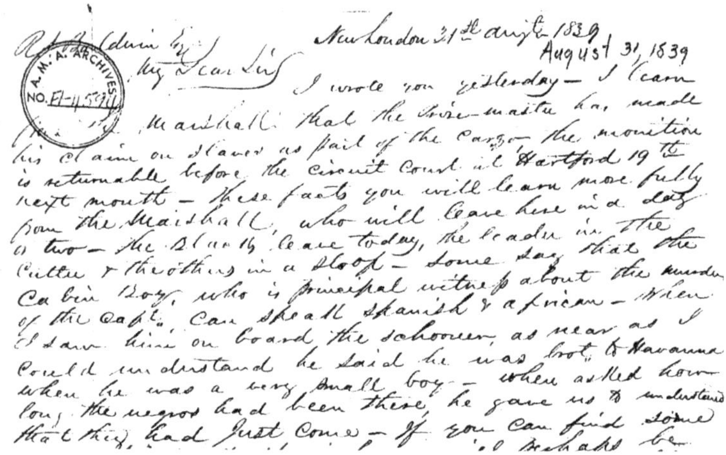
R. S. Baldwin Esq.
A. M. A. ARCHIVES NO. FI-4594
New London 31st Augt 1839
August 31, 1839
My Dear Sir
I wrote you yesterday — I learn from the Marshall that the Ship-master has made his claim on slaves as part of the Cargo — the monition is returnable before the Circuit Court at Hartford 19th next month — these facts you will learn more fully from the Marshall, who will leave here in a day or two — the Blacks leave today, the leader in the Cutter & the others in a Sloop — Some say that the Cabin Boy, who is principal witness about the murder of the Capt., can speak Spanish & African — When I saw him on board the schooner, as near as I could understand he said he was brot to Havanna when he was a very small boy — when asked how long the negros had been there, he gave us to understand that they had just come — If you can find some ... perhaps be

Figure 1.2 AMA Archives FI 4594, The *Amistad* Research Center, New Orleans, Louisiana, USA.

A sense of urgency inspired Janes to write again to Leavitt on September 2, 1839,[50] insisting on securing effective counsel for the Africans and on finding an interpreter: "Can't you find some person in N.Y. who can speak African [*sic*] and send him up to New Haven? Perhaps I overrate the importance of this affair, but I believe all the abolitionists here feel as I do."[51] Janes prophetically understood the crucial connection between having an interpreter and the historical impact of this "providential act." For this reason, he pressed Baldwin in hopes of recruiting him as one of the three attorneys-of-record. In the words of another fellow abolitionist, Mr. W. Bolles, who cosigned his last letter, stressing the importance of this case in the overall movement against slavery:

> The case of the slaves attended to in the above letter of Mr. Janes I think will involve several important questions, and I hope will receive a thorough investigation. The discussions consequent on such a trial would be highly beneficial to the cause of freedom in the States. We want something to wake the people up as well as to get justice for the sufferers.[52] (refer to Figure 1.3)

[50] AMA files date this letter "September 22, 1839." Handwriting and content analysis strongly suggest September 2, 1839, as the accurate date.
[51] AMA Archives FI 4594, The *Amistad* Research Center, New Orleans, Louisiana, USA.
[52] AMA Archives FI 4594, The *Amistad* Research Center, New Orleans, Louisiana, USA.

Aware of all the discrepancies revealed at this hearing, Janes sought to enlist sympathizers to the anti-slavery cause. The arrival of these defendants, fanned by the accounts published in local newspapers, alerted the abolitionists to the need for mobilizing and organizing in favor of the *Amistad* Africans. Abolitionists based these actions on their interpretation of the biblical calling to "love their neighbor" and "the foreigner among them."[53]

The arrival of the Mende Africans was timely; the "[USA] was experiencing a widespread reform movement that, on the surface at least, exalted the common man [*sic*] and emphasized equality of opportunity."[54] Part of this reform involved coming to terms with the two key positions against slavery—that of the abolitionists and that of the anti-slavery supporters. Both agreed on the elimination of the institution of slavery. However, their loyalties and methods for achieving this goal differed. As foreseen by Janes, the *Amistad* case prompted those along the anti-slavery spectrum to join forces with the abolitionists. Sinha expounds on the coalescing effect of the *Amistad* case as envisioned by Janes, Bolles, and others: "The revolt . . . not only galvanized the abolition movement but also, because of the protracted legal proceedings, became a forum for abolitionists to make their case against the national recognition of slavery and to draw attention to the prolific illegal African slave trade."[55] Notes accompanying the financial offerings on behalf of the Africans demonstrate this fusing effect of the pro-*Amistad* organizing among the different factions of the movement. Inside an envelope enclosing three dollars for the cause, a handwritten note by Warrimer read:

> P.S.: You are aware that I am not an Abolitionist in the popular sense of the term, yes, I hope slavery will soon cease in the U.S. and throughout the world. I think the slave owners have rights as well as the slaves; and that compensation (at least in part) should be made to the owners; and for myself I would cheerfully pay my proportion of a tax to free the slaves in the South at once. . . . But I do not intend to argue the question, as I fear we shall not agree.[56]

[53] Unfortunately, at the same time, their theological–liberation actions resulted in their imperial-Christian pursuits to bring the Gospel to Africa, to Christianize the incarcerated Africans, and to assimilate them culturally and linguistically, a common practice among Christians that combined contradictory and racist outcomes. This will be discussed in other chapters.

[54] Jones, *Mutiny on the Amistad*, 31.

[55] Sinha, *The Slave's Cause*, 407.

[56] AMA Archives FI 4622, The *Amistad* Research Center, New Orleans, Louisiana, USA.

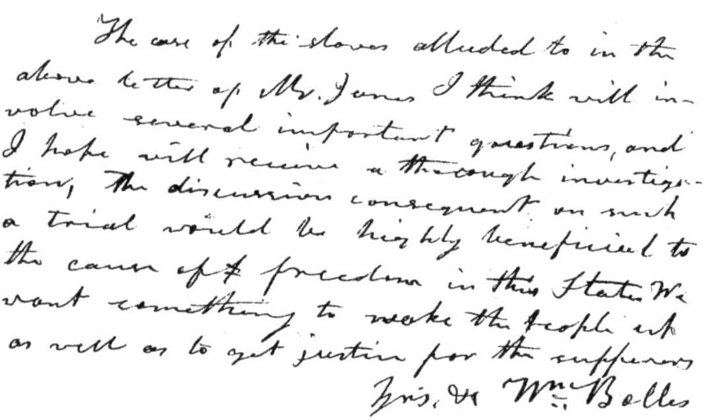
The case of the slaves alluded to in the
above letter of Mr. Janes I think will in-
volve several important questions, and
I hope will receive a thorough investiga-
tion, the discussion consequent on such
a trial would be highly beneficial to
the cause of freedom in this State. We
want something to wake the people up
as well as to get justice for the sufferers
Yrs. &c Wm. Bolles

Figure 1.3 "Janes to Leavitt." AMA Archives FI 4594, The *Amistad* Research Center, New Orleans, Louisiana, USA.

Warrimer summoned the courage to identify himself as a signatory. Others preferred anonymity as a cautionary measure against repressive actions from pro-slavery followers. A note, this time, evinced how this case and the public and religious narratives drew anti-slavery followers on the fringes of the abolitionist movement. Though he was not an abolitionist, the author of the following note expressed a slight inclination toward the abolitionist movement enough to summon his financial support:

Anonymous
Sept 6, 1839
Enclosing $2 for the Africans
One who is almost persuaded to be an abolitionist.
"May you prosper."

Even when the two bands were inclined to side with the *Amistad* Africans, the abolitionists and anti-slavery camps definitely disagreed in their approaches and beliefs. Both shared the moral conviction that slavery, a social evil, should come to an end. But the methods for achieving this exemplified their opposing views. Warrimer's note accentuated this difference. The anti-slavery movement believed in remuneration for slaveholders in compensation for releasing their enslaved population. They claimed that this action generated a "profit loss." The loss was much greater for the millions of humans losing their lives, wages, health, language, and a truncated dignified quality of life. Abolitionists adamantly opposed a financial trade in exchange for freedom, taking a more radical posture. These activists, however, did not contemplate compensating the enslaved for their generations of forced labor. Warrimer's citation exemplifies the anti-slavery position, which predominated when Great Britain compensated slaveowners in order to abolish slavery. Later, the 1817 treaty between Great Britain and Spain also compensated the Spanish Empire for signing this treaty in an attempt to abolish its international slave trade. Yet, as the saying goes: "*quien hace la ley hace la trampa*"—those who make laws create the pathway to violate them. Spain's involvement in the transatlantic-enslaving trade increased with the signing of the 1817 and 1835 anti-transatlantic-enslaving treaties with England. But they were not alone. The USA, along with other imperial nations, actively joined forces with Spain in this transatlantic endeavor.

Though US abolitionists had existed back in the eighteenth century in smaller numbers, their growth increased at the juncture of a reformist movement and a religious fervor after the 1830s. Still, they remained a relative minority, estimated to be composed of around 200,000 people.[57] Reformers wanted greater educational opportunities for young people, more rights for women and for those suffering from mental illnesses, and greater assistance for the poor.[58] At the same time, churchgoers increasingly wanted to eliminate sin and build a nation pleasing to God. The abolitionists took advantage of this moment to appeal to the reformists for their support.

"Christian abolitionists" became a synonym, almost pejoratively, for abolitionists; sometimes they were even called ultra-abolitionists. The "Christian" adjective added to their name highlighted how their theology and scriptural interpretation steered their anti-slavery beliefs. The abolitionists proposed a radical end to slavery in contrast to the gradual end promoted by the anti-slavery, many of whom were also Christian. For them, slavery was an abomination, a sin that contravened Christian doctrines and corrupted the moral fiber of society. Therefore, the abolitionists criticized their anti-slavery counterparts because:

> Even in the states in which slavery is not tolerated, the great majority of the people are its apologists and supporters. Many, while they acknowledge that slavery is an evil, seem quite unconscious that to keep

[57] Zeinert, *The Amistad Slave Revolt*, 37.
[58] Zeinert, *The Amistad Slave Revolt*, 36.

> men [*sic*] in bondage is a sin. They pity the unfortunate slaveholder but have no sympathy for the wretched slave.[59]

A religious abolitionist tract of the time called slave keepers or slaveholders, apostates.[60] As a sin, its end was deemed to be imminent. To grow internal and external support, abolitionists formed associations that solidified their objectives. Disseminating information through the printed press, and especially newspapers, served as a key and efficient medium for feeding the movement, gaining adherents, and calling for action. In 1831, *The Liberator*, a newspaper name that echoes the name of the "Great Liberator" of Latin America, the General Simón Bolívar, printed its first issue.[61] In 1833, the American Anti-Slavery Society (AASS) was formed along with its newspaper, *The Emancipator*, for a second time since 1820. In 1827 and 1837, two African American newspapers began to publish their voices and vision in the struggle to abolish US African slavery: *Freedom's Journal*[62] and *The Colored American*, respectively, both printed in New York City. Additionally, dozens of anti-slavery societies sprung up as organizing tools through the Northeast and other northern cities, including the Massachusetts General Colored Association in 1826 and the numerous female anti-slavery societies

[59] "The Abolitionist: Or Record of the New England Anti-Slavery Society (1833–1833)," 1, no. 1 (January 1833): 1, https://www.proquest.com/docview/124719797/879CB3F8A0194B90PQ/2?accountid=1517 (accessed through ProQuest. July 24, 2023).

[60] Benjamin Lay, *All Slavekeepers that Keep the Innocent in Bondage, Apostates* (Philadelphia: Printed for the author, 1737), Pdf, https://www.loc.gov/item/66038906/.

[61] *The Liberator* began circulating in 1831, one year after the passing of "The Great Liberator," widely known as the General Bolívar in transatlantic abolitionist circles. In that same year, his memoirs were published in London and circulated around the world, entering the libraries of many activists engaged in the liberation struggles from enslavement or colonization from European countries. Given the historical proximity of Bolívar's death and the birth of *The Liberator*, it is possible that this newspaper title was inspired by this transatlantic liberationist.

Bolívar's name also came up during the *Amistad* trials. In his testimony, John Ferry—the *Amistad* interpreter—stated that Gen. Bolívar liberated him at La Güaira. While it was not until 1851 that Black slavery was abolished through the Gran Colombia territory, as early as 1809 Bolívar attempted to eliminate the enslaving practice when "the Junta abolished . . . the imposition upon slaves." However, this year coincides with the approximate year of Ferry's birth. In 1816, a decree promoted freedom for the enslaved who joined the Bolívar army, following a promise Bolívar made to Alexandre Pétion, Haiti's president. This leaves us with two additional dates for consideration: 1821, when Bolívar liberated his slaves from his *Hacienda*, and 1824, when an emancipation decree yielded such a commotion that it made Bolívar seek refuge in Haiti. Any one of these last three decrees paved the way for Ferry's historic linguistic contribution to the lives of the *Amistad* Africans.

[62] O. Alexander, *Freedom's Journal (1827–1829)*. BlackPast.org. (January 4, 2011), https://www.blackpast.org/african-american-history/freedom-s-journal-1827-1829/.

formed by white Europeans, People of Color, or Black women abolitionists, for instance, the Utica Female Anti-Slavery Society and the Philadelphia Female Anti-Slavery Society.

However, it seems that some abolitionist and anti-slavery movements suffered from a single-track organization emphasis, lacking the ability to support parallel struggles and ask questions that would unmask their systemic shared nature. Arthur Tappan, along with others, adamantly advocated for the freedom of the Mende Africans. At the same time, though, he vehemently opposed women speaking and voting in the AASS. His objection eventually provoked a fissure in the movement that created the American and Foreign Anti-Slavery Society in 1840. This myopic perspective prompted activists to organize around single issues, instead of seeing the intersectionality of similar oppressive matters and committing to support different marginalized groups simultaneously. A diversity of opinions within the movement promoted the full integration of colored communities, their right to vote, interracial marriages, rightful employment, and women's active participation. Others pleaded for a limited extension of these rights. To date, *Amistad*-related archives don't attest to abolitionists being engaged in the land advocacy and sovereignty of the First Peoples in the early years of the USA republic.[63] I speculate as to why. Abolitionist pursuits echoed imperial expansionism within and without the USA. In order to invade other people's lands, geographic usurpation was a prerequisite that also involved the violation of their human rights. All of this stood in contradiction to their liberating views in regard to slavery, which largely explains their absenteeism for the Native American causes. A pro single-focus cause breeds other limitations to effecting change. Being against one injustice does not automatically build a path to a reality free of all oppression. This monotonal objective also had many ramifications after the nineteenth-century emancipation process. Abolitionist and anti-slavery activists lacked an integration plan for those freed from enslavement. Others in both movements favored repatriation as the best alternative for African-descent people instead of struggling for integration into the US society. Without an encompassing holistic plan, similar oppressive conditions proved to be an obstacle for the enslaved to thrive and rebuild their lives.

[63] Khalil Anthony Johnson Jr.'s research uncovers the names of other nineteenth-century abolitionists committed to both causes. From his paper, "Rev. Samuel Hopkins and the 18th Century Missionary Origins of the Federal Indian Boarding Schools," read at the Forty-Fourth Annual Meeting of the Society for Historians of the Early American Republic, July 14, 2023.

By September 4, 1839, a week after the Mende Africans arrived in New England, the AASS formed the *Amistad* Committee to enlist supporters from all parts of the religious and political spectrum on behalf of this forced-immigrant group now incarcerated in New Haven jails. Simeon Jocelyn, Joshua Leavitt, and Lewis Tappan, staunch abolitionists, founded this committee. The committee's announcement was published in newspapers, initially in *The Emancipator* and *British Emancipator* and later spreading to others. Their announcement stated their desire to collect funds to ensure the rights of the Mende defendants, starting with employing "interpreters, able counsel, and tak[ing] all necessary means to secure the rights of the accused."[64]

Faith-based and political organizing for the abolitionists came with a cost. Abolitionists who were criticized for their radical measures suffered persecution. William Lloyd Garrison, the founder of the AASS and the newspaper *The Liberator*, was almost hanged in Boston; Elijah Lovejoy met his death when he insisted on printing articles in support of the liberation of the enslaved; Prudence Crandall followed her vocation to teach Black students even though the school where she taught was set on fire because of her commitment; and for the heads of the Tappan brothers, a $100,000 reward was issued, payable anywhere in the South.[65] The cost was also paid with the lives of the brown and Black people who rallied against slavery and imperializing enterprises, fighting for their rightful place in society within and outside the USA. Abolitionism began with them: the overwhelmingly nameless people who resisted at all stages of the enslaving journey. The *Amistad* Africans, their interpreters, and their translators joined this resistance movement hoping for concrete changes. Despite the hostile environment in Congress thwarting the possibility of bringing forth to Congress any anti-slavery discussion, the *Amistad* case provided an opportunity "to rally support for the Abolitionists' causes," for "having moral rectitude [to] influence legal justice," and for "all to unite under a single banner."[66]

The success of "the Abolitionists' movement [in the USA] lay in making real for people in Britain and America that the ships carrying slaves were pervasive and utterly instrumental terror, which was indeed its defining feature."[67] The *Amistad* afforded them just such a chance to inject into the discussion a first-hand testimony of the alarming truths of the enslaving process: from capture to the Middle Passage, to landing in Spanish colonies

64 *The Emancipator*," September 5, 1839.
65 Zeinert, *The Amistad Slave Revolt*, 42–5.
66 Osagie, *The Amistad Revolt*, 8–9.
67 Rediker, *The Slave Ship*, 8.

and the newly created empire. It was hoped their testimonies would help to shake the legal and religious foundations of the institution of slavery to accelerate the end of slavery in the USA. They needed a catalyst—"a dramatic event . . . to awaken their countrymen [*sic*] to the sordid nature of slavery"[68]—precisely what the *Amistad* offered for "such a time as [that] one."[69]

Most leaders of the abolitionist *Amistad* movement, across the racialized spectrum, had received formal training as ministers and attorneys. They were cognizant of racism as a pillar for slavery, though not all agreed on issues of equality and on what steps to follow to dismantle this institution. The enslavement chain was complex, involving the complicity of some African nations, partially as a result of their internalized oppression. Racism and the justification of slavery, in this historical period, rested on the principle that darker skin pigmentation predisposed people to subjugate themselves for the profitable benefit of others with lighter skin tones. Those supporting this racialized financial system believed that people with darker skin tones were less than human and inferior in intellectual abilities. Though these racist attitudes were not resolved in the actions and narratives of those opposing slavery, including the abolitionists, this latter group hoped that if they "demonstrated that color was not a legitimate obstacle to a person's natural right to freedom, they would lay the basis for a major assault on slavery that might vindicate their larger aims."[70] Something else characterized them; they were mostly men.

Women's leadership in the public sphere of the abolitionist movement, inside or outside of the church, appears limited. The women's issue, inexplicably, divided the anti-slavery movement. The Garrisonians promoted equal participation of women of all backgrounds in all spheres, in opposition to Lewis Tappan, who vehemently oppossed any women's participation and right to vote. Tappan received and sent most of the *Amistad* letters up to this point in the narrative, but very few women featured as the recipients or signatories on those letters. Perhaps the names of women were omitted for protection or the letters containing their names vanished. Notwithstanding, their support was palpable throughout the *Amistad* case. Lucretia Mott, an abolitionist and feminist leader, met with Baldwin and his daughter in Philadelphia, Pennsylvania, USA, to talk about the case, a stop he made on his way to Washington, D.C., to file a dismissal petition at the Supreme

[68] Jones, *Mutiny on the Amistad*, 35.
[69] An allusion to a poignant dialogue in the Book of Esther in the Hebrew Scriptures where her uncle challenges her to intervene on behalf of their people and to use her privileged position in the King's court for "such a time as this."
[70] Jones, *Mutiny on the Amistad*, 32.

Court.[71] Mrs. Emily Baldwin and Elizabeth Baldwin, their daughter, corresponded about this encounter and shared their own views on the legal arguments, merits, and significance of the *Amistad* case. Dozens of women of color and white women sent their offerings to the *Amistad* Committee. Yet, women seem disproportionately unnamed in the *Amistad* movement.

US African Americans in the *Amistad* Case

A dozen or so abolitionists of European descent actively led and organized on behalf of the *Amistad* Africans, but they were not the only ones. US African American abolitionists also advocated for their freedom in substantial ways. A New York City newspaper, *The Colored American*—edited by Charles B. Ray, the sole proprietor, and Samuel Cornish[72]—regularly published articles about the status of the Africans, the progress of the case, and collections taken. US African American churches in New England welcomed the *Amistad* Africans to speak about their liberation journey after the trial. They also organized fundraising events on their behalf during the trial and raised financial support to fund their trip back to Africa, which began the Mende Mission. The Reverends James W. C. Pennington and Joel Hawes preached about their return to Africa in fundraising events. Christopher L. Webber, Pennington's biographer, surmises that it is very likely that Pennington moved from New York City to Hartford, Connecticut, anticipating that he would offer his support to the *Amistad* Mendes.[73]

The September 14 issue of *The Colored American* republished the announcement on the creation of the *Amistad* Committee soliciting "interpreters and able counsel." From the early stages of the *Amistad* saga, US African Americans financially endorsed their liberation from captivity. In the following issue, the newspaper published a note from abolitionists Jocelyn, Tappan, and Leavitt in acknowledgment of the receipt of $84.25 from these African American churches in support of the "sacred cause" (see Figure 1.5). As a result of financial challenges and other political issues, however, the newspaper took a hiatus from toward the end of 1839 to March 1840.

71 "Letter by Elizabeth Baldwin," The Baldwin Family Papers (MS 55), Manuscripts and Archives, Yale University Library.

72 Rev. Cornish published, in 1820, the first known African American newspaper, *Freedom's Journal*.

73 Christopher L. Webber, *American to the Backbone: The Life of James W. C. Pennington, the Fugitive Slave Who Became One of the First Black Abolitionists* (New York: Pegasus Books, 2011), 125.

Once reincorporated, Ray continued to publish information on the *Amistad* judicial proceedings.

These US African American communities "continued to send money to the *Amistad* Committee . . . providing defense lawyers for the Africans and taking care of their physical needs."[74] Black women's participation in the life of the church—via collections, coordinating refreshments and meals, assisting public events, or gathering clothing for the jailed—should be considered abolitionist acts on behalf of the *Amistad* Africans. In December of 1840, the Colored Citizens of Cincinnati sent $90 to the committee. Dozens of women identified in the financial records by the prefixes "Mrs., Miss, and widows," named and unnamed—to avoid possible reprisals—contributed to this cause from January to December of 1840.[75] Funds from people who came from all walks of life and US geographical locations were sent to the different *Amistad* committees or anti-slavery societies from as far as Michigan, Ohio, Vermont, and New Hampshire, especially in the year 1840, in preparation for the appeal and the Africans' possible return to Africa.

An important contribution to the *Amistad* story came from Robert Purvis, Esq., a well-to-do Black abolitionist from Philadelphia who commissioned painter Nathaniel Jocelyn to paint a portrait of "Cinque."[76] Nathaniel was Simeon Jocelyn's brother, one of the three founders of the *Amistad* Committee. Purvis hired a prominent white artist to memorialize the figure of Sengbe Pieh, the leader of the *Amistad* revolt, as a "symbol of black resistance and moral fortitude." The painting was unveiled weeks before the Supreme Court began deliberations in the appeals process of the *Amistad* case to build public pressure and visibility. Counsel Purvis kept the painting in his house, which was a stop on the Underground Railroad. This painting, an emblem of resilience and triumph, inspired Madison Washington to lead the rebellion on board the Creole schooner. Washington stayed at Purvis's house on his way to the South to free his family after escaping from slavery

[74] Jessica A. Gresko, "Coming to the Aid of the *Amistad* Africans," In *African American Connecticut Explored*, ed. Elizabeth M. Normen (Middletown: Wesleyan University Press, 2014), 129.

[75] Someone by the name of "Sarah Parker" appears as one of the donors. There is a likelihood that it may refer to the Salem Black abolitionist Sarah Parker Remond who eventually moved to London to pursue a medical degree denied to her in the USA and later settled in Italy, where she was a very influential person.

[76] Kim A. Silva, Sign Language historian and interpreter, has led The *Amistad* Tour sponsored by the Farmington Congregational Church in Farmington, CT. After the Supreme Court decision, the *Amistad* Africans lived in Farmington, a stop on the Underground Railroad, hosted by this church and its members until their return to Sierra Leone, Africa. Silva has written on the linguistic connection between the *Amistad* story and Sign Language interpreting, which informed this research.

Figure 1.4 "Cinque," painting by Nathaniel Jocelyn, part of the permanent collection at the New Haven Museum. The original is a color painting.

himself. Looking at the painting hung on the wall, he learned about the victorious *Amistad* rebellion.[77] In the painting, Sengbe resembled a Greco-Roman deity, which aimed to contradict the racist perceptions undermining Africans' intelligence, leadership, and social standing in a slavery-centered world. Purvis's artistic commission pursued a racialized, humane depiction of Sengbe and the Africans, more palatable to people of European descent who were brought up with this venerated historical mythology, in hopes of enlisting more of them to the *Amistad* cause. Replicas of this painting were sold at $1 apiece to raise funds for the *Amistad* Committee and the liberation of the Mende Africans.[78] In May of 1841, Purvis offered "to engage to provide comfortable quarters"[79] [emphasis in original] to provide lodging for the liberated African-Mende in their visit to Philadelphia. Purvis also assured the committee that he thought that "thousands of colored folks would give 25¢ to them."[80] Palpable support came from US African American churches to the *Amistad* Africans. They supported this cause as a sign of the liberation to come for those chained by slavery and racism. It was a beacon of a new kind of relation between people of different ethnic backgrounds in the newly formed USA (refer to Figure 1.4).

77 Richard J. Powell, "How Cinque Was Painted," *The Washington Post*, December 28, 1997, https://www.washingtonpost.com/archive/lifestyle/style/1997/12/28/how-cinque-was-painted/64bcb5bd-bae9-4db4-9be8-52352c21a829/?utm_term=.c9b94ff237e2.

78 Quarles, *Black Abolitionists*, 177.

79 AMA Archives FI 4998, The *Amistad* Research Center, New Orleans, Louisiana, USA.

80 AMA Archives FI 4998, The *Amistad* Research Center, New Orleans, Louisiana, USA.

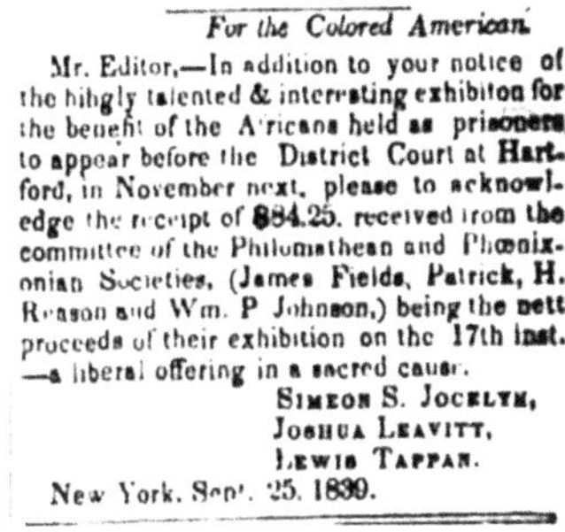

For the Colored American.

Mr. Editor,—In addition to your notice of the hihgly talented & interesting exhibiton for the benefit of the Africans held as prisoners to appear before the District Court at Hartford, in November next, please to acknowledge the receipt of $84.25. received from the committee of the Philomathean and Phoenixonian Societies, (James Fields, Patrick, H. Reason and Wm. P Johnson,) being the nett proceeds of their exhibition on the 17th inst.—a liberal offering in a sacred cause.

SIMEON S. JOCELYN,
JOSHUA LEAVITT,
LEWIS TAPPAN.

New York, Sept. 25, 1839.

Figure 1.5 *The Colored American*, September 28, 1839.

Additionally, during the early period of William Lloyd Garrison's newspaper, *The Liberator,* 75 percent of his contributors were of African descent.[81] His publication intentionally offered a platform for their voices on behalf of their freedom from slavery and racism. Garrison also supported women's right to speak and to vote and often published articles by Black and women writers, whether identifiable by their own names or not. These included Charles Lenox, the brother of Sarah Parker Remond.

Abolitionist Theological Principles

Across racial lines, US abolitionists' theological precepts fuelled their movement. Christian abolitionists, professing radical biblical hermeneutics, "were the most fiery group among the antislavery people."[82] An anti-slavery hermeneutical lens differentiated their biblical text selection from their pro-slavery counterparts who gravitated toward texts that reinforced enslaving ideologies. In fact, both sides shared a similar scriptural approach: both used as their compass their ideological beliefs to find biblical passages that would justify what they already believed in. For the faith-based pro-slavery sector, a prominently pro-slavery Bible represented an easy task selecting slavery-prone narratives between the Hebrew Scripture and the New Testament.

[81] Donald M. Jacobs, "William Lloyd Garrison's Liberator and Boston's Blacks, 1830–1865," *The New England Quarterly* 44, no. 2 (1971): 260–1, https://doi.org/10.2307/364529. According to Donald M. Jacobs, leading Black and wealthy abolitionists, such as James Forten from Philadelphia, and James G. Barbadoes, John Hilton, and other important leaders in Boston, sent large monetary donations for the printing of this paper. In 1834, 75 percent of the paper's subscriptions came from the Afro-descendant communities in Boston, New York, and Philadelphia. Shirley Yee notes that Barbadoes was responsible for the subscription office of *The Liberator* (66).

[82] Kromer, *Amistad: The Slave Uprising*, 41.

By contrast, their anti-slavery counterpart faced a greater challenge as they perused through the Bible. The Christian abolitionists leaned on Jesus's preferential option to equate human rights with divine law, calling to accountability of the powers that be, organizing in support of those views, and the fundamental principle of the US Constitution that "all men [*sic*] were created equal." Slavery as a sin unto God, unequivocally, stood against the values of the kingdom of God and thwarted the manifestation of a spiritual evolution. This group was convinced that slavery stood against human nature and the Will of God.[83] Some of their theological writings quote the successful escape of the Israelites from Egypt in the book of Exodus; or the text in Galatians affirming that in Christ Jesus there is no "free or slave"; or the well-known verse in the Gospel "love your neighbor as yourself." In their assemblies, abolitionists approved motions against allowing slaveholders' participation, entry into churches, or supporting them in any way. They did not shy away from condemning their actions, especially those who professed the Christian faith.

Unfortunately, with the same angst, abolitionists launched their evangelizing practices with the Mende captives. Their missiology responded to a theological framework which voiced Christian, linguistic, and ethnic superiority. In an effort to increase support from those on the fringes of the anti-slavery movement and the public at large, abolitionists recruited an array of volunteers as English and Sign Language teachers: students from the Yale seminary; and the oral language interpreters, John Ferry and James Covey. English instruction for the African prisoners, along with Christian indoctrination, occupied four to five hours of their time every day. For them, language and Bible learning went hand in hand to make the captives look "civilized" while advancing their African mission field. It was not an either-or situation. English language could have equipped the Africans with greater agency to tell their truth. Through the voice of an interpreter, the Mende leader expressed: "Cinque says he wants to learn the language and will apply himself. He says, 'if you were in my country and could not talk with anybody, you would want to learn our language; I want to learn yours'"[84] For him, it was a matter of hospitality, survival, and linguistic courtesy in a situation of power imbalances. As part of a US linguistic minority, Cinque's circumstances also forced him to add another language to those he already

[83] Despite the contradictions in the North, this geographical region yielded a fertile ground for the movement to thrive and to strategize. Newspapers such as *The Colored American*, *The Liberator*, *The Emancipator*, and *The Congregationalist* sustained a platform for them to theologize and to keep the readers abreast of anti-slavery pursuits at home and abroad.

[84] AMA Archives FI 4660, The *Amistad* Research Center, New Orleans, Louisiana, USA.

spoke to maneuver his surroundings. English and the Mende language did not find themselves on an equitable playing field. Fighting for their rights should not have required Christian conversion, only the conviction of their right to human rights by their supporters and allies. Acting on Christian anti-slavery principles should not have been entangled with forcing Africans into this triune faith or English-language acquisition, which carried imperial and colonizing overtones. After two years in the Northern states, Cinque preferred to retell his story of liberation in his vernacular, Mende.

After the release of the *Amistad* Africans, the abolitionists selfishly delayed sending them back to Africa as a means to further mobilize their movement. The ruling upheld by the US Supreme Court from the lower court made the US executive branch responsible for returning the Africans to their homeland. However, they did not follow through with this mandate. The US president at the time, along with the secretary of state, had previously assured the Spanish Empire via its Washington, DC, minister that they would transport the *Amistad* Africans back to Cuba. They were confident that the Supreme Court would overturn the ruling of the trial court.[85] In a surprising turn of events in favor of the *Amistad* Mendeans, it was left to the USA-based abolitionists to raise the financial funds for the return to Africa aboard the *Gentleman*. While this task offered greater security that they would be returned to freedom and not to bondage, it also provided the Christian activists with more time to organize at the expense of the Africans who yearned to be home.

With these theological underpinnings, Christian abolitionists' leadership sought a trustworthy court interpreter among their faithful networks. Despite the Africans' willingness to learn the English language, their need for translation and interpreting remained consistent from the time of their arrival until after the *Amistad* trial ended in January 1840.

The Abolitionist Movement in Cuba

Wherever enslaved people lived, there were transatlantic abolitionist movements seeking to eradicate this horrific institution. The enslaved, on sea or land, were the first ones to rebel in multiple ways. Previously enslaved women, men, and children, especially those who were ill-treated despite manumission, were eager to lead liberating revolts, even though they were

[85] Legajo 1272, no. 49909: 31–2, Fondo Gobierno Superior Civil, Archivo Nacional de La Habana, Cuba.

often only partially successful, or their efforts led to torturous consequences.[86] Other non-African people, moved by humanist ideas or religious principles, also joined forces. Within this larger context, the abolitionist movement in the Southern Hemisphere combined various pro-independent aims. Those charged with conspiracy in favor of independence from Spain or other European empires also advocated for an end to human enslavement. After Haiti's independence from France and Bolívar's initial decrees, beginning in the 1820s the region experienced how Argentina, Chile, Bolivia, and Uruguay abolished slavery as they gained their independence from Spain.[87]

Cuba, a Spanish colony,[88] delayed abolishing slavery until late in the 1800s. However, slave uprisings, *criollos*'s[89] conspiracies to overthrow the colonial government, and abolitionist's activities abounded during the first half of the nineteenth century.[90] Acts of Black resistance[91] and *cimarrón*[92] activities proliferated in the Caribbean and Latin America. The enslaved arduously manifested their unwavering commitment to change their inhumane conditions. Some of the most notable revolts during this period were: *la Conspiración de Aponte* (1811–12), *la Rebelión de Guamacaro* (1825), and in 1843, *la Conspiración de la Escalera*.[93] The *cimarrones* effectively organized to

[86] See the research by Cuban historians, such as Gloria García Rodríguez, *Conspiraciones y Revueltas: La actividad política de los negros en Cuba (1790–1845)* (Santiago de Cuba: Editorial Oriente, 2003) ISBN 978-959-11-0389-5 and Gloria García Rodríguez, *La esclavitud desde la esclavitud: La visión de los siervos* (México: Centro de Investigación Científica Ingeniero Jorge L. Tamayo, 1996), ISBN 968-29-9097-1.

[87] María Julia de Vinatea, "Las Aboliciones de la Esclavitud en Iberoamérica: El Caso Peruano (1812–1854)," *Revista Historia de la Educación Latinoamericana* 16, no. 23 (2014): 187–204, https://doi.org/10.19053/01227238.3069.

[88] Cuba and Puerto Rico were the last two Spanish-colonized islands to abolish slavery.

[89] According to Garcilaso de la Vega in *Commentarios reales*, as cited by Ada Ferrer in her article "Unfixing Race," the term "criollo" was created by the African-descent people to identify one of them born in the Americas. From there, it evolved to include both Spaniards and Africans born in the Americas. (K. Burns, "Unfixing Race," in *Histories of Race and Racism: The Andes and Mesoamerica from Colonial Times to the Present*, ed. L. Gotkowitz (Duke University Press, 2011), 61. https://doi.org/10.2307/j.ctv11hpnf1.5).

[90] Jorge Castellanos e Isabel Castellanos, *Cultural Afrocubana 1: El negro en Cuba (1492–1844)* (Miami: Ediciones Universal, 1988), 187.

[91] The Chinese also resisted the enslaving context and practices, as well as the Irish, who were brought to "Whiten" the racialized equation in Cuba.

[92] *Cimarrones* denotes previously enslaved people through the Americas that escaped their enslaving condition to create independent communities known as *palenques* or *quilombos*. Research suggests that the word "*cimarrón*" derives from "*simara*" an Arawak word meaning arrow. (José Arrom, "Cimarrón," in Gabriel de Avilez Rocha, "Maroons in the Montes: Toward a Political Ecology of Marronage in the Sixteenth-Century Caribbean," in *Early Modern Black Diaspora Studies*, ed. C. L. Smith (2018), 19, https://doi.org/10.1007/978-3-319-76786-4_2.

[93] Osvaldo Manuel Álvarez Torres, "La conspiración de La Escalera: Una visión histórico-jurídica," *Justicia y Derecho* 10 (Enero-Diciembre 2022): 17–18.

free themselves and others and to create remote communities, although their efforts may have been thwarted. The abolitionist movements in Cuba—and also in Puerto Rico—were not able to secure the privileged spaces occupied by their counterparts in the northern USA. Neither were they as prolific in their publications, through which they attempted to enliven the movement during the early part of this century. Yet, they did exist.[94] On May 18, 1841, a representative to the Spanish Crown who was updating the local Cuban authorities on the status of the *Amistad* case informed them that it was likely that the abolitionists would liberate the African captives imprisoned "in a section of the English-American territory where the abolitionists exert a lot of influence as we have seen."[95] This letter did not deny the presence of the Cuban abolitionist movement, but remarked on the high level of influence in contrast to the movement in the Spanish-speaking Caribbean colonies. Later that year, in the months of July, September, and November, Royal Decrees—*Reales Órdenes*—were issued to hinder the proliferation of literature promulgating "abolitionist ideas that may be circulated among the people of color of this island" who "were always keen to rebel."[96] These official orders speak to the literacy and resilience of the free non-White communities that were displeased with the status quo. The second decree informed the Maritime, Commerce, and Governing authorities that newspapers "full of anti-slavery ideology from *Haytí*"[97] were being trafficked. The decree forbade vessels from "Santo Domingo"[98] from anchoring along the coast and asked for increased vigilance in the region. These anti-slavery decrees are evidence of the existence of percolating abolitionist forces.

The *Amistad* rebellion contributed to anti-slavery momentum both in the USA, Cuba, and very likely beyond. Afraid of the impact on the enslaved, the freed people of color, and the Cuban reformists, the Spanish Crown made every attempt to squelch the success of the *Amistad* movement. Word must have spread in the Caribbean islands of this successful rebellion that ended in liberation and the return to the African motherland, instead of execution.

[94] In 1852, Andrés Avelino de Orihuela translated Stowe's influential novel, *Uncle Tom's Cabin*, in a way in which translation was used as tool of anti-slavery resistance in the Spanish-speaking world. Orihuela also wrote a Cuban-based anti-slavery novel *El Sol de Jesús del Monte*, also published in 1852. See the translation of this novel by David Luis-Brown, *The Sun of Jesús del Monte: A Cuban antislavery novel* (2022).

[95] Legajo 1272, no. 49909, Fondo Gobierno Superior Civil, Archivo Nacional de La Habana, Cuba. Translated by the author from the Spanish original.

[96] Legajo 1272, no. 49909, Fondo Gobierno Superior Civil, Archivo Nacional de La Habana, Cuba. Translated by the author from the Spanish original.

[97] Legajo 41, no. 16, Fondo Asuntos Políticos, Archivo Nacional de La Habana, Cuba. Honoring the spelling found in the archival source.

[98] What is known today as the Dominican Republic.

Through the enslaved communities of Captain Ferrer, the enslavers Ruiz and Montes, and eavesdropping, news of the *Amistad* event also must have travelled via the enslaved crew of the Cuban *Golondrina* Schooner,[99] who were ordered to seize the *Amistad* Schooner and arrest the *Amistad* Africans. The *Amistad* event nurtured in many hopes of liberation in the US and Spanish territories.

Court Interpreting in the Nineteenth Century in Spain, Colonized Territories, and the USA

For centuries, Spain had vast experience in hiring interpreters within and outside of courts. By the fifteenth century, Catholic royalty under King Carlos V had institutionalized a means of responding to the multilingual and multicultural nature of the empire, which demanded the translation of diplomatic correspondence and experienced linguists in negotiations. By the sixteenth century, the courts in the Spanish Empire enacted laws establishing court-interpreting standards. This need fostered the creation of the *Secretaría de Interpretación de Lenguas*, known today as the *Oficina de Interpretación de Lenguas* (The Office of Language Interpretation) within the Ministry of Foreign Affairs, a necessary pioneering step at the time.[100] *La secretaría* translated official correspondence, such as peace and war treaties, agreements, and royal decrees.[101] As the empire expanded, so did the types of religious and top secret documents in Turkish, Arabic, German, Flemish, Portuguese, Greek, and Persian, to mention only a few.[102] Although not listed as one of the official languages, English must have featured as well, considering the diplomatic workings and international–imperial relations between England, Spain, and the USA during this period.

[99] This represented one of the various vessels sent by the Spanish maritime division to intercept the *Amistad* vessel. Despite all efforts, the results were fruitless, as these ships only explored the coastal region, not imagining that the plan involved sailing northward and eastward.

[100] Ingrid Cáceres-Würsig, "Breve historia de la secretaría de interpretación de lenguas," *Meta: Journal des traducteurs* 49, no. 3 (2004): 624.

[101] Cáceres-Würsig, "Breve historia de la secretaría de interpretación de lenguas," 610. Latin and French represented the written *lingua francas*, while Italian and Spanish became the oral *lingua francas*.

[102] Native People's languages are missing from this list, a crucial mishap. This fact points toward the lack of diplomatic acknowledgment and international standing by the colonizing Spanish Empire to those initially inhabiting the many lands now being usurped.

On this other side of the Atlantic, from its genesis, the DOS established diplomatic offices in many countries, including Spain, Gran Colombia, and Venezuela. John Forsyth, for instance, served as foreign minister in Madrid prior to occupying the post as DOS secretary during the early *Amistad* period. The DOS was in charge of the Spanish to English diplomatic correspondence through this case. Inherently, Forsyth represented another Spanish/English bilingual officer in this story's thread. Translation of *Amistad* letters from English to Spanish for the perusal of the Spanish authorities were commissioned to the personnel for the Spanish diplomatic offices in New York, Boston, and Washington, D.C. In contrast, interpretation services for the Spanish nationals involved in the *Amistad* judicial case or Antonio, the cabin boy, were not provided by either the Spanish diplomatic offices, the DOS, or the courts. Instead, Ruiz and Montes pleaded through the newspaper their undoubtful right to the *Amistad* cargo and Africans aboard to the Spanish audiences, while criticizing the abilities of the Mende interpreter and the veracity of their interpretation.

As early as the end of the sixteenth century and in contrast with the USA, Spain enacted laws that required the presence of interpreters in colonial judicial hearings to facilitate Native People bringing their grievances to court as a consequence of living and working in *las encomiendas*.[103] Beginning in 1529 and promulgated within a span of a hundred years, these laws stipulated the rights and responsibilities of interpreters at least until the late eighteenth century, when *las encomiendas* were abolished. "The Law of the Indies" envisioned the provision of language access to non-Spanish speakers appearing in court and addressed issues pertaining to qualifications, skills, interpreter's traits, and preferred professional standards.[104]

Interpreters, or *lenguas*, as they were referred to in these ordinances, played a pivotal role in the colonization and Christianization of the southern American continent. Yet, their level of impact did not rise to receiving the necessary training or being respected by the system. They "did not enjoy high prestige or recognition for the service they provided. They were not trained or instructed in any way and were often drawn from the domestic staff of the conquistadores or were held in *encomienda*."[105] At the same time, the

[103] *Las encomiendas* were a legal system in the Spanish colonies whereby the Spanish Crown granted colonizers land where Native Peoples already lived. Colonizers exacted taxes and were required to engage in Christian evangelizing practices, while expected to protect the indigenous people. In time, the system grew into a corrupt enslaving system that took over their lands and exploited the Native Peoples. *Las encomiendas* were finally abolished at the end of the eighteenth century.

[104] Giambruno, "The Role of The Interpreter," 33.

[105] Giambruno, "The Role of The Interpreter," 33.

existence of these ordinances in the Spanish colonial courts in the sixteenth and seventeenth centuries exemplified the importance of establishing standards and protocols for interpreters to safeguard the needs of the court and land-usurping agents, the needs of interpreters and, hopefully, those of the multilingual societies being served. Professional standards and protocols displayed concerns and solutions that resonated with twenty-first-century preoccupations. Interpreters in these courts were drawn from the *encomiendas*, the same Indigenous communities who sought assistance from the courts. As in the *Amistad* trials, these interpreters shared a sociocultural proximity to the defendants or the claimants they served.

Explanation of the law underlined the importance of interpreters assuming their tasks with impartiality "*favorecer más a uno que a otro*" (without favoring one of the parties over the other).[106] As a deterrent against impartial actions, Law VI warned interpreters against discussing legal matters with "Indians" in their homes, "*ni fuera de ellas*" (or anywhere else).[107] This law specified that these matters should be brought before the court, otherwise steep penalties were set for the interpreters who infringed upon the law. Professionals in the field, then and now, were discouraged from offering advice. In addition, they should avoid the appearance of "partiality." The fact that the redacted law penalized interpreters who discussed judicial matters with those serviced suggests the opposite as a common practice, hence the need to establish a norm to curtail this type of behavior. The interpreters and the claimants shared a common background and some of them may even have been neighbors. Whether through a physical, linguistic, or cultural closeness, both parties may have gravitated naturally toward each other within an adversarial system, as will be seen with the "knives incident" in the *Amistad* case. The need to procure "an adequate number of interpreters in the courts" suggests a high demand for interpreters and a mismatch between their numbers and the needs of the court and its claimants.

Such written ordinances did not guarantee implementation by all officers, interpreters, and parties to the cases. Their promulgation reflected the multilingual composition of the colonized geographical area: most of the inhabitants did not speak the imposed language of the Spanish courts. Despite the intentions behind these ordinances, they attempted to respond to the judicial needs and the need to hear the complaints of the colonized

[106] A similar concern is expressed in Canon 2—Impartiality and Conflicts of Interests of the NAJIT Code of Ethics and Professional Responsibilities for court interpreters: court interpreters and translators are to remain impartial and neutral in proceedings where they serve and must maintain the appearance of impartiality and neutrality.

[107] Giambruno, "The Role of The Interpreter," 33.

peoples, which grew with the systemic oppression of the empire. In providing access to the courts, the system aimed to tame civil discontent and unrest among the Indigenous peoples in a point-of-no-return situation created by the Spaniard geographical expansion. Contrary to their counterparts in the northern English-speaking states, the Spanish Empire adopted advanced judicial measures that established court-interpreting protocols.

The institutionalized experience of Spain with interpreters was vast, especially against people they have subjugated. When the Spanish Inquisition was established between 1478 and 1834, interpretation "was crucial" for related activities to the tribunal, including oral testimony in trials, interpretation of edicts in the colonized regions, and translators for documents needed to be rendered into or from Castilian, the language of the Empire.[108] This type of tribunal sought interpreters in the languages of those under the Spanish expansion, for example Arabic, Catalan, Basque, Italian, and Berber. When the Inquisition travelled to the Americas and the Pacific region, the list of languages grew to include to the Indigenous languages of Native Peoples and the languages spoken by the enslaved.[109] Inquisition courts were established in Mexico and in *Cartagena de las Indias*. As the Protestant church gained more adept interpreters, a new group of interpreters were sought who spoke the language of those professing the newer faith in the European region, for instance, Flemish and German.[110] According to Sarmiento-Pérez, there were thousands of interpreters who volunteered their skills coming from all walks of life, for example, members of religious orders, consuls, traders, artists, sailors, and even children that interpreted for their parents.[111] Consuls, traders, and sailors placed themselves in contexts where they could practice, and acquire languages like *Amistad* African interpreters, Covey and Pratt. So, when the editor of the newspaper *Noticioso de Ambos Mundos* remarked that in Cuba "the interpreters provided would be as legal or more than those they have had,"[112] there was some truth in this statement.

In the 1839 Spanish–Cuban colony, translation and interpreting continued to be essential. *La Aurora: boletín oficial y diario de gobierno de Matanzas*[113] published consecutively on November 17, 18, and 22, 1839, a Royal Decree to be read and complied by the "interpreters and those hiring or interacting

[108] Marcos Sarmiento-Pérez, "Interpreting for the Inquisition," in *New Insights in the History of Interpreting*, ed. K. Takeda and J. Baigorri-Jalón (Amsterdam: John Benjamins, 2016), 48.
[109] Sarmiento-Pérez, "Interpreting for the Inquisition," 57.
[110] Sarmiento-Pérez, "Interpreting for the Inquisition," 51.
[111] Sarmiento-Pérez, "Interpreting for the Inquisition," 68.
[112] *Noticioso de Ambos Mundos*, 23 de noviembre de 1839.
[113] Translation, *The Dawn*: the official news and daily bulletin of the government of Matanzas.

with their services." The adoption of official regulations for the interpreters in all provinces in the Cuban island speaks to the need for standardization of nonofficial services prevalent in different segments of society. It sheds light on the probable difficulties with administrative, fidelity, and interpreting and translation practices of both professional and ad hoc interpreters and translators. This decree detailed not only the manner in which interpreters should conduct their businesses but also specified expected payment for services in different languages. Translations of pages containing twenty lines per page in French, English, Italian, and Portuguese were compensated at *2 pesos* per page. The amount increased for Latin, German, Flemish, Dutch, or any other Northeastern European language to *3 pesos.* In contrast, for documents written in Greek, Turkish, or any other Asian language, translators were paid an additional *peso* per page. Commercial and political relations with the corresponding countries generated the need for translation and interpreting services in the various segments of society, including the colonized ports and the judicial courtroom. African and Indigenous languages are excluded from this list as they were devoid of political leverage or linguistic rights by mainstream society, though profitable in all accounts. Yet, despite suppressive maneuvers, their ethnic and societal influence gained momentum in cultural and historical ways through the resistance movement.

2

Translated Racial and Ethnic Issues in the *Amistad* Case

How They Mattered

Throughout the duration of the *Amistad* trials from 1839 to 1845, Spanish documents and translations abounded. Newspaper articles and legal debates increased after the civil trial that took place on January 7, 1840. The exchange of diplomatic letters, Grand Jury hearings, and witness testimony in court during the fall of 1839, already envisaged their primal importance to the case. Spanish/English translation issues extended to diplomatic letters to and from the US Department of State (DOS), the Executive Branch, and Spain[1], and to abolition treaties signed by Spain that were reviewed by the 26th Congress. Other letters also took center stage, such as those from Ruiz and Montes published in Spanish newspapers and translated in English papers, or letters from English-speaking abolitionists translated for a Spanish readership. Court files and newspapers hid the translators' names. In all public or judicial instances, the official translator's name was unknown and omitted from the translation, but not completely absent from the archives. But other archival materials, like the personal papers of John Quincy Adams (JQA), contained missing names of the *Amistad* translators. And of all documents, the *licencias* and their racialized translations resulted in the most contentious reactions.

The abolitionists' initial strategy for disproving the validity of the *licencias* centered on a vision of the defendants telling their counter-story in court through an able interpreter via testimonial evidence, contrary to the other party's documentary evidence. For this reason, they searched assiduously for a court interpreter for their non-English-speaking clients to dismantle contentions by the opposite side.[2] The other side, composed of the Spaniards'

1 The referred archival letters will be the focus of future articles.

2 Zaragoza-De León, "The Search for a Mende Court Interpreter" (TFM). "The search for a Mendi-court interpreter in The *Amistad* Case in order to challenge the institution of slavery." M.A. Thesis, Universitat Jaumé I.

legal team, the prosecutor, and the US government, understood the danger of turning up the volume on the *Amistad* voices and adopted two strategies: to impeach James Covey, their interpreter; and to concentrate their litigation efforts on trying to validate their documentary evidence. Spaniards relied on admissibility of the *licencias* to dissipate suspicion about their purported retention of the Africans.

A Spanish-experienced translator to produce and decipher the controversial textual matters was badly needed, after the abolitionists learned of the widespread prevalence of document falsification throughout the Spanish colonial system. Nonetheless, what added "*leña al fuego*" (fanning of the fire) was the publication of the manipulated translation of these official travelling documents by US Congress, in collusion with Spanish authorities. The translation of documents in the *Amistad* slavery and anti-slavery continuum uncovered pertinent and surprising matters requiring professional translation skills: to decipher translation-manipulation strategies; to identify pro-slavery translation techniques; to expound on translation theories; to review diplomatic translations; and to translate racial diatribes in newspapers. The dire condition of those on the anti-slavery side, especially for the Africans relocated from chattel slavery to incarceration—their new type of enslavement—required experienced translators.

In contrast, the search for a translator did not involve a laborious search. An inherent characteristic of the formally educated during nineteenth-century USA, including those in public office, held the solution. A culture of translation practices permeated the schooled elite across the racial spectrum as well as the anti- and pro-slavery continuum. The licit and illicit migratory influx and outflow of people from around the globe through New York City and other coastal ports, the Spanish and French geopolitical influences, and the already-existent multilingual-ethnic communities through the northern continent shaped the multilingual identity of this newly formed imperial country. Multilingual skills provided the venue to have a seat at the table with other existing empires, to advance colonial endeavors, and to gain power status. This gave a way for trained abolitionists-Spanish interlocutors versed in the written and oral versions of this language to corroborate the Spanish/English translations and interpreting activities, the Spaniards' testimonies, and eavesdropping on conversations that might proffer useful insights for their defense. The opposing side also depended on bilingual and translation skills to attempt to sway the public sentiment to their side.

The *Amistad* Committee trusted that the bilingual skills displayed by the *Amistad* abolitionists and their trustworthy network sufficed. For instance, JQA, Esq., an experienced translator and polyglot, from his privileged position advocated in US Congress by creating the subcommittee in this legislative branch to investigate the alleged fraudulent translations in this judicial matter. Judge William Jay contributed with his bilingual expertise to further demonstrate the inaccurate target translation of the *licencias*, which further implicated all branches of government in the misuse of dual languages. However, the research unveiled additional names of translators.

On the Evidentiary Documents: The *Licencias*

Unlicensed with *Licencias*

During the first *Amistad* court hearing on August 29, 1839: "Several bundles of letters were produced, saved from the *Amistad* and . . . read including two licenses signed by the Governor of Havana, Gen. Ezpeleta. . . . Regular passports were produced, allowing the passengers to proceed to their destination."[3] English constituted the language of US courts. Hence, if they were "read," an interpreter absent from the archival materials converted the Spanish-printed information into an oral interpretation, or sight translation, a commonly known technique in the interpreting field. Lacking a Mende interpreter, the production of the falsified *licencias* proved detrimental to the Africans, since these documents alleged that they had lived in Cuba for over twenty years, which was far from the truth. Linguistic privilege voiced through an English-speaking interpreter favored José Ruiz and Pedro Montes, supporting the false allegations penned in the *licencias* that would be disproven in the months to come. As a result, the Mende were incarcerated and the Spaniards were released into society, but not for long. The litigation team on behalf of the Africans filed a suit against them for false imprisonment, which generated a warrant executed for their arrest in the City of New York, in November of 1839.

Licencias were required visa-like documents issued to all persons, enslaved or not, departing or entering Spanish colonial ports during the century in question. According to the Spanish dictionary of "1817 *Academia Usual*," the formal definition of *licencia* referred to "the right or permission to do something," or "the extreme liberty assumed by someone to do or

[3] This observation suggests that the several documents written in Spanish were sight translated for this judicial proceeding. Barber's account does not disclose those responsible for sight translating these *licencias* for the record. Perhaps, either "*Señor Don José Ruiz*," who spoke English, Lieut. Meade, who spoke Spanish, or one of the abolitionists versed in this European language assisted the court in this task. Barber, *A History of the Amistad Captives*, 6.

say something."[4] A working definition of this term defined the authorizing document with a particular intent, a "*licencia*," a term translated into "license" or "permit." *Amistad*-related documents switched between "permit" and "passport," depending on the power dynamics in display manifested in the enslaving relationships. Dr. Richard Robert Madden's testimony, in the November 1839 court hearing, referred to these documents as "*traspasos*." This term appertains to dual definitions. The first one, "transfers," refers to authorizing the transport of people from one place to another, a popular usage and understanding. In contrast, the official entry in the 1817 dictionary defined a *traspaso* as a violation, indeed also applicable in this case. Neither was the term *traspaso* part of the linguistic-Cuban heritage in the local dictionary of the *Diccionario Provincial, casi razonado, de Voces y Frases Cubanas, por el autor Hon. de Marina*, by D. Esteban Pichardo, of 1836. A *traspaso* provided an explanation of the extent (and limits) of geographic mobility in a form that would be accepted in locations where the *traspaso* was accepted.

Passport versus Permits

During this period, issuance of *licencias* and passports by Spanish governmental authorities was customary. Spanish passports, in the early nineteenth century, served as a type of licensing document that allowed foreigners and nationals to travel within a province, its ports, or outside the state. The 1817 *Academia Usual* dictionary defines "*pasaporte*" as "*licencia ó despacho por escrito que se da para poder pasar libre y seguramente de un reino á otro, ó de una á otra parte*."[5] While this definition allows for both terms to be employed, outside and inside a territory, the different usages in the *Amistad* case point to other perspectives and realities. The term "passport" mainly was reserved for when the Spaniards were being referred to, but translated as "permit" when it referred to the enslaved Africans. The usage of the term "passport" signalled the freedom granted to Spaniards in contrast to the limited mobility of the enslaved in this colonial system. According to US-based *Black's Law Dictionary*, a passport is "a formal document certifying a person's identity and citizenship so that the person may travel to and from

4 "Facultad ó permiso para hacer alguna cosa. La demasiada libertad que alguno se toma para hacer ó decir alguna cosa," Real Academia Española, *Mapa de diccionarios académicos* (2013), https://apps2.rae.es/ntllet (accessed February 17, 2023).

5 "*Pasaporte*" (Translation: a permit or written document granting authorization to travel from one kingdom to another, or from one place to another), Real Academia Española, *Mapa de diccionarios académicos*.

a foreign country."[6] At the same time, the "permits" recall the denial of the rights of citizenship to those who are racialized and unempowered in this context. It is possible that this difference in translation was used as a strategy to spotlight the hidden truths of the *licencia* as well as the power differential between the freed and enslaved in a particular society. These distinctions became part of the court record inked on the back of these evidentiary documents by the expert witness for the defense, Dr. Madden, an abolitionist.

While their size and content layout varied through the century, the issuance of *licencias* was consistent throughout the Caribbean, including the Cuban port of La Habana. The *Amistad licencias* consisted of a two-page license sealed with red wax. They measured roughly 8 by 6 inches, while passports[7] issued on the Spanish–Iberian Peninsula were twice that size. The header on the *licencias* designated space for the date and the name of the city granting permission to travel. The bottom was reserved for signatures and duties to be paid ("2 *reales*").[8] The back stated the travelling vessel, in this case the "*Goleta Amistad*" (the Schooner *Amistad*), the destination port, date, and authorizing signature. The front of the second page— signed by Ezpeleta, governor of the island of Cuba—included the city of issuance, date, tariffs, and authorization to proceed to the destination.

The left-cropped section, "*Filiación*" (personal data), recorded the main physical features of the holder; height, age, color—as in skin tone—and eyes, nose, mouth, hair, eyebrows, and beard, left blank in the case of all of those aboard the *Amistad*. Similarly, passports, in lieu of pictures, contained this same section. The center section included "*Concedo licencia á*" [*sic*], "I grant permission to," followed by the name(s) of those authorized on the vessel. The crux of the translation controversies in the *Amistad* case concern information contained therein. (see Figures 2.1 and 2.2.)

Additional comments handwritten, post-June 1839, became memorialized on these evidentiary documents preserved in the court files. On the *licencias* pertaining to the *Amistad* Africans, "R.R. Madden" signed his name on the left-bottom corner, "in front of counsel," per his on-the-record testimony. Furthermore, *licencias* were numbered—No. 1 to No. 5—for the benefit of referring to evidence in court proceedings and related correspondence. On January 7, 1840, in a letter addressed to Mr. Baldwin, and signed by Mr. Holabird, *Amistad* Case District Attorney, Mr.

6 Garner, *Black's Law Dictionary*, 1233.

7 Although corrupt procedures characterized local colonial provinces regarding the usage and issuance of these permits, during this same period, distinct documents identified as "passports" circulated in Spain for internal as well as international travel. Perhaps these became "local passports" in faraway lands.

8 A "*real*" was the Spanish coin at the time.

Ingersoll, clerk of Connecticut, mailed the five (5) *licencias* in contention in the *Amistad* case—"List of papers sent @ A Ingersall, Esq [illegible] in the Case of the US v Schooner *Amistad*"—No. 1—for Pedro Montes, No. 2 for the African girls, No. 3 for José Ruiz, No. 4 for the African men and boy, and No. 5, the license for the *Amistad* Schooner. Despite the textual nuances in the central section, I will concentrate on the ideological issues relating to translation displayed in the *licencias* for the *Amistad* African men and boys, and the *Amistad* girls. Documentary evidence presented on behalf of Montes and Ruiz was submitted as "passports" instead of adopting the parallel cognate, "license." Penned during Dr. Madden's expert witness testimony, on the backs of the Spaniard's passports was similarly stated, ". . . passport from Príncipe to Havanna." The translation decision recognized class, race, and privilege, raising the status of the Spaniards over the Africans in a white colonial and enslaving society. By contrast, Ruiz's permit authorizing the transfer of the *Amistad* men read, "Don José Ruiz Permit to transport slaves from Havanna to Príncipe." The back of license "No. 4" equated the term *Ladinos* to "slaves." But an anonymous pen favoring the pleadings of the *Amistad* Africans inserted the term *Bozales* on the *licencias*, echoing Madden's testimony. Court clerks by the order of the Court carried the responsibility for labelling evidence, as in most judicial proceedings. *Amistad*-altered exhibits assisted in telling additional nuances of the story.

Obtaining the *licencias* for Spaniards or anyone travelling from one port to another complied with a legal process. However, after 1820, for sequestered *Bozales*, who only spoke African vernaculars, the Spanish system established an illegal process.[9] This process involved bribing the Spanish authorities, who gladly became complicit in the inhuman slave trade by changing their African-given names to Spanish names, and changing their status to *Ladinos,* a term contained in the center section of the permits. In short, during the researched period, the term *Ladinos* described Africans who had lived anywhere in the Spanish colonies or the Spanish–Iberian peninsula long enough to assimilate culturally and linguistically. These falsified and counterfeited documents created a pathway for transferring enslaved people between Cuban ports. Unlicensed to transport the Africans with the fraudulent *licencias*, the Spaniards forced the Mende Africans onto the schooner *La Amistad*, bound for Puerto Príncipe, an Eastern Cuban seaport (refer to Figures 2.1 and 2.2).

[9] Zaragoza-De León, "Los abolicionistas cristianos contratan a un intérprete judicial para los Mende-africanos en el caso Amistad para desafiar la institución de la esclavitud en los EE UU del siglo XIX," *Revista Iberoamericana de Lingüística*, no. 12 (2017): 67–82.

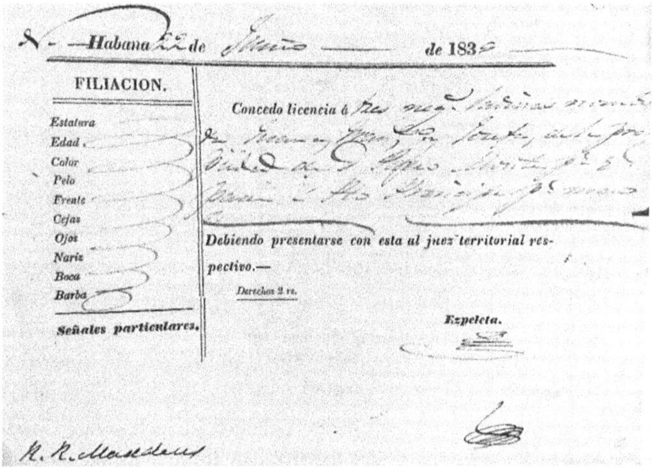

Habana de de 183

FILIACION.

Estatura
Edad
Color
Pelo
Frente
Cejas
Ojos
Nariz
Boca
Barba

Señales particulares.

Concedo licencia á

Debiendo presentarse con esta al juez territorial respectivo.—

Derechos 2 rs.

Ezpeleta.

Figure 2.1 *Licencia* for *Amistad* Girls (front).

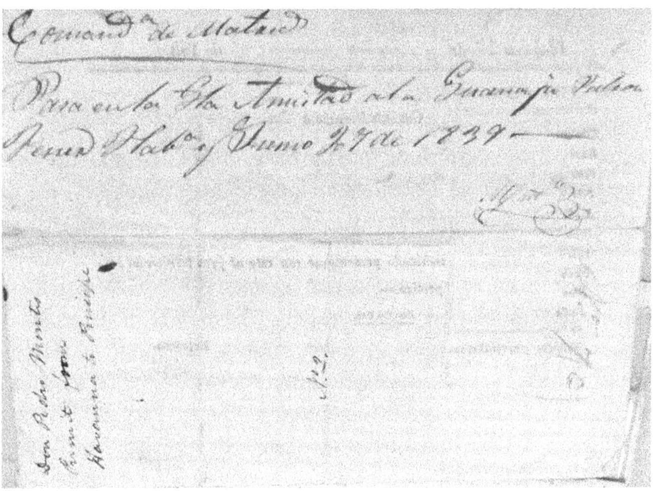

Figure 2.2 *Licencia* for *Amistad* Girls (back).

Ladinos or Not *Ladinos*, That Is the Question

On January 16, 1840, *The Emancipator* published the transcripts of the *Amistad* trial, indicating that the US Attorney submitted "the schooner's papers . . . with a translation of them." But by then, the translation issues had become front and center in the trial. After Dr. Richard Robert Madden's deposition as a material witness for the defense, on November 20, 1839, linguistic and translation discrepancies lodged in the *licencias* quickly attracted everyone's attention and concerns. His job, as a British commissioner for the Office of Superintendent of Liberated Africans for the mixed Court of Justice for Britain and Spain, offered him the vantage point of an eye witness in the trial.[10] From his post, he monitored the illegal slave-trading sea activities in the Atlantic Ocean and Caribbean Sea, and often visited the *barracones* in the capital of La Habana, the sardine-like lodging of the enslaved while they were targeted for another involuntary transfer.[11] Madden's statements offered a counter-story to the Spaniards' version. In his testimony, the terms *Ladinos* and *Bozales* bolstered the contentions of the abolitionists. He stated that the term *Ladinos* was "a term totally inapplicable to newly imported Africans," for the adults and especially the children aboard the schooner.[12] Madden's response brings to light the fraud involved in these visa-like documents and demonstrated the collusion between local authorities in Cuba and this unlawful practice:

> Any negroes [*sic*] [that] landed in the island since 1820 and carried into slavery have been illegally introduced and the transfer of them under false names such as calling *Bozals* [*sic*], *Ladinos,* is necessarily a fraud. Unfortunately, there is no interference in the part of the local authorities. They connive at it and collude with the slave traders. The governor alone at the Havana received a bounty or impost on each negro they illegally introduced for 10 dollars a head.[13]

As it happened for court testimonies and transcripts as well, Madden's sworn testimonies were published in newspapers. The weight of his expertise as eyewitness to the smuggling of the slaves in Cuba was sustained throughout legal interrogation. Neither was his testimony devoid of public scrutiny after he returned to Cuba days later. Contention on the veracity of his testimony was publicized in the documents generated by the US Legislative and

[10] "Dr. Madden's Court Testimony," *Thomas R. Gedney v The Schooner Amistad*, US District Court for the District of Connecticut, National Archives at Boston.

[11] "The Buzzard" brig that employed James Kaweli Covey and docked in the NYC harbor, sailed the seas to capture slave-carrying ships engaged in illicit transactions in violation of international treaties.

[12] "Dr. Madden's Court Testimony," US District Court for the District of Connecticut, National Archives at Boston.

[13] "Dr. Madden's Court Testimony," US District Court for the District of Connecticut, National Archives at Boston.

Executive branches. As late as June 24, 1846, Madden's devastating testimony to the Spaniards' untruths that the *Amistad* Africans lived on the Caribbean Island before 1817 showed how it crumbled to pieces. A congressional document entitled "Schooner *Amistad*" for the 29th Congress, 1st Session, Rep. No. 753, for the Committee on Foreign Affairs recounted the colonizing and racialized dilemma of the *Amistad*. In response to his testimony on the *licencias*, a letter published therein argued the following:

> [The *Amistad*] papers were indisputable. Without Madden to cry fraud, one negro vagabond to swear to it, another to swear that he believed the first, and a professor of African dialects to give his opinion that the fifty negroes were not slaves, the whole fabrication of fraud on which American courts, less respectful of authentic document than the most arbitrary commander of a sloop-a-war, was baseless suspicion without proof.[14]

Instead of aligning with the truth of the fraudulent nature of the *licencias* to uphold the human rights of the enslaved—always the viable option—the opposing parties opted to succumb to an anti-blackness attack on the interpreter and *Amistad* Africans' supporters, as Prof. Gibbs alluded to. Common for justice-seeking movements, allies were also targeted for standing with their conscience in favor of race, class, linguistic, or gender equality. Profs. Gibbs and Madden, both of European descent, became the objects of this letter writer who could not believe his own lies. The disputable nature of the Spanish documents evoked a racist response trying to suppress the truth from emerging. Racial references attacked Covey's blackness and African heritage in an attempt to discredit the other side of the story and to prevent him from serving as an interpreter for the Africans. This response represented a typical anti-liberation response that aimed to invalidate individuals and to deviate public opinion from supporting the *Amistad* captives. The pro-enslaving side failed to sustain their own lies even as they tried to hide the unavoidable truth. Despite a colonizing and racist ideology, the submitted evidence in court corroborated Madden's testimony and the hypothesis from the abolitionists. News among the enslaved and free populations travelled from coast to coast on ships, on printed literature, whispers, eavesdropping, and counter-stories to all levels of the enslaving colonial society. The impending news on the *Amistad* rebellion echoed hope on the island of Cuba upon Madden's return. US-Spanish ministers' imperial

[14] Rep. No. 753, 12.

desperations drove them to question the US judicial system, naturally favoring white supremacy, class, male, and racial privileges. As would be proven, the transferring documents signed by a Don Joaquín Ezpeleta y Enrile, governor of Cuba at the time, did not stand up to rigorous judicial scrutiny.[15]

These pivotal evidentiary documents migrated from one file to another from 1839 before being finally lodged in the 1843 *Amistad*-related trial. Along with the original *licencias* found in the 1843 Thomas Gedney *Amistad* case file, an official "Translation" filed for the African *licencias* remained in the court files (refer to Figure 2.3). The English translation of these official records offered a less inflammatory version compared with the one published by sources outside the US government, as in the case for Congress in Doc. 185 discussed in this section. This version provided a less accurate translation and a more ambiguous one as it related to the decisive issues in this case.

Aside from the section on the general characteristics of the *licencia*'s template, the document records general aspects on both its front and back. For the African men, the term *Ladinos* remained in the official translation. Omission characterized the Black girls' *licencias*, which referred to them only as "three black females." Someone reinforcing the testimony of witnesses Madden or Covey, added "*Ladinas*" on top of this phrase as a corrective note (see Figures 2.1, 2.2 and 2.3.) The last sentence in both of these main sections translated the word *licencia* as "permit," instead of "passport."

As discussed earlier, Dr. Madden's testimony informed the court about two distinct ways of existing as an African-descent enslaved person in the "New World": one was as a *Ladino* o *Ladina*[16] and the other as a *Bozal*. Both terms carried "centuries" of enslaving and linguistic history. By the time they were printed in an 1836 Spanish–Cuban dictionary, the terms signified particular ethnic and corporal conditions. These acceptations were at the heart of the translation issues. The 1836 *Diccionario de Voces Cubanas* defined *Ladino* as follows:

> *Ladino, na—El Negro ú negra africanos, que ya está bastante instruido, esperto ú civilizado, y habla ó entiende suficientemente el castellano.*[17]
>
> (Ladino, na—A female or male Black African who is well educated, proficient and civilized and speaks and understands enough Spanish.)

[15] *Diario de La Habana*, martes, 1ero de enero de 1839. Biblioteca Nacional José Martí, La Habana, Cuba.

[16] The term *Ladino* also described culturally and linguistically assimilated immigrants living in Spain during this period. This term also described people of Jewish descent during another period.

[17] Esteban Pichardo, *Diccionario provincial de voces cubanas* (Matanzas, Cuba: Imprenta de la Real Marina, 1836), 152.

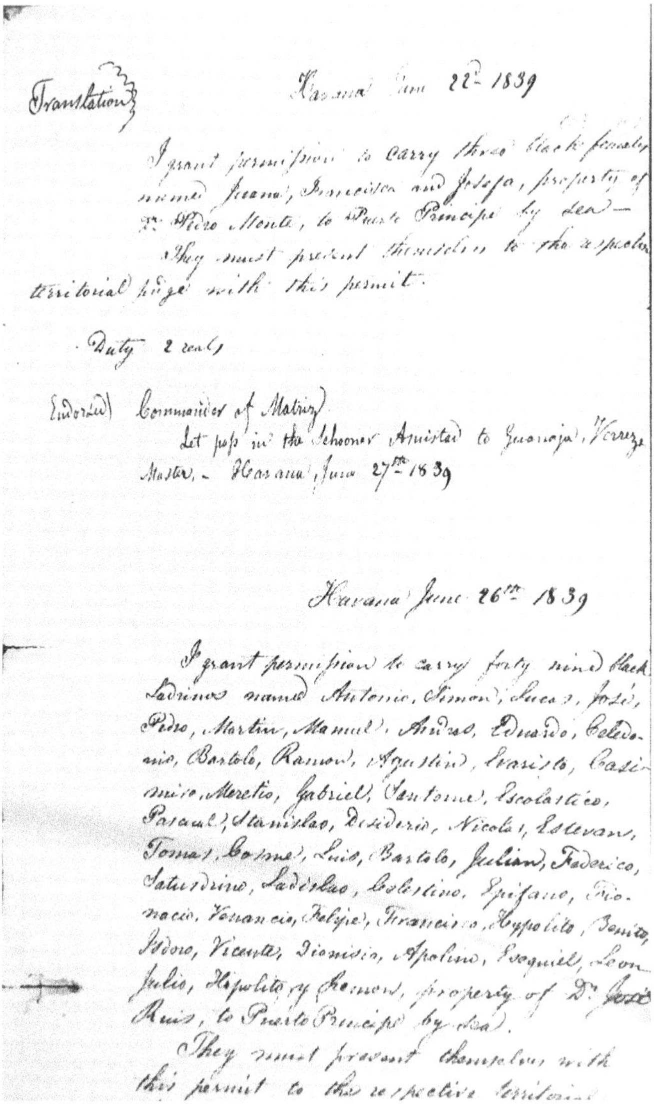

Translation

Havana June 22d 1839

I grant permission to carry three black females named Juana, Francisca and Josefa, property of Dr. Pedro Monte, to Puerto Principe by sea—

They must present themselves to the respective territorial judge with this permit.

Duty 2 reals

(Endorsed) Commander of Matriz
Let pass in the Schooner Amistad to Guanaja, Ferrer, Master, — Havana, June 27th 1839

Havana June 26th 1839

I grant permission to carry forty nine black Ladinos named Antonio, Simon, Lucas, José, Pedro, Martin, Manuel, Andres, Eduardo, Celedonio, Bartolo, Ramon, Agustin, Evaristo, Casimiro, Merced, Gabriel, Santorne, Escolastico, Pascual, Stanislao, Desiderio, Nicolas, Estevan, Tomas, Cosme, Luis, Bartolo, Julian, Federico, Saturdino, Ladislao, Celestino, Epifanio, Dionacio, Venancio, Felipe, Francisco, Hypolito, Benito, Isidoro, Vicente, Dionisio, Apolino, Esequiel, Leon, Julio, Hipolito y Ramon, property of Dr. José Ruis, to Puerto Principe by sea.

They must present themselves with this permit to the respective territorial

Figure 2.3 Official *Licencia* translation, *Amistad* case files. "Translation of *Licencia* in Court Files," *Thomas R. Gedney v. The Amistad Case*, US District Court for the District of Connecticut, National Archives at Boston.

A *Bozal*, on the other hand, identified someone who could not speak the colonizing language or be understood in theirs. Contemporary definitions equate "*bozal*" with a "muzzle." Back then, a "*Bozal*" referred to the reins of a horse maneuvered by the rider to control the direction and pace of the four-legged animal: "*el lazo de soga que asegura el hocico del caballo para manejarle*." A few centuries apart, both definitions encapsulated the linguistic, physical, and racialized subjugations of African-descent people in the Americas. Pichardo's lexicographical work seconded the definition used by the abolitionists, an African Black recently arrived from the continent—"*el negro recien llegado de su país*"—but specified that in the "*isla*," it referred to a person born in Africa, regardless of how long ago they had emigrated.[18] Both definitions seemed applicable to the *Amistad* Africans, except when considering the time frame of their unwanted arrival to Cuba. In the *Amistad* story, the term *Bozales* recalls: the chaining irons from kidnapping from the internal regions of the continent and through the Middle Passage; the muzzling of counter-stories and rebellious voices; the linguistic muzzling taking away their right to testify in their vernacular without a court interpreter; and the muzzle attempted on Covey. These were muzzling actions caught among anti-slavery, pro-slavery, and racist ideologies: all actions taken to suppress the truth.

Pichardo's Spanish–Cuban local dictionary contradicted Madden's first-hand knowledge of the enslaving patterns in the Caribbean Island in conspiracy with slave traders in Africa, Europe, and the USA. This dictionary mirrored local transatlantic realities. *Bozales*, on paper, were disguised as *Ladinos* for the convenience of the authorities that continued to feed the transatlantic slave trade route. The working definition for the term "*Ladina*" supported the witness testimony of R. R. Madden and others in the *Amistad* movement. The same dictionary proffered two definitions for the term "*Bozal*," of which one aligned with the routes of enslaving activities. Madden testified in court that the appropriate term to use for the *Amistad* Africans was *Bozal* and not *Ladino* as tendered by the initial definition.

The *bozal* personified those forced to assimilate linguistically and culturally to the imperial Spanish ways for survival. The latter identified those "muzzled" subalterns who could not speak the imperial languages or navigate the cultural mores of an enslaving system. Identifying newly sequestered Africans as *ladinos/nas* in the *licencias* covered for Spanish authorities signing off on these inauthentic documents and realities.

The official US government and legislative translation of these documents aligned itself with the pro-slavery group. The term *ladinos* became translated to

[18] Pichardo, *Diccionario provincial*, 39.

"sound negroes" in an attempt to obscure the illicit transactions of the Spanish *licencias*. The adjective "sound," commonly used at the time, evoked certainty, confidence, trust, and even the healthy status of the noun modified, all assayed to eliminate any doubt. As the investigation unfolded, the DOS translator was exonerated of providing the negligent translation, and instead it fell into the hands of US Congress' publishing house's editor to be discussed further. The fraudulently obtained permits, compounded with these manipulative activities, supported the institution of slavery, which in turn fuelled an orchestrated-abolitionist movement in favor of the *Amistad* Africans.

All communications underwent a close analysis along the continuum of class, ethnicity, and positionality, by abolitionists or pro-slavery advocates. "Doc. 185" also incorporated written communication that bridged the diplomatic relations between the Spanish minister, the US DOS secretary, the *Amistad* prosecutor, and the US president. The original letters and their translations, from Spanish to English and vice versa, were published for the benefit of representatives in US Congress. This action continues to highlight how diplomatic, judicial, and cultural translations occupied an important role in the shaping of the geopolitics and cultural development of the nineteenth century for the newly formed USA republic. This research shies away from engaging in a textual analysis of these letters or the possible mistranslations that may exist. Instead, I prefer to scrutinize the racialized polemics revealed in both original and produced translations of the *licencias* and through these letters. For decades since 1817, these falsified documents concealed the inhumane treatment of African-descended people forced to cross the Atlantic in which too many perished.

One of the primary matters discussed in these diplomatic letters pertained to the authenticity of travelling *licencias*, because both empires depended on the hidden trades behind the translations. Spanish representatives, abroad and in the USA, denied any possible manhandling or irregularities from Ruiz and Montes. Although the letters authored by US representatives seem to express an objective inquisitorial stance, in the end their actions endorsed the opinions of the Spanish authorities, which, in turn, echoed their own. This three-party validation process demonstrated collusion among these branches of the US government with a judicial process that affirmed the pleas of the Spanish Crown on behalf of the *licencia* holders.

Part of the abolitionists' strategy to use language advocacy for racial equity was to have a Mende interpreter assist the Mende Africans in disproving the fabricated claims embedded in the *licencias*. It was complicated, if Antonio, enslaved by Captain Ferrer as the cabin boy, testified in favor of the Spaniards, in Spanish. According to certain accounts, he served as an interpreter for the *Amistad* Africans. New written and oral evidence needed to be produced in court to refute the bogus evidence by the opposing, more privileged side. In addition to the Spanish documents filed as evidence, "anything offered in court to prove the truth or falsity of a fact in issue,"[19] or public English translation of the *licencias* published for the benefit of the legislative branch, caused unexpected havoc, that favored the *Amistad*-abolitionist cause. They contended that this English-translated version demanded skilled translators and translation experts to unpack the vital word "*Ladinos*" hidden in the racially charged phrase "sound negroes." Where would the translation expertise come from for analyzing the evidence on the abolitionist side?

Spanish native and trained speakers were common at this time in US history. In contrast, finding someone who could understand both English and a few African languages represented a greater challenge. In 1839, there were more than thirty newspapers printed in New York City, four of which were printed in Spanish, appealing to a wide Spanish-reading community. A Spanish readership pointed to the multilingual nature of the New England coastline and the desire of English speakers to attain Spanish-language competency. For instance, *Amistad* lawyers Theodore Sedgwick and John Quincy Adams had trained formally and informally as Spanish connoisseurs. At the age of eleven, Sedgwick had read both volumes of *Don Quixote*, in Spanish, and by the time of the trial he had developed oral Spanish abilities sufficient to serve as an interpreter in the *Amistad* trial. Adams had accumulated translation expertise in various modern and old languages, including Spanish. The search for a competent Spanish translator remained within the abolitionist circles for safety reasons. They avoided a wider search for a Spanish translator, since collectively they possessed the necessary skills to evaluate the quarrelsome Spanish letters and *licencias*.

Translation Issues from Connecticut to Congress, from the Judicial to the Executive Branch

After Judge Judson's positive verdict in favor of the *Amistad* defendants, the House of Representatives passed a resolution presented to the floor by John Quincy Adams on March 23, 1840, "requesting the President to communicate to that House . . . any demand made by the minister or other diplomatic representative, of belonging to, the vessel called the *Amistad;* and of all correspondence between this Government and the said minister or diplomatic representative." This mandate yielded a seventy-six-page pamphlet for the Twenty-Sixth Congress, First Session, for the House

[19] Julian R. Hanley and Wayne W. Schmidt, *Legal Aspects of Criminal Evidence*, 3rd ed. (Berkeley, CA: McCutchan Publishing, 1984), 4.

of Representatives and the Executive branch, known as "Doc. No. 185," comprising thirty-seven documents: fifteen diplomatic letters between Spain and the USA, ten of them translated from Spanish into English, enclosures, memoranda, plus all transcribed *licencias* and their translations.

Beginning on September 23, 1839, shortly after the Spaniards found resistance in the USA to regaining control of their boat, cargo, and slaves, diplomatic correspondence hinted at the problems of the authentication of this document. John Forsyth, US Secretary of State at the time, wrote to Ángel Calderón de la Barca, Spanish minister based in New York City at the time, petitioning additional documents to legitimize the *licencias* and the information contained therein. Forsyth's due diligence masqueraded their support for the return of the Africans to Cuba. In response to Forsyth's letter, the Spanish minister pledged his political support to Montes and Ruiz, whose activities exemplified what occurred rampantly through the Americas, in violation of the signed treaty of 1817:

> Sir: In the examination of the case of the Spanish schooner "*Amistad*," the only evidence at present within reach of this department is that presented by the ship's papers. . . . If you have any other authentic documents relating to the question, or evidence of facts which can be useful to a proper understanding of it, I have the honor to request, by the direction of the President, that you will communicate them to me with as little delay as practicable.[20]

Six days later, Mr. Calderón replied in Spanish:

> *En contestación, me apresuro á manifestar a V.S. ahora que tengo tiempo para ello [. . .] que no hay en poder la legación de S.M., documentos algunos mas que la declaracion jurada de Montes y Ruiz; puesto que los papeles del buque, de cuya legitimidad no parece haya motivo de dudar, están en el tribunal mencionado.* [Diacritical marks or lack thereof reflect the original][21]

The English version of the response published under the heading "[Translation]," without an identified translator, reads:

> In reply, I hasten to assure you, now that I have time for that purpose . . . that there are not in the possession of the legation of Her Majesty

[20] U.S. Congress, House, H. Doc. 185, 11.
[21] U.S. Congress, House, H. Doc. 185, 12.

> any documents, besides the declaration on oath of Montes and Ruiz; inasmuch as the papers of the vessel, of the lawfulness of which there appears to be no reason for doubt, are in the court above mentioned.[22]

Two reactions occurred at the same time. Via the *Amistad* legal team, the abolitionists raised appropriate legal concerns about the legitimacy of these documents that drew both public and private attention from all branches of government. Adams, strategically using his privileged governmental position, broadcasted the bi-branch collusion active on stage and behind the scenes. On paper, US officials appear on some level to question the legitimacy of these documents, while behind the scenes the *Grampy*, a US military vessel anchored in the New Haven port, was ready to take the *Amistad* Africans back to Cuba. Reading between the lines of this diplomatic and formal missive raises various questions: Why would the US executive branch serve as custodian of evidentiary documents of a legal case under the jurisdiction of the judiciary branch? This was most certainly an atypical chain of custody, even for this century. This paragraph corroborates the involvement of the executive branch, which was forced to understand, or at least pretend to understand, the core issues in this case embedded in the *licencias*. The data thus far lacks confirmation of whether or not Mr. De la Barca, as well as other Spanish officials, were complicit in the rampant illegal sequestration of Africans into the Americas. Yet, applying a hermeneutics of suspicion makes it difficult to assume that they were unaware of what was hidden in plain sight in the fabrication of the *licencias* at La Havanna. There was much "reason to doubt," as the abolitionists and others suspected, particularly after Dr. Madden's validation in court, prompting the DOS to inquire further.

On September 23 of the same year, Mr. Forsyth, Secretary of State, wrote to Mr. Holabird, US District Attorney for the Connecticut District, requesting "the ship's papers" so that the US president may arrive at a "just decision." Furnishing the papers represented a challenge. The Spanish side of the equation delayed fulfilling the diplomatic request from their political ally. On October 13, Mr. W. S. Holabird concluded: "I have used every reasonable endeavor to possess myself of the papers of said schooner, without yet being able to obtain them, they having been retained by José Ruiz . . . the facts regarding the matter were not as fully disclosed at the court of inquiry as they afterwards were before the grand jury, at the circuit court."[23] The court of inquiry referred to the court proceeding after the September proceedings. It is questionable why these material case documents were not surrendered

22 U.S. Congress, House, H. Doc. 185, 12.

23 U.S. Congress, House, H. Doc. 185, 41.

to the court early in the judicial process, when the first hearing took place aboard Brig *Washington*. Eventually they were, and they still remain in the *Amistad* case files at the National Archives in Waltham, Massachusetts.[24]

The diplomatic written exchange attests to the solicitation for assistance by the new Spanish minister, Pedro Alcantara Argaíz, to the DOS for another pressing matter. The *Amistad* Africans via the *Amistad* abolitionists secured the arrest of their captors by the New York courts to appear in "the proper tribunal, to answer for wrongs alleged to have been inflicted by them upon the personas of said Africans."[25] While not unique to the *Amistad*, there were not many instances where enslavers were brought to justice for their crimes against Africans or Native Americans. This represented another accomplishment of the abolitionists advocating for the cause and creating a public upheaval. Unfortunately, Ruiz and Montes did not spend many nights in jail. Forsyth, on behalf of the US president, pledged his support by instructing the US attorney in New York to offer his counsel in case there were measures that could be put to use to secure their release and indemnity.[26] While indemnity was not possible, their bail was lowered to an amount they could post and be released from prison.

It was not until November 5, 1839, that Mr. Holabird complied with the request made by the DOS, with the "*Copia de los papeles encontrados a bordo de la Amistad*."[27] There were eight documents in total: four *licencias*—for Don José Ruiz Carrios, Don Pedro Montes, the "*cuarenta y nueve negros Ladinos*," and "*tres Negras Ladinas*"—two protections for Celestino Ferrer and Jacinto Verdagué—the ship's registration, and the custom permit for the shipping of goods. As discussed earlier, the translation of the phrases "*cuarenta y nueve negros Ladinos*" and "*tres Negras Ladinas*," which caused the greatest commotion among the anti-slavery and abolitionist movement, prompted them to print their own annotated and abbreviated version of the same congressional document. These transcribed and translated evidentiary folios further disclosed the colonial and enslaving enmeshment of the nineteenth-century political systems of the USA and Spain. In response, the *Amistad* abolitionists employed their privileges on behalf of this cause, regardless of the cost. Initially, it seemed as if manipulating translation strategies of

[24] Case files, additionally, contained some transcribed copies, diplomatic letters, and two translations of the *licencias* for the *Amistad* Africans. Responsible translators and transcribers of these linguistically mediated documents, to date, are unnamed. However, the US DOS Language Department seemed to have produced the English translations of the diplomatic correspondence received at the DOS offices, but this cannot be ascertained.

[25] U.S. Congress, House, H. Doc. 185, 14.

[26] U.S. Congress, House, H. Doc. 185, 17.

[27] Eng. Trans.: copy of the documents found on board the *Amistad*.

addition and omission orchestrated the contentious translations. Arguments in favor and against the choices established clear lines of support for either pro-slavery or anti-slavery positions.

The one-page introduction addressed "to the people of the United States" explained the reason for reprinting:

> For the use of Members of Congress and their constituents, omitting only some of the ship's papers, and the originals of letters of which the translations were published in the original document, with explanatory and critical notes, &c. Otherwise, it is an exact copy of the document printed by order of the House of Representatives.[28]

Twenty-eight pages make up for the total printed in contrast to the seventy-six-page original congressional document. The outrage of the anti-slavery movement surpassed translation discrepancies raised by the choice of words in the center section of the *licencias*. Abolitionists were flabbergasted at the collusion between these three main governmental branches, the judicial, legislative, and executive, against the rights of those seeking racial justice. This collusion protected the interests of Ruiz, Montes, the widow of Captain Ferrer, and the claims of the Spanish diplomats in their communication on behalf of their own Spanish citizens. The editor commented:

> The attention of the free people of this country is invited to the contents of this public document, and they will not fail to notice with astonishment the attempt of the executive to interfere with the regular administration of justice. The Government of a free people should protect defenceless [*sic*] strangers[29] thrown, by the providence of God after a successful struggle for liberty, upon their shores, and not give them up to foreign claimants unless imperiously required to do it by treaty. But in this instance, it will appear that instead of interposing the national Aegis to shield the weak and oppressed, our government has lent all the aid and facilities, at its command to have them placed in the hands of the Spaniards with certain knowledge that many of them would be put to death! [All emphasis in original][30]

[28] U.S. Dept. of State, *Africans Taken in the Amistad: Congressional Document: Containing, the Correspondence, &c.: In Relation to the Captured Africans.* [Reprint of the House of Representatives document no. 185, 26th Congress, 1st sess.] (New York: Anti-Slavery Depository, 1840), 2.

[29] In this quote, a "stranger" signifies someone not from the USA, more specifically, the *Amistad* Africans.

[30] U.S. Dept. of State, *Africans taken in the Amistad*, 2.

This abbreviated congressional version dismissed most Spanish originals, except for the *licencias* pertaining to the *Amistad* Africans; girls, a boy, and the men. It includes four editorial notes stating the anti-slavery ideology of the abolitionist editors, two of these addressing translation matters. Instead of opting to distinguish the terms "passports" and "permits," the unnamed *Amistad* translators preferred to even the racial and social positioning playing field to honor the *Amistad* Africans' rights to citizenship by adopting the term "passport" as a translation for "*licencia*" for both litigants. In the context of the controversy around these translations, this choice refocused the issue to the racial and historical linguistic matters of the terms *Ladinas* versus *Bozales*, instead of distracting the reader with discrepancies in the translation of the term *licencia*. Furthermore, this intentional preference championed their rights as human beings—their human rights—as it recognized *Amistad* Africans as citizens with inherent rights to freedom from sequestration and enslavement.

For starters, the abolitionists took offense to the translation of the license for the African girls. The abbreviation "Neg.~," meaning "Negras" (Black

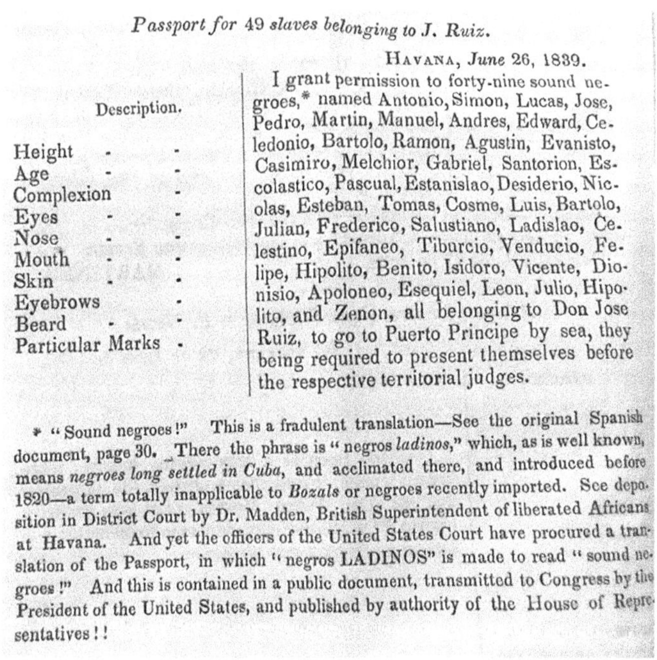

Passport for 49 *slaves belonging to J. Ruiz.*

Havana, *June* 26, 1839.

Description.

Height -- -
Age -- -
Complexion -
Eyes -- -
Nose -- -
Mouth -- -
Skin -- -
Eyebrows -
Beard -- -
Particular Marks -

I grant permission to forty-nine sound negroes,* named Antonio, Simon, Lucas, Jose, Pedro, Martin, Manuel, Andres, Edward, Celedonio, Bartolo, Ramon, Agustin, Evanisto, Casimiro, Melchior, Gabriel, Santorion, Escolastico, Pascual, Estanislao, Desiderio, Nicolas, Esteban, Tomas, Cosme, Luis, Bartolo, Julian, Frederico, Salustiano, Ladislao, Celestino, Epifaneo, Tiburcio, Venducio, Felipe, Hipolito, Benito, Isidoro, Vicente, Dionisio, Apoloneo, Esequiel, Leon, Julio, Hipolito, and Zenon, all belonging to Don Jose Ruiz, to go to Puerto Principe by sea, they being required to present themselves before the respective territorial judges.

* "Sound negroes!" This is a fradulent translation—See the original Spanish document, page 30. There the phrase is "negros *ladinos*," which, as is well known, means *negroes long settled in Cuba*, and acclimated there, and introduced before 1820—a term totally inapplicable to *Bozals* or negroes recently imported. See deposition in District Court by Dr. Madden, British Superintendent of liberated Africans at Havana. And yet the officers of the United States Court have procured a translation of the Passport, in which "negros LADINOS" is made to read "sound negroes!" And this is contained in a public document, transmitted to Congress by the President of the United States, and published by authority of the House of Representatives!!

Figure 2.4 Doc. number 185—"Sound Negroes."

females), described the noun "*Ladinas*." Omission of the term "*Ladinas*" and substitution with the term "sound women" led to a great commotion. Ample court documents and witness testimonies contained in writs of *habeas corpus* attested to the fact that the Black females were not women but minors between the ages of seven and eleven.[31] The abolitionists petitioned the court to release them as they clearly did not arrive in Cuba prior to 1820. In another attempt to prove that the *Amistad* Africans arrived in Cuba before the abolition of the Spanish transatlantic slave trade, the patriarchal English translations denied the girls' actual ages and identities. They were not women, but girls; not owned by Montes, but belonging to their families and communities. The translation imposed adulthood and a truncated childhood, as often happened in the enslaving trade. Inclusion of the term "sound" veiled, in writing, the visual reality of the *Amistad* girls and the rest of the *Amistad* Africans. The middle section of the two *licencias* encompasses the disputed terms. The first one falsified the African girls' given names, bestowed by their families:

> *Concedo licencia á tres neg.~ Ladinas nombradas Juana, Francisca, y Josefa, de la propiedad de Don Pedro Montes, para que pasen á Puerto Príncipe por mar, debiendo presentarse con esta al juez territorial respectivo.* (*US v Amistad* Case).[32] (refer to Figures 2.1 and 2.2)

Similarly, the English translation for the African men's *licencias* contained forty-nine falsified Spanish names and the inaccurate term "sound negroes," in substitution for the original Spanish *licencia*, read "*cuarenta y cinco Ladinos*" (trans. "forty-five *Ladinos*"). The translation added "sound negroes," eliminating "*Ladino*" from the official translation, for a final product of "forty-five sound negroes." Based on the historical background presented, I propose that "sound negroes" represented another way in which the Spanish colonial ideology colluded with US racist ideology. The term "negroes" was commonly used, pejoratively, in the US context to refer to descendants of Africans forced to migrate from their native lands. Incorporated into the

[31] According to Benjamin N. Lawrance, the 1830s fell within the high point for the child-enslaving period from Africa, "boy children between the age of eight and twelve years were among the 'most favorite cargoes.'" Girls featured less prominently in slave cargoes than boys, possibly because "their acquirers in Africa valued their potential as bearers of children and did not sell them to Europeans." Lawrance, "*La Amistad's* 'Interpreter' Reinterpreted," 35.

[32] Span to Eng trans.: I grant license to three Black *Ladinas* named Juana, Francisca, and Josefa, property of Mr. Pedro Montes, for them to travel to Puerto Príncipe by sea. They must appear before the appropriate administrative regional judge.

translation, "negroes" evoked contextual similarities between the Mende Africans on Cuban soil and US African descendants. By "translating" their racialized condition to a common racialized status understood in the US context, the pro-slavery translation editors hoped to close the public controversy and enlist more supporters. The term "sound" attempted to muddle the transatlantic interpretations on the translated paper, but it did not (refer to Figure 2.4).

Anti-slavery advocates who joined the efforts by Christian abolitionists were apprised of the political motivations behind these word choices. *"Ladino or Ladina"* and *"Bozal"* represented critical terms in this case that were deleted in the official court translations and substituted by the term "sound negroes." "*Negras Ladinas*" and "sound negroes" may have conveyed to slavery-supporting readers that nothing was amiss. Translation addition and omission choices concealed the real stories of the fifty-three Africans (girls, boy, and men) on board the *Amistad*. Abolitionists maintained that the Mende Africans introduced to Cuba after 1820 had additional legal protection under international agreements to bear arms in defense of their freedom. Therefore, any other term or translation deliberately misled the court about their racialized origins and masked these hidden illegalities. The *Amistad* defense litigation strategy questioned the validity of both original and translated versions as presented by pro-slavery proponents, finally proving the obvious lie in both the Superior and Supreme Courts.

"There Is a Scandalous Mistranslation!": John Quincy Adams and the Department of State's Involvement in the *Amistad* Translation Matters

By May 10, 1840, Baldwin and Tappan insisted that Adams be briefed on the "scandalous translations" of the *licencias*. One of Adams's three diaries chronicled this affair:

> Mr. William L. Storrs, a member of the house from Connecticut, who had yesterday given me a Letter, to read from R. S. Baldwin, the leading Counsel of the Africans of the *Amistad*—I cannot suppress, and yet must controul [*sic*]. There is a scandalous mistranslation of one of the Spanish papers, in the Document N. 185. Noticed by Mr. Baldwin . . . which I received this day a Letter from Lewis Tappan of New York.

This was not the first time that Adams had heard news about the *Amistad* trial. As early as September 23, 1839, Ellis Gray Loring, another Boston abolitionist previously acquainted with Adams, insisted through letters and personal visits that Adams cast his "opinion upon the knotty question involved in the case of the Spanish ship *Amistad*."[33] Adams's initial response in writing was not positive. Based on prior judicial decisions, he opined that a dismal and fatal end awaited the *Amistad* Africans. Loring would not take "no" for an answer, and so Adams requested copies of the file for his perusal. Beginning on February 10, 1840, Adams introduced various resolutions in Congress on behalf of this case, despite the Gag Rule on slavery matters passed on January 28 of that same year. Adams, as well as other abolitionist leaders, catapulted on the *Amistad* case in the spaces they had access to in order to advance the anti-slavery cause; Congress represented one of those spaces. Most resolutions voiced by Adams did not find a voting majority, except for two key ones: creating a subcommittee to investigate the translation matters in the *Amistad* case and the printing of the *Amistad*-related documents. It had taken a year for abolitionists to recruit Adams to represent the case on appeal. It was not until October 27, 1840, that Adams agreed to represent the case of the *Amistad* Africans before the Supreme Court.[34] The following month, Adams acquiesced to requests from the prisoners and the abolitionists to travel to Hartford and meet with the prisoners and Baldwin in jail, without Covey present.

Translating Slavery and Liberation via the *Amistad* Missives

Evidence of translation reference tools also suggests that written-linguistic Spanish–English mediation was a common practice in New York City as well as in other areas of the North American continent, like Louisiana.[35] On April 4, 1840, the editor of the newspaper *Noticioso de Ambos Mundos* reviewed a bibliographical resource for those engaged in Spanish/English translation

[33] September 23, 1839, v. 42, John Quincy Adams Digital Diary, v. 42 [electronic edition], Adams Family Papers: An Electronic Archive. Collection of the Massachusetts Historical Society. http://www.masshist.org/digitaladams (hereafter cited as date, volume, John Quincy Adams Digital Diary).

[34] October 27, 1840, v. 41, John Quincy Adams Digital Diary. Collection of the Massachusetts Historical Society.

[35] During the nineteenth century, New Orleans became a haven for the liberal creoles from Cuba who had not yet succeeded in their independence movements (Coronado 2013, 368 and 527). Travel from the Caribbean, Louisiana, and Texas seemed fluid and constant during this time, contributing to a rich Spanish language and cultural growth. Raúl Coronado further cites the work of Kirsten Silva Gruesz who describes the multilingual literary intellectual culture during this period in New Orleans, contextualizing the production of this translation resource.

activities entitled, "The English translator, or a practical and theoretical guide to learn how to translate from the Spanish to the English language." Dr. Cubí had just published his second edition as assistant professor at the College of Louisiana.

This reference assisted both "*al principiante*" (the beginner) and others more advanced in this linguistic task. It offered assistance with Walker's rules for pronunciation, adverbial clauses, explanation of idiosyncrasies of the English language, interlinear format to illustrate examples, presented translation challenges when tackling difficult passages, and suggested why and how to avoid literal translations. Translators or editors could have availed themselves of these types of resources to complete Spanish/English translations to satisfy a linguistic need during the timeline of the *Amistad* case.

Translation in dual languages served to air passionate sentiments regarding pro-enslavement or pro-liberation stands. Redacted letters and published pamphlets from appalled abolitionists charge the US governmental agencies for their complicity in perpetuating the unjust incarceration of the enslaved *Amistad* Africans in connection with the translation issues present in the *Amistad* case. An anonymous author, on May 4, 1840, wrote a letter to Baldwin, counsel for the Africans, that focused on "an important error in the translation of a Spanish document."[36] Three pages out of the four-page letter addressed the translation problem in the *licencias*: another anonymous, skilled translator. The author of the missive alludes to the decision of Judge Judson in the *Amistad* case, who found that "said passports do not truly describe the said persons shipped under same."[37] As previously protested by Jay and the anti-slavery pamphlet, the unidentified writer reiterated the controversial translational issues of the passports. The letter writer transcribed one of the *licencias* in the original Spanish language and cited Dr. Madden's testimony in his distinction between "*Ladinos*" and "*Bozales*." He treaded carefully to avoid insulting the attorney general, who decided to authenticate the *licencias* as presented by the Spaniards: "this vessel cleared out from one Spanish port to another Spanish port, with papers regularly authenticated by the proper officers at Havana."[38] Translation issues surfaced in the outgoing process of the duration of the case. The writer gives the benefit of the doubt to the attorney general for his decision, "probably not being aware of the diversity in the description of the property [sic] authorized to be transported, and of

[36] "Anonymous," The Baldwin Family Papers, Manuscripts and Archives, Yale University Library.

[37] "Anonymous," The Baldwin Family Papers, Manuscripts and Archives, Yale University Library.

[38] U.S. Congress, House, H. Doc. 185, 58.

the men who were actually shipped seems to regard the passport signed by the colonial governor as 'conclusive' as to the propriety interest in the thing in question."[39] The same author, probably a lawyer himself, cites two cases—Case of the Odin and Case of the Eugenia—in which the court decided not to be bound by documents that were false in nature. This correspondence, along with Judge Judson's letter to Baldwin, alerted authorities about problems and offered litigation strategies for the appeal's case.

Letters disclosed in newspaper articles broadcasted sentiments springing from such an "exciting" case to outmost dismay between English and Spanish interlocutors. The fervor of this case permeated newspapers "across the nation," including the Spanish newspaper, *Noticioso de Ambos Mundos*, which also noted the widespread interest in the events and matters of the "*Goleta Amistad*" (*Amistad* Schooner): "*vemos como era de esperarse, que con este motivo se ha suscitado una cuestion en que todos los periódicos de esta vasta república van tomando parte con el calor propio de asunto tan interesante*" (trans. as expected, we see how this matter has elicited a response from all newspapers of this vast republic, which have taken sides based on the inherent nature of this interesting issue).[40] This interest extended to articles as well as publication of letters on both sides, particularly between *el Señor* Lewis Tappan and Don José Ruiz, the latter, according to this Spanish newspaper, who "was our friend . . . and nephew of Don Saturnino Carrios."[41] The concepts of patronage and agency regulated the translations of letters in newspapers alongside ideological fidelity. Whether it was the *Noticioso*, a pro-Spanish Crown and enslavement paper, *The Emancipator*, or *The Colored American*, pro-liberation and anti-slavery papers each promoted news catered to their respective audiences. Letters of each band found voice in the other; however, editorial comments swayed the reader to opine within the ideological commitments of each newsprint.

One of the first letters published in newspapers, from either ideological inclination or linguist manifestation, was "A Card" written by Ruiz and Montes, on August 29, 1839, three days after their arrival in New London, USA, in *The Emancipator*. The "card" expressed their gratitude for the "rescuing" efforts of the Navy officers from the alleged "ruthless gang of African buccaneers." The article does not specify whether it was written originally in Spanish or in English. Their expressed gratitude surfaced in response to the palpable anti-slavery sentiments perceived among the

[39] "Anonymous," The Baldwin Family Papers, Manuscripts and Archives, Yale University Library.

[40] *Noticioso de Ambos Mundos*, 7 de septiembre de 1839.

[41] *Noticioso de Ambos Mundos*, 31 de agosto de 1839.

general public. Ruiz and Montes reminded readers of the USA alliance with the imperial Spanish nation, and how actions on their behalf would be most appreciated by the Queen of Spain. Shortly after this co-authored publication, two short articles strongly criticized the "Card," disputing the racist ideology to hide the scheme from which they frame their description of the Africans "as a ruthless gang of African buccaneers."[42]

One article called the Spaniards, *los señores y los dones*,[43] "brutish beasts," reverting to the racist terms used to describe people of African-descent, but, in this instance, to those who dehumanized and treated the Africans as less than human. Harsh and criminal depictions of the Spaniards was common in these anti-slavery newspapers, regarding them sometimes "as villains" for their illegal enslaving activities and inhuman trafficking actions. The author illustrated the absurdity of the events, inviting the reader to ponder what would have happened if the reverse had been true; if those enslaved had been white captives by a crew of African descent. This twist, which formed part of the middle *Amistad* story, steered readers to reflect on the imbalanced power dynamics of those of darker skins in a system privileging white systemic and ideological values and morals. While the North participated in the enslaving system in some subtle and not so subtle ways, the writer celebrated that a northern jury would offer better chances for the captives to experience freedom. This editorial article showed complete solidarity with the Africans:

> Can it be possible, that as this day a man, merely because he is from Africa, has no right to the exercise of self-defense? . . . Just reverse the picture, make the crew *black* and the captives *white*. Think ye, they would be called "a ruthless gang of African buccaneers"? Oh! Indeed the word African has all the charm. We say again, these have committed no crime against the law of nations, the least violation of the law of God, or any act which an enlightened conscience will not fully approve. Thanks to the Providence that directed them to a northern port, were they are to be tried by a northern jury.[44]

As expected in the racialized letter diatribes, the Spaniards' side contested, vehemently, that US courts did not represent an appropriate jurisdictional venue to judge whether Spanish subjects had violated their own laws. If Ruiz and Montes had been in violation, this matter should have been heard in the appropriate judicial forum, in Spanish territory, they claimed. They

[42] *Noticioso de Ambos Mundos*, 31 de agosto de 1839.
[43] The Meussrs and Dons.
[44] "From the Conneaut Gazette," *The Emancipator*, September 26, 1839.

demanded that schooner, Africans, and cargo be surrendered without haste and transported to Cuba for justice to be administered. Before and after the *Amistad* case, this appeared to be practiced. But the *Amistad* movement resisted this *modus operandi*. The abolitionists supported the principle of the Africans to exercise their right for self-determination by bearing arms toward their freedom. Justice should not be lopsided, especially for a country that fifty years ago used arms to free themselves from colonial ruling. On the other hand, the Spaniards alleged that a crime committed on the seas under another country's flag when Captain Ferrer was killed by those considered "property" of another should be judged by that flag. The lengthy article portrayed a very unlikely reality: justice for the *Amistad* Africans in the Spanish courts. They argued that even if it were true that they had the right to bear arms, "*solo á tribunales españoles les corresponde juzgarlo; en ellos los negros podrán alegar causas atenuantes, y aquellos tribunales las admitirán si son admisibles; y los intérpretes que se les dén serán tan legales ó mas que los que aquí han tenído*" (trans. It is only the duty of Spanish courts to determine whether this can be proven. In these courts the Africans will be able to present mitigating causes, and those courts will find if they are or not admissible. And the interpreters provided will be as legal or more legal than the ones they have been provided here).[45] Spaniards affirmed the competency and fairness of their courts and asserted the better qualifications of their own judicial interpreters. Underneath these "legal" claims, the Spaniards trusted that their courts would favor them, not the Africans.

As has been elaborated thus far, the abolitionists and other anti-slavery voices relied, mostly, on witness testimony for their defense, in contrast to the Spaniards' approach, which was centered on documentary evidence, such as treaties and the schooner papers. The *Noticioso* hesitated to proclaim or deny the validity of the *licencias* divulged in court proceedings and other forums. To this effect, the second *Amistad* article published in the same Spanish newspaper stated:

> *Se adelantan muchos á decir sin embargo, que los esclavos en cuestión, no lo son legalmente, por haber sido comprados en la Habana donde dicen que han sido introducidos recientemente en aquella isla en contravención de las leyes españolas. De esto repetimos, no les toca juzgar á las autoridades de este pais; ningun tratado tiene esta nacion con España sobre abolicion del tráfico de esclavos, y este tráfico no es contra el derecho de jentes, y solamente es una infracción de las leyes de algunas naciones, y así solo*

[45] "Goleta Española *Amistad*," *Noticioso de Ambos Mundos*, 23 de noviembre de 1839.

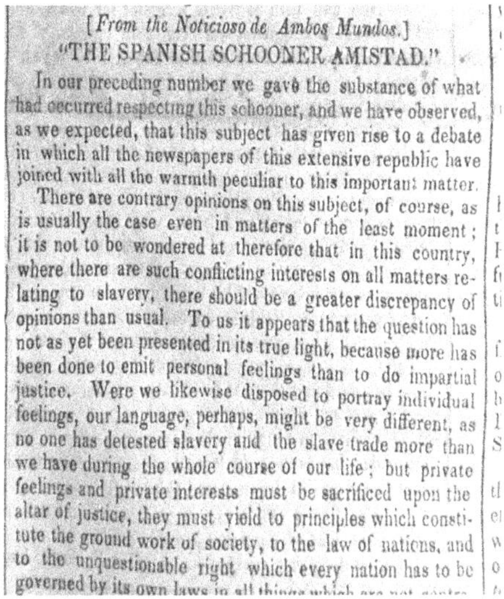

[*From the Noticioso de Ambos Mundos.*]
"THE SPANISH SCHOONER AMISTAD."

In our preceding number we gave the substance of what had occurred respecting this schooner, and we have observed, as we expected, that this subject has given rise to a debate in which all the newspapers of this extensive republic have joined with all the warmth peculiar to this important matter.

There are contrary opinions on this subject, of course, as is usually the case even in matters of the least moment; it is not to be wondered at therefore that in this country, where there are such conflicting interests on all matters relating to slavery, there should be a greater discrepancy of opinions than usual. To us it appears that the question has not as yet been presented in its true light, because more has been done to emit personal feelings than to do impartial justice. Were we likewise disposed to portray individual feelings, our language, perhaps, might be very different, as no one has detested slavery and the slave trade more than we have during the whole course of our life; but private feelings and private interests must be sacrificed upon the altar of justice, they must yield to principles which constitute the ground work of society, to the law of nations, and to the unquestionable right which every nation has to be governed by its own laws [illegible]

Figure 2.5 *Noticioso de Ambos Mundos*, September 19, 1839 (translation) in *The Emancipator*, November 23, 1839.

> *á ellas corresponde castigar á los súbditos suyos que las hayan violado.*[46]
> [Spelling and diacritic accents or lack thereof per the original]

Translation kept the news flowing to Spanish- and English-speaking communities alike in the newspapers through the course of the *Amistad* period. The same Spanish article was translated into English to be published in *The Emancipator* in the September 19 edition (see Figure 2.5).

On November 23, one of the most notable exchanges of letters published in the *Noticioso* related to the *Amistad* event exemplified the role of translation in this multilingual and multicultural case. The heated exchange began with a communique entitled "*¡Todavía mas acerca de la goleta Amistad!*" (trans. Still more regarding the Schooner *Amistad!*). In a feigned welcoming tone, a letter sent by "*el Señor* Lewis Tappan" to the editor of the *Noticioso* was printed along with a response. No translator mentioned, consistent with all newspaper publications. The beginning of the article strove to even the playing field by highlighting commonalities between the anti-slavery group and the Spaniards. "We," the narrator's voice of the article, stated that they also echoed Tappan's philanthropic interests in the cause. They acknowledged "that people of color have a soul" and wished for the Africans to enjoy the

[46] *Noticioso de Ambos Mundos*, 7 de septiembre de 1839.

salvation they have been granted. A salvation based on a Christian faith voided of the principles of equality that characterized Jesus's ministries and baptized by the marriage of two empires, the Catholic Church and the Spanish empire. Enslavers' and racists' perspectives continued to percolate in the missives. Their statements, emblematic of the enslaving system, undermined the intelligence, critical skills, and abilities of the African captives and of their interpreters, Covey and Pratt, also of African birth. The impassioned letter styled with exclamation points signaled cynical and condescending comments, attempting to appeal to Tappan's logic:

> *Seámos francos Señor Tappan . . . Los negros ignoran, no lo dude V., todo el efecto que habian de causar sus declaraciones, ignoran igualmente el valor que tiene la cruz con que han señalado sus declaraciones, y sino son ciertamente ellos los que demandan contra Montes y Ruiz . . . ¡Quien ha dicho á V. Que esos dos intérpretes que han hallado. Vds. en el Buzzard saben igualmente bien la lengua de los africanos y el inglés? ¡Basta para la legalidad que ellos lo digan!*[47]

The Spaniards questioned the entire US judicial process, because it did not align with the Spaniards' desires and framework. For example, they did not support the linguistic competencies exemplified by the interpreters recruited by the *Amistad* Committee. Ruiz and Montes doubted the credibility of the testimony of the Africans. The mention of "*la cruz*"—a religious symbol—refers to the sign used by letter writers and witnesses, interpreters included, when they could not sign their name on official documents, using the Latin alphabet. The Spaniards measured their credibility with their writing skills, their role in an enslaving society, and the color of their skins. Their opinions reinforced their language oral and written privileges. They bet on this advantage to bring the Africans and the *Amistad* Schooner back to Cuba.

On November 21, 1839, another letter, translated from Spanish into English and published in *The Emancipator* as well as *The British Emancipator* and *The Cincinnati Gazette*, revealed how the Spaniards' suspicions of the linguistic competencies of the interpreters and the credibility of the Africans were based on other nonlinguistic proclivities, such as racism, religious

[47] *Noticioso de Ambos Mundos*, 23 de noviembre 1839. (Eng. trans.: Let's be honest, Mr. Tappan . . . don't you doubt for a second that the Blacks do not know the consequences of their declarations. They also are not aware of the importance of the Cross which they have affixed to their statements, and they are the ones suing Montes and Ruiz . . . who told you that those interpreters that you have found in the Buzzard know well the same language of the Africans and English? It was only enough for the court for them to say so!)

bias, domination, and class and pro-slavery ideology. The long diatribe between both sides started with the translated sentence, "in what country do we live?—such is the inquiry of every impartial man upon learning the imprisonment of Messrs. Ruiz and Monte." It continued midway with the following observations regarding interpreting issues:

> Where is the sanction of the oath of men who are in the first-place notorious murderers, and in the second-place savages ignorant of the existence of the divinity, and without more idea of the Holy Bible than we have of what has never existed? In the next place who can believe that the language and meaning of these negroes, who speak none of the cultivated languages, and whose depositions have been taken through another negro interpreter, picked up by the abolitionists, Lord knows where, have been truly and faithfully interpreted?[48]

The impartial ideology purported in this quote denotes the Africans as "savages" for being ignorant of the European God and biblical texts, but knowledgeable of the right to defend their freedom. The author ascribed to a theology professed by the religion of the colonial and enslaving empire. The author claimed partial views through impartial perspectives. The Africans and the allied abolitionists would not be heard "objectively" in their courts of law with the Catholic blessing complicit with the institutions representing Spain.

A nameless translator converted the decision of Judge Judson from English to Spanish in the article printed on February 15, 1840, in the *Noticioso*. It pointed to translation issues and quoted portions of the decision in English. This article was signed by "*UN ESPAÑOL*" (trans. a Spaniard). With such high stakes, anonymity exercised by writers and translators on both sides offered a layer of protection from public accusations, ostracizing, or persecution. The public controversy must have been such that this writer/translator preferred to stay anonymous, even from the other side of the issue. Preferences for anonymity extended to informants who knew the negative consequences of revealing the truth. In another article that criticized how slaveowners bypassed the international treaties abolishing transatlantic slavery in Spain, the writer specified that the informant chose to remain unknown, "for obvious reasons." He is "a gentleman of responsible character, who enjoys ample opportunities of knowing the customs of Cuba, but who, for obvious reasons, does not choose to give his name to the public."[49] A

[48] Ibid.

[49] *The Emancipator*, September 26, 1839.

similar reason may have guided the translators on both sides to remove their names and forgo credit for the work.

In this nineteenth-century case, responsibility for translations resided within institutions, whether the DOS, Congress, or newspapers. This stands in contrast with interpreters whose names and identities were given full visibility. The *Amistad* interpreters suffered greater risks and racialized attacks than the *Amistad* translators who remained publicly anonymous. In a high-profile case such as the *Amistad* case, translators utilized alternatives to hide inconspicuously behind the printed words, an option not available to those offering oral interpretations in public hearings, depositions, and interviews.

3

The *Amistad* Translators

John Quincy Adams, One of the Four *Amistad* Translators

By the time John Quincy Adams (JQA) became ingrained in the *Amistad* matter, he had been trained as a translator and knew how interpreting matters intermingled with international policy and relations. In 1817, Adams was appointed as secretary for the US Department of State—the first department "to be established under the Constitution"[1]—after an international experience in Paris, Great Britain, the Netherlands, Germany, and Russia.[2] Since the creation of the DOS, translation and language matters became essential activities of this bureau. John Hay, his predecessor, was responsible for incorporating the role of interpreters/translators as part of this office. Jay convinced Congress to authorize him "to appoint an interpreter so that in the future all papers written in a foreign language which might be communicated to Congress from the Department of Foreign Affairs should be accompanied with a translation into English."[3] By then, printing duties of approved congressional resolutions and other documents fell within the scope of the DOS. These pamphlets were to be delivered to each senator, representative, and state governor, which, in the case of the *Amistad* issues, augmented the visibility of the *Amistad* conundrum for all sides and opened the door for the printing of the "N. 185" that revealed the mistranslations.

Adams's eight-year tenure inherited the practice of hiring multilingual translators and interpreters for high-level linguistic tasks. As early as in 1789, the DOS hired French interpreters for $250 a year, and others for $150.[4] Since then, other translators and interpreters served in the department, such as Robert Greenhow, who came to work as DOS translator for a yearly salary of $1,600. Additional tasks were added to his linguistic role: that of

1 Graham H. Stuart, *The Department of State: A History of His Organization, Procedure and Personnel* (New York: MacMillan Co., 1949), 15.
2 Stuart, *The Department of State*, 52.
3 Stuart, *The Department of State*, 7.
4 Stuart, *The Department of State*, 7.

the keeper of the archives and library, which Adams reorganized during his time as secretary. From the beginning of the formation of the US, language mediation was at the heart of US political dealings and cultural imperial ventures. Forced to contend with three main imperial powers: England, France, and Spain, the US depended on diplomatic translations and linguistic mediations to negotiate colonial expansion and secure geopolitical presence. Spanish, a lingua franca at the time, represented one of those key languages. Before Adams exited as secretary, a bill was passed before the House of Representatives to appoint a "keeper of the archives" who possessed Spanish-language knowledge. Greenhow, the *Amistad* translator, was appointed to this task.

Adams's educational, personal, and political background suited him for his post as DOS secretary in many areas, but particularly on the linguistic front. As a polyglot and as an experienced translator, he continued developing these skills for decades, translating biblical verses, comparing literary texts, reviewing international treaties, and using sight translation as a language-learning tool.[5] Adams often translated from the biblical Greek and Hebrew, during or after attending church services. From the French, he translated the *Fables of La Fontaine*, which he compared to others published at the time. From German to English, he translated *Oberon* which was published posthumously 100 years after the arrival of the *Amistad* Africans. Translation skills from and to various languages offered a venue for practitioners to acquire linguistic competency, as it did for Adams, and the educated elite in US educational institutions. His diaries account for the numerous times that Adams employed these skills, "attempting" to translate: Horace's *The Odes*, the *Letters on Silesia*, Auger's French translation of *Oration*, and *Ovid's Epistles*. Other times, he requested to see the originals of Spanish, Italian, and French documents with their respective translated copies to contrast and review. His experience with Spanish documents extended to treaties with Spain, Mexico, and, notably, his own translation of a section of Las Casas's witnessing of the cruelties of the Spaniards with the Indigenous populations: "I made this morning a translation from the works of Las Casas, of his statement respecting the use of bloodhounds by the Spaniards in the island of Hispaniola, against the Indians."[6] It stands as a contrast that his sympathies

[5] Also known as "Sight Interpreting," this technique combines both professional translation and interpretation skills. The translator or interpreter reads a text while rendering an oral interpretation in another language. This was a common practice at DOS to review translations used by Adams with his granddaughters to teach them French while sight translating English biblical verses.

[6] April 4, 1840, v. 42, John Quincy Adams Digital Diary. Collection of the Massachusetts Historical Society.

against the atrocities to the Native Americans in the newly formed USA were absent from his daily reflections and, in fact, his political and personal actions. Furthermore, as DOS Secretary under the presidency of Monroe, Adams played an instrumental part in the drafting of the Monroe Doctrine, a prelude to the contemporary overall colonial relationship between the US, the Caribbean, and Central and South America.

When Adams compared the original Spanish *licencias* to their English translations, he was a competent translator. His decades of multilingual translation experience in the private and political sphere prepared him to develop perspectives on translation theory and methodology. This theoretical and professional background informed his opinion on the *Amistad* "scandalous mistranslations." Consideration of contextual clues have been in the purview of those perfecting their translation skills for centuries. Another translation technique commonly utilized involves inserting words to make a translated text more comprehensible to the audience. Adams encountered a myriad of opportunities to employ both methods, such as when reflecting on the translation of the biblical verse of Mark 7:11:

> There appears to be no difference of opinion as to the meaning of the passage but in the original the sentence is incomplete, and all translators interpolate words to make it intelligible. There is some obscurity with regard to the import of the word Coban, which is used in no other passage of the Bible—but the meaning is to be settled by the context.[7]

Additionally, to some of the readership of translated texts, the translation activity may result in procedural gains and losses. Adams commented on some of the losses when translating Chapters 54 and 55 of the prophetic book of Isaiah in the Bible. After elaborating on the historical and contextual elements of this book, he pondered: "the power in the original Hebrew can be conceived only by reflecting how immeasurably all poetical beauty withers in any translation."[8] A paraphrasing preference instead of a word-to-word translation has also been defended in translation circles for centuries. JQA commented in 1804 on his unpublished translation of Jean-Baptiste Rousseau's "Ode to Fortune" and on how to translate historical texts: "the

[7] June 11, 1839, v. 41, John Quincy Adams Digital Diary. Collection of the Massachusetts Historical Society.

[8] March 14, 1841, v. 41, John Quincy Adams Digital Diary. Collection of the Massachusetts Historical Society.

allusions to ancient history . . . must be rendered rather by paraphrase than by translation."[9]

Despite his accumulated expertise that he applied for the benefit of the *Amistad* Africans, Adams was dissatisfied with the myriad tasks that occupied his hours in a day, preferring to devote his time to developing one: "I had made extracts, copies, translations, quotations more perhaps than any other man living, without ever being able to pack up my knowledge or my labour in any methodological order."[10] By the time that John Quincy Adams used his high level of influence in advocacy of the *Amistad* translation controversy, his extensive experiences along with his abolitionist stances informed his opinions. This background foregrounded Adams when he met with Robert Greenhow.

JQA, Robert Greenhow, the Second *Amistad* Translator, and the Creation of the 1840 Congressional Subcommittee to Explore the *Amistad* Translation Matters

For nine years, Greenhow was a DOS clerk working as a translator, aka a "dragoman." In this role, he encountered translation challenges similar to the ones posed by the *licencias*. JQA's diary entries alternated between the terms "translator" and "dragoman" when referring to the DOS translators and interpreters. The Turkish-derived term "dragoman" appertains to a translator, interpreter, and/or diplomatic negotiator of multiple languages within the Ottoman Empire. Dragomans filled a high-level linguistic need of a vastly populated multilingual geographical area. Children or prisoners were trained in the responsibilities and language skills required to hold these diplomatic positions, often inherited from familial structures.[11] Along with the privileges inherent to the dragoman, their role exposed them to dangerous and precarious situations, often even life-threatening. Older empires than the USA around the world had long experience in the training and employment

[9] October 5, 1841, v. 41, John Quincy Adams Digital Diary. Collection of the Massachusetts Historical Society.

[10] September 5, 1841, v. 41, John Quincy Adams Digital Diary. Collection of the Massachusetts Historical Society.

[11] Moira Inghilleri, "Translation and Violence," in *The Routledge Handbook of Translation and Politics*, ed. Fruela Fernández and Jonathan Evans (London; New York: Routledge, 2018), 150–1.

of dragomans. In need of diplomatic linguistic tradition, the US adopted the usage of this term to identify their DOS translators.

When John Quincy Adams met with Robert Greenhow to inquire about his translation methodology on December 9, 1840, Adam's extensive experiences as a translator informed his opinions and actions. Adams compared Greenhow's translation with the one printed on Doc. No. 185 several times prior to the congressional hearing on the matter. The established procedure involved two steps: DOS translating, followed by DOS sending both original and translations to the congressional office in charge of printing. Adams walked to the DOS offices on December 19 with three objectives in mind: to notify Greenhow that he was to attend the Congressional Translation Committee in two days; to speak with John Forsyth, current DOS Secretary; and to compare once more Greenhow's translation with the copy of the *licencias* of the *Amistad* captives sent by Holabird, the district attorney in the case.

In the meeting with Adams, Greenhow argued vehemently in his favor, complaining "that he had been unjustly charged with making a false translation" in Jay's letter.[12][13] Greenhow avouched that he retained the preferred technique of transferring the same term from the original document to the translated text when a suitable term in the recipient's context or language did not exist. He further insisted that his technique was sound, inserting the term "*Ladino*" in his official translation.[14] To prove it, he brought copies of his translations.[15] Concerned for both his reputation and future employment with the DOS, he petitioned Adams to intervene to clear this matter and for "the House

[12] December 9, 1840, v. 41, John Quincy Adams Digital Diary. Collection of the Massachusetts Historical Society.

[13] In her book, *The Unsettlement of America* Anna Brickhouse examines how Greenhow "produced patently false translations for the U.S. government, manipulating long-standing tensions between literature and history to lay the legal groundwork for national expansion into the hemisphere." (Anna Brickhouse, *The Unsettlement of America: Translation, Interpretation, and the Story of Don Luis de Velasco, 1560–1945* [New York: Oxford University Press, 2014], 192.) To date, *Amistad* archival materials do not draw connections to mistranslations of the *licencias* to Greenhow. On the other hand, Adams's role in the unveiling of the mistranslations issues of the legislative branch and the role of the *Amistad* African interpreters support a perspective argued in her book of the "unsettling" resistance-like actions during the colonial-imperial expansion of the nineteenth century.

[14] December 9, 1840, v. 41, John Quincy Adams Digital Diary. Collection of the Massachusetts Historical Society.

[15] Adams's diary attests to having read Greenhow's translation; however, I have not been able to locate an original or copy of the translation. December 21, 1840, v. 41, John Quincy Adams Digital Diary. Collection of the Massachusetts Historical Society.

to exonerate him."[16] This meeting spawned the congressional resolution presented to form the subcommittee to investigate the scandalous translation. Adams did not miss this opportunity to launch another attempt to abolish the Gag Rule passed early in the year. In collaboration with another member of the House, they proposed to "reconsider the vote for printing 15,000 copies" of the controversial pamphlet containing the translational disputes. The more printed copies, the greater the visibility for struggles congruent with that of the *Amistad* Africans. Both propositions were quashed, but the creation of the five-member subcommittee was approved and was composed of the following House representatives: James M'Kay, William Medill, Daniel Barnard, John Dennis, and Adams, the latter appointed as the chair. With this action, Adams demonstrated that he acted "to exonerate [Greenhow] entirely from all blame in the matter."[17]

At 10:00 a.m., on December 21, 1840, the "Committee on the Falsified Documents N. 185" began their hearing. They examined under oath the two deponents: Robert Greenhow, DOS translator, and Thomas S. Geddes, proofreader of *The Globe*. Geddes worked at the printing office of "Blair and Rives," editors under contract with Congress to produce *The Congressional Globe*, which published extracts and summaries of congressional proceedings and debates. Geddes declared that "he set the types according to the manuscript, and that the word 'sound' was substituted for Ladino, and Ladina, by the direction of the proofreader, marked on the proof."[18] Greenhow came prepared to prove his inculpability with the finalized translation and other DOS-related *Amistad* court files in hand.

Robert Greenhow was deposed regarding his translation methodology. As part of his hearing, he showed his original documents demonstrating how he maintained the Spanish terms, *ladinos/ladinas*, as part of his translation process. Greenhow charged with his expertise indicating that "there was no possible sense in which the word *sound* was a correct translation"[19] of the terms in question. This testimony dismissed him from the mistranslation. The editor of the publishing house was also deposed in the committee stating that he could not remember "who" instructed him to record the change

[16] December 9, 1840, v. 41, John Quincy Adams Digital Diary. Collection of the Massachusetts Historical Society.

[17] December 10, 1840, v. 41, John Quincy Adams Digital Diary. Collection of the Massachusetts Historical Society.

[18] John Quincy Adams Digital Diary, v. 41, December 21, 1840. [electronic edition], Adams Family Papers: An Electronic Archive, Collection of the Massachusetts Historical Society. http://www.masshist.org/digitaladams.

[19] John Quincy Adams Digital Diary, v. 41, December 21, 1840. [electronic edition], Adams Family Papers: An Electronic Archive, Collection of the Massachusetts Historical Society. http://www.masshist.org/digitaladams.

in the final copy. Similarly, Geddes's explanation removed him from any responsibility in the switching of these terms. Yet, the question remained: Who or what entity was responsible for this "sound" pro-slavery mistake? Complicity in the stance against freedom and human rights penetrated various layers of the governmental bodies, including subcontractors.

The committee adjourned without a final decision on the matter, until December 24, on Christmas Eve. They would meet twice before arriving at a decision. The deponents present were sworn in and questioned regarding a "small slip of paper" attached to the written-translated document. Other mistranslations involving the *licencias* made it to printed page, but without any major consequence to the main issue at hand. The hearing yielded a plausible story. Trendholm, the printing office proofreader, assumed responsibility for the "sound negro" exchange in response to the information contained in the "small slip of paper." He testified that someone instructed him to make the change but could not recall the reason for his note. Trendholm withheld the name of the one who instructed him from Congress. Although this situation leaves more questions than answers, the committee members at that meeting—Adams, M'Kay, Medill, and Barnard—were satisfied with the findings and continued deliberations on the contents of the report. M'Kay and Medill opposed any reference that would incriminate the proofreader or the DOS. No consensus was reached except on one issue: to designate Adams to draft the committee's falsification report.[20]

Amistad-related entries in Adams's diaries for the month of December 1840 constitute a third of all his daily chronicles, around fifteen in total for that month. His January 1841 entries reflect a similar number. After the Christmas Eve meeting, Adams called for another meeting for December 31. Still no agreement was reached between M'Kay, Medill, and the Chair. The former insisted that the subject of the report should be limited to the facts and should not include opinions. Adams disagreed with a "tight-laced" approach and proceeded to prepare the report accordingly. However, the report was not approved. M'Kay and Medill wanted to produce a report exonerating the "proofreader of all bad intention and the house printers of all responsibility [and] the administration of all knowledge or participation in the wrong."[21] In other words, to exonerate them of any intentional collusion. Even though this translation did not represent the official one in the court files, the exposure of this "sound" mistake could leave lasting impressions on the readers and

[20] December 21, 1840, v. 41, John Quincy Adams Digital Diary. Collection of the Massachusetts Historical Society.

[21] December 31, 1840, v. 41, John Quincy Adams Digital Diary. Collection of the Massachusetts Historical Society.

the anti-slavery and pro-slavery continuum. All parties were guided by their individual principles and ideologies, even though these were in opposition to each other. At the end, Adams's reporting principles prevailed.

To aid in his defense, this report provoked Trendholm to pay Adams a visit expressing his angst about the report and pleading to insert a sentence on "his exposition of his reasons for changing the words *Ladino* and *Ladina* in the manuscript to *sound*."[22] Adams did not acquiesce: "I assured him that his new paragraph was not necessary; but that if it was, I could not authorize the alteration of an iota from the manuscript."[23] Was the proofreader trying to inculpate someone else, was he compensated for the change, or was he trying to offer some linguistic competency licensing him to effectuate the change on the manuscript? These questions remain unanswered. However, Trendholm's reaction elicits the gravity and impact of the editorial, purposeful mistake and points to other parties being rescued from further accountability, most likely pro-slavery supporters in cahoots with congressional members. Chairing the committee and preparing for the upcoming Supreme Court appearance consumed Adams for a considerable amount of time, and his daily tasks were largely set aside.

The *Amistad* matter brought to the forefront international-political maneuvers that were troublesome for Adams. He followed up with Attorney General Henry D. Gilpin, relating to him the position of the executive branch in this case. Gilpin related that the president of the USA did not support the dismissal of the case before the Supreme Court, largely "because the Spanish Minister insisted on the delivery up of the men as slaves to be sent to the Havana."[24] Adams pressed Gilpin with his arguments in favor of dismissal, to no avail. President Van Buren masqueraded his pro-slavery ideology, succumbing to the international pressure mounted by the Spanish Empire in the voice of the Spanish Ministers located in the USA. This bi-branch collusion, in addition to the mysterious instructions to the proofreader, troubled Adams:

> with deep anguish of heart, and a painful search of means to defeat and expose the abominable conspiracy executive and judicial of this Government against the lives of these wretched men—How shall the facts be brought out? . . . with temper—with calmness—with moderation—

[22] January 8, 1841, v. 41, John Quincy Adams Digital Diary. Collection of the Massachusetts Historical Society.

[23] January 8, 1841, v. 41, John Quincy Adams Digital Diary. Collection of the Massachusetts Historical Society.

[24] December 11, 1840, v. 41, John Quincy Adams Digital Diary. Collection of the Massachusetts Historical Society.

> with firmness—with address—to avoid being silenced, and to escape the imminent danger of giving the adversary the advantage in the argument, by overheated zeal.[25]

William B. Hodgson: The Backstage Translator in the *Amistad* Congressional Saga

Despite Greenhow's attempts to prove his innocence in the mishandling of the final printing of the translation of the Africans' *licencia*, rumors circulated about his possible dismissal from office as DOS translator and librarian. William B. Hodgson—a prior DOS translator and current DOS dragoman—informed Adams of his precarious situation. They became acquainted under Adams's presidency in the 1820s when he began his service as dragoman.[26] During their encounter, Hodgson expressed that, in case Greenhow's dismissal materialized, he wished to be reinstated in his previous post as translator at the Washington office. Hodgson feared he may be sent "to Constantinople as Dragoman,[27] and in that event Commodore [David] Porter,[28] will either kill him or in some way accomplish his ruin."[29] Hodgson further asked Adams to intervene with the DOS on his behalf. It is difficult to ascertain whether the rumors had weight, if Hodgson was avoiding a dangerous assignment by Porter, or if he just wanted take Greenhow's post. Greenhow continued working at the DOS even as late as 1852, and Hodgson returned to the Mediterranean in 1841 as consul general of Tunisia.

Hodgson joined the translation team as the third backstage *Amistad* translator. Prior to his request to work in the DOS language office, Hodgson wrote to JQA on December 16, 1840, to offer his expertise on the usage of the term *Ladino* when he lived in South America as part of his DOS duties (refer to Figure 3.1). Adams trusted Hodgson perhaps more than he trusted Greenhow, seeking a second opinion. He consulted with Hodgson on the definitions of the terms *Bozales* and *Ladinos*. At his request, Hodgson geared

[25] December 12, 1840, v. 41, John Quincy Adams Digital Diary. Collection of the Massachusetts Historical Society.
[26] Charles J. Johnson, "William Brown Hodgson 1801–1871," https://www.georgiaencyclopedia.org/articles/history-archaeology/william-brown-hodgson-1801–1871/ (accessed March 15, 2023).
[27] Emphasis in original.
[28] Porter served in Constantinople as Chargé d' Affaires, leading a diplomatic mission at the capital of the Ottoman Empire.
[29] April 8, 1841, v. 41, John Quincy Adams Digital Diary. Collection of the Massachusetts Historical Society.

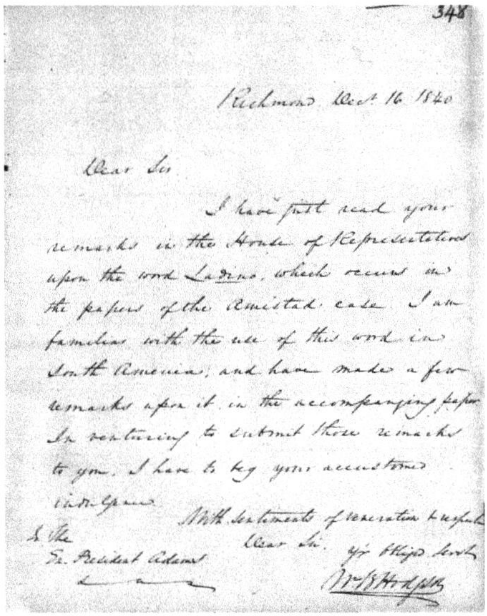

348

Richmond Decr 16 1840

Dear Sir

I have just read your remarks in the House of Representatives upon the word Ladino, which occurs in the papers of the Amistad case. I am familiar with the use of this word in South America; and have made a few remarks upon it in the accompanying paper. In venturing to submit these remarks to you, I have to beg your accustomed indulgence.

With sentiments of veneration & respect
Dear Sir. yr obliged servt
Wm B Hodgson

To the
Ex-President Adams

Figure 3.1 "Hodgson to Adams." MHS P 54 Reel 516, WBH to JQA 12-16-1840 Richmond. Collection of the Massachusetts Historical Society.

into action. In February 1841, Hodgson forwarded a letter, in Spanish, to Adams from Mr. Martín on the term "*Ladino*" in contrast with the term "*Bozal*." Martín based his conclusions on two Spanish literary works: *El Cid*, from the twelfth century, and *Don Quixote*, from the seventeenth century. His exposition confirmed the racialized and cultural significance of these terms, now contextualized to the *Amistad* situation. *Ladino*, he abounded, derived from "*latino*," which refers to moors or Blacks who spoke with ease the lingua franca spoken by Christians.[30] *Bozales*, on the other hand, spoke only their modern tongue. Adams applied his Spanish-language skills, once more, to read this letter as a second source from Spain to widen his sources, in hopes of strengthening his arguments. The extended relationship between Hodgson and Greenhow encompassed the *Amistad* translation concerns.

Adams's sphere of influence in government through the *Amistad* period was sound. As he joined the *Amistad* movement, however, he was concerned. Still, he felt unprepared to present his arguments even after the many hours devoted to the task. His frustration turned into despair when he envisioned a fatal end for the *Amistad* Africans. He could only think of one solution:

[30] Reel 517, Record 31180, John Quincy Adams Digital Diary. Collection of the Massachusetts Historical Society.

"the best thing . . . make up a purse and pay for them and then send them to Africa."[31] In 1828, Adams pardoned Ho-Chunk defendants sentenced to be executed because the court failed to provide a suitable interpreter during their murder trial. He was aware of "the decisive and potentially prejudicial role that interpreters played in courts organized by a colonizing power."[32] The *Amistad* case displayed a different outcome. Competent interpreters assisted the Africans to testify in court substantiated by the favorable decision issued by the trial judge. He continued preparing for the hearing before the Supreme Court that had been postponed until March of the same year, allotting him more time to pen his arguments.

William Jay, Esq., the Fourth *Amistad* Translator

Other friends of the *Amistad* Africans objected to the translation choices in the congressional document, the December 1840 edition of *The American and Foreign Anti-Slavery Reporter, Extra*, published "Documents relating to the Africans taken in the *Amistad*." Except for the opening letter addressed to Lewis Tappan, Esq., from Jurist William Jay, 1808 Yale graduate, the other printed documents were excerpted from the same official Doc. No. 185 published for the 26th Congress, 1st Session, dated April 15, 1840. In his letter presented before Congress regarding those responsible for translating the *licencias* from Spanish into English, Judge Jay asserted:

> The documents from which I have quoted, were laid before Congress by the President, in March last. On such occasions, it is usual to give *foreign* documents in their own language, *verbatim* with English translations. These last, it is understood, are made in the Department of State. Among the documents submitted, are the *Amistad* papers in Spanish, with translations. They include two permits, granted at Havana, for the transportation of the slaves belonging to Montes and Ruiz. . . . From the Havana fraud, let us turn to an extraordinary falsifications of papers, perpetrated, probably, in the department of State.[33]

Judge Jay dedicated close to half of the content of his editorial letter to elaborating on the problems of the translations, specifically of the Spanish

[31] January 4, 1841, v. 41, John Quincy Adams Digital Diary. Collection of the Massachusetts Historical Society.
[32] See Foreword in this book.
[33] *The American and Foreign Anti-Slavery Reporter*, December 1840, 4.

licencias. The jurist summarized the story and judicial issues of the case, following the affirmative decision of Judge Judson on behalf of the *Amistad* Africans on January 7, 1840, trial that was being appealed to the US Supreme Court. Regarding the *licencias* and the decision of the district attorney for the federal government, Jay indicated:

> The court decided that the Spanish papers . . . were false and fraudulent; that the men were *Bozals* [*sic*], or native Africans, illegally imported, and were not slaves; and that they should be sent back to Africa by the President, under the act of 1819.
>
> [. . .]
>
> Having now contemplated with me, the cruelty, hypocrisy, and chicanery of the Federal Government with regard to these men, let me next ask your attention to a bold, palpable and wicked FRAUD.[34] [All emphasis in original]

The Spanish *licencias* were so crucial that after Judge Judson issued his decision in the case, he wrote to Mr. Baldwin, Esq., on June 24, 1840, advising him to include them as part of the appeal brief: "Sir, I have made some slight corrections in the findings drawn up by you, and still think it proper to incorporate in the record the two passports, which will be filled [*sic*] in by the clerk"[35] [all emphasis in original]. From when Judge Judson dismissed the case of Margaret Crandall, whose school for Black girls was burned down by anti-Black supporters, his views had experienced a significant transformation. His decision in favor of the Africans showed a change of heart from his prior biases, "the political partialities . . . and the zeal he had sometime before exhibited against the Abolitionists."[36] This letter, in turn, reflects his partnership with counsel for African defendants. The "passports" Judson refers to are the two *licencias*, pertaining to the transport of the "forty-nine African males" and the "three Black girls" that had been discussed on previous pages. These also comprised the same two documents that were the object of discussion in Judge Jay's letter.

William Jay's exposition on the matters of the Spanish *licencias* was comprehensive.[37] Not only did he analyze the problematic issues in the usage of the terms *Ladinos, Ladinas*, and *Bozales*, but also quoted portions of Dr.

[34] *The American and Foreign Anti-Slavery Reporter*, December 1840, New York, 3.
[35] Baldwin Family Papers (MS 55). Manuscripts and Archives, Yale University Library.
[36] *The American and Foreign Anti-Slavery Reporter*, December 1840, 4.
[37] William Jay was an acting judge who wrote about the *Amistad* case but did not preside in these proceedings.

Madden's affidavit submitted as evidence in the November 1839 proceeding, for which he sailed from Cuba to the USA, on his way to Spain to engage in abolitionist efforts with another Spanish side. Jay quoted Madden to reinforce the reasons why a governmental document produced in Cuba would utilize the term *Ladino* instead of *Bozal*:

> Africans recently introduced cannot legally be held as slaves, and are called *Bozals* [*sic*]. Now the *Amistad* negroes had been introduced only about ten days before the date of the permit. How come [*sic*] they then to be designated as *Ladinos* in the document? The explanation is given by Dr. Madden. "The object of giving the name of *Ladinos* to *Bozals* [*sic*], in the permit or *traspasso* [*sic*], is to prevent capture by British cruisers on the coast of Cuba."[38]

Judge Jay continued to elaborate beyond evidence presented at trials. His linguistic comments suggest his personal translation skills in Spanish and French. He cited extensively other linguistic sources as the basis for his opinion on the grammatical attributes of nouns and adjectives in the translations. Analyzing the treatment of the term "*Ladinos*," he explained: "Observe that *Ladinos* is used in the permit as a substantive; as the specific name of a class of men—the translator has made it an adjective, although there is no substantive which it qualifies."[39] His arguments demonstrate his tacit knowledge of grammatical Spanish issues and of the translation process of research and analysis. In this exposition on the pivotal terms and their meaning, he quoted the definitions of the terms "*Ladino*" and "*Esclavo Ladino*" included in both the Spanish dictionary of *La Real Academia Española* and the French–Spanish dictionary, *Nunes y Taboada*, respectively. Right below each term, the Spanish is inserted followed by the Latin equivalent, plus an English translation of the term. He commented, "we thus find that the original meaning of the term, is one who speaks a foreign language."[40] Jay focused on the different translation of a phrase contained in both *licencias*, namely "*de la propiedad de*" [of the property of], which was translated as "belonging to," per the same congressional document. He explained, "the expression 'all belonging to' constituted, in the opinion of our government lawyers, such irrefragable evidence of title, as in a case of a life and death, to be beyond all investigation!"[41] His perspectives bolstered the notions that the Africans

[38] *The American and Foreign Anti Slavery Reporter*, December 1840, 4.
[39] *The American and Foreign Anti-Slavery Reporter*, December 1840, 4.
[40] *The American and Foreign Anti-Slavery Reporter*, December 1840, 4.
[41] *The American and Foreign Anti-Slavery Reporter*, December 1840, 4.

could not "belong" to the Spaniards as a result of their illicit trading and had the right to exercise self-defense. Jay's perspectives and actions demonstrated how translators as allies exerted key roles in this case as translators.

Judge Jay objected to the translation of the term *ladinos*, or "sound negroes," in the official US congressional document as was duly elaborated in the annotated version of this document by the Anti-Slavery Depository. He was not shy about voicing his direct opposition to the employment of this term, "this is rendered in the official translation submitted to Congress, 'I grant permission to forty-nine SOUND NEGROES'. . . . Thus, a passport for Africans imported prior to 1820, is, by state necromancy, converted into a bill of health for forty-nine negroes. . . . Now, is this translation a blunder or a fraud?"[42] [all emphasis in original]. Concerning the utilization of the word "negroes," he commented, "this interpolation of negros [*sic*], if accidental, is certainly no less convenient than extraordinary, since it renders the translation, at least, grammatical, by furnishing a substantive to which the adjective 'sound' may apply."[43] For Jay, there was only one possible culprit to the fraudulent translation: the DOS translator. He asserted: "The documents from which I have quoted, were laid before Congress by the President, in March last. On such occasions, it is usual to give *foreign* documents in their own language, *verbatim* with English translations. These last, it is understood, are made in the Department of State."[44] This statement propelled Greenhow to go to Adams to explain his innocence.

The pressure exerted by the translation issues in these Spanish documents resulted in a more accurate translation of the *licencias* printed by the Supreme Court as part of a seventy-page document published as part of the appeal process. The controversial phrases were translated to "three black *Ladinas*" and "forty-nine black *Ladinos*," an English translation more "faithful" to the original Spanish, but not to the reality of the transatlantic trade activities.

Manipulations in translations have been the focus of study for scholars from the School of Manipulation. Their scholarship has identified the forces and ideological tendencies twisting the source meaning of literature and contorting the resulting translation. Both individuals and institutions can use such translation tactics to sustain cultural and ideological principles, often under the term of "patronage." Patronage, according to Lefevere, refers to the lack of leverage of a translator in publishing her/his translations when commissioned by individuals in positions of authority or by powerful

42 *The American and Foreign Anti-Slavery Reporter*, December 1840, 4.
43 *The American and Foreign Anti-Slavery Reporter*, December 1840, 4.
44 *The American and Foreign Anti-Slavery Reporter*, December 1840, 4.

institutions.[45] Quincy Adams suspected that the manipulation of the term "*Ladinos*" happened under the patronage of the US Department of State for the consumption of another patron, US Congress. Lefevere points out the cultural role of these translation strategies: "translation can be studied as one of the strategies cultures develop to deal with what lies outside their boundaries and to maintain their own character. [It is] the kind of strategy that ultimately belongs in the realm of change and survival, not in dictionaries and grammars."[46] The manipulated translation of the *licencias*, adding the word "sound" and omitting the term "*ladinos*," reflected the support of an enslaving USA culture during a gag period in Congress to divert readers from the legislative branch from any doubts they might have had.

The commotion stirred by William Jay and by the altered translated version motivated the Hon. John Quincy Adams to "[move] an inquiry, by a select committee" to look into the possibility of a fraudulent translation. The article was published in the *Journal of Commerce* and reprinted in *The Liberator*, on December 18, 1840. Adams informed Congress that "someone" had falsified public documents—the *licencias*—during the last congressional session of the *Amistad* matter. He further wanted to investigate if the omission of the term "*negros Ladinos*" was based on "ignorance or in fraud." Regarding the inquiry on the matter, the journalist reported:

> The translator of the State Department gave the original words, "*negros ladinos*," but, Mr. A. [John Quincy Adams] alleges that it was subsequently translated and rendered, "sound negroes." If the negroes are "*ladinos*," they were imported prior to 1820, and are slaves even under the law of nations. But Mr. Adams states that this was a fraudulent designation given them at Havana. If they are "*negroes Bozals* [*sic*]" they were imported since the slave trade was prohibited, and are free under the stipulations of a treaty existing between Great Britain and Spain.[47]

Mr. Adams became the chair of the inquest committee (refer to Figure 3.2), where he would "sift matters to the bottom." The investigated matter was considered very relevant to the case, especially as Adams and the abolitionists

[45] André Lefevere, *Translation/History/Culture: A Sourcebook* (London: Routledge, 2002), 19.
[46] Lefevere, *Translation/History/Culture*, 10.
[47] "Congress," *The Liberator*, December 18, 1840. Collection of the Massachusetts Historical Society.

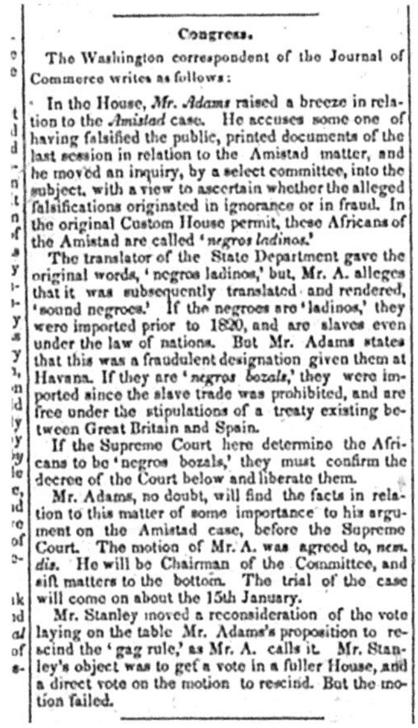

Congress.

The Washington correspondent of the Journal of Commerce writes as follows:

In the House, *Mr. Adams* raised a breeze in relation to the *Amistad* case. He accuses some one of having falsified the public, printed documents of the last session in relation to the Amistad matter, and he moved an inquiry, by a select committee, into the subject, with a view to ascertain whether the alleged falsifications originated in ignorance or in fraud. In the original Custom House permit, these Africans of the Amistad are called '*negros ladinos*.'

The translator of the State Department gave the original words, 'negros ladinos,' but, Mr. A. alleges that it was subsequently translated and rendered, 'sound negroes.' If the negroes are 'ladinos,' they were imported prior to 1820, and are slaves even under the law of nations. But Mr. Adams states that this was a fraudulent designation given them at Havana. If they are '*negros bozals*,' they were imported since the slave trade was prohibited, and are free under the stipulations of a treaty existing between Great Britain and Spain.

If the Supreme Court here determine the Africans to be 'negros bozals,' they must confirm the decree of the Court below and liberate them.

Mr. Adams, no doubt, will find the facts in relation to this matter of some importance to his argument on the Amistad case, before the Supreme Court. The motion of Mr. A. was agreed to, *nem. dis.* He will be Chairman of the Committee, and sift matters to the bottom. The trial of the case will come on about the 15th January.

Mr. Stanley moved a reconsideration of the vote laying on the table Mr. Adams's proposition to rescind the 'gag rule,' as Mr. A. calls it. Mr. Stanley's object was to get a vote in a fuller House, and a direct vote on the motion to rescind. But the motion failed.

Figure 3.2 "Congress," *The Liberator*, December 18, 1840.

prepared to argue the appeal before the Supreme Court on January 15, 1841, as the article pointed out: "[Mr. Adams] will find the facts in relation to this matter of some importance to his argument on the *Amistad* case." Translation issues in the *Amistad* case took center stage in newspapers and congressional forums.

4

The Recruitment

The *Amistad* Recruitment Strategies

Meritorious reasons propelled the recognition for a court interpreter as part of the defense strategy. The distinct, yet, multifaceted background of the nineteenth-century *Amistad* case prescribed particular strategies for recruiting the ideal interpreter. They generated a sui generis approach. Lacking court mandates regarding interpreting rights and without a Mende interpreter in proximity, the impassioned abolitionists, eager to defend the captured Africans and the unheard incarcerated Africans desiring to be set free, built an effective game plan. Added factors, such as the racially charged national and international context, the unfriendly threats against the lives of those on the pro-African side, and the influential hidden diplomatic agreements between Spain and the USA in the judicial process shaped the design for recruiting interpreters. The abolitionists' clear objective of hiring a judicial interpreter forged an impromptu method for answering two basic questions that had remained concealed: What languages were the African prisoners versed in? Where in Africa were they from? In response, the *Amistad* abolitionists established a dual process: the first step was to gather glossaries used to test the Africans in an attempt to identify their spoken languages, and the second was to bring African-speaking candidates to the jail who might be able to converse with the prisoners and identify those languages. To a certain extent, both searches depended on each other. Both paths sought confirmation through the manifestation of physical, oral, and emotional responses signalling a linguistic match.

Gathering Vocabulary Lists

Glossary lists aided in both pursuits. The Christian abolitionists activated their intimate networks in order to identify "trustworthy"[1] speakers of African and European languages; the responses began to be mailed from Boston, and Washington, D.C. Clues came from all venues. Lists of possible languages were received based on (1) historical facts—languages of the colonizers and their interactions with enslaved peoples along the African coast; (2) geographical knowledge—ethnic customs that would provide a connection to their places of birth, such as teeth sharpening, circumcision, and other ethnic traditions in Western Africa; and (3) the different languages spoken by Africans who lived on the African continent or on board vessels with fellow Africans and non-Africans. Lexicon lists included Spanish, Arabic, Portuguese, Mandingo, Mandingo Goulah, Gissi, Kissi, Lasso, Bambarra, Yimmanee, Sousou, Lambar, Mah-heé-no, Ah-ne-gó, "African," and Congolese. The search continued.

On September 20, 1839, Ellis Gray Loring from Boston wrote to the Tappan brothers in New York City reporting that "[he] sent yesterday to Hartford, an account of a young man here who can speak Spanish, English (very well) and three African languages viz. Ah-ne-gó, Mandingo, and Mah-heé-no." The letter closed with a task list: "I have requested a friend there to make a short vocabulary from his lips, and to send it to Hartford, directed to Lewis Tappan, or R. S. Baldwin."[2]

A letter from abolitionist Isaac Parish to Joshua Leavitt contained a list of mainly edible items: Tobacco-Yamba, Bread-Tammee, Munko, Rice-Malo or Bainda, Meat-Soubee, Fish-Yucka, Yeo, Palm bit-Turik Baby, and White Man-Torteny[3] (refer to Figure 4.1). The process involved reading these lists to the Mende Africans in hopes that they would recognize some of the terms and alert their support team of a possible linguistic and interpreter match. Among the lawyers and ministers, two key linguists belonged to this team: Professor (Rev.) Josiah Williams Gibbs,[4] a Hebrew scholar and philologist from Yale University in New Haven, Connecticut; and Dr. George E. Day, a

[1] AMA Archives FI 4606, The *Amistad* Research Center, New Orleans, Louisiana, USA.

[2] AMA Archives FI 4631, September 20, 1839, The *Amistad* Research Center, New Orleans, Louisiana, USA.

[3] AMA Archives FI 4613, September 12, 1839, The *Amistad* Research Center, New Orleans, Louisiana, USA.

[4] References to Gibbs who served as an expert witness in the trial on behalf of the *Amistad* Africans, and Day, abound in the letters from this period. Even Covey, during his deposition, stated that he had "conversed with these Africans separately in the presence of Mr. Gibbs."

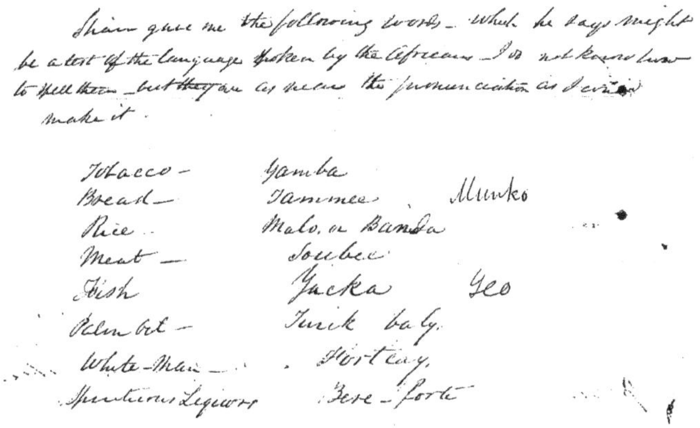
Shain gave me the following words – which he says might be a test of the language spoken by the Africans – I do not know how to spell them – but they are as near the pronunciation as I can make it.

Tobacco –	Yamba
Bread –	Tammee, Munko
Rice –	Malo, or Bamba
Meat –	Soubee
Fish	Yacka Yeo
Palm oil –	Turik baly
White Man –	Fortay
Spirituous Liquors	Bere – forte

Figure 4.1 "Shain's Voc. List." AMA Archives FI 4613, the *Amistad* Research Center, New Orleans, Louisiana, USA.

Sign Language teacher and interpreter who worked for the New York School for the Deaf and Dumb [*sic*].

Other tools were used in a similar fashion for language identification and the recruitment process. Energies were employed in securing published resources toward these pursuits. Several books circulated during this time period that proved useful. The search team dedicated time and resources into locating and furnishing a specific glossary of African words entitled *Travels through Central Africa to Timbuctoo, Vols. 1 and 2*, by Jomard René Caillié, which was considered an excellent source of African languages and was available in French and English. John Pickering informed L. Tappan:

> There are few vocabularies of the Mandingo language. . . . The most extensive one that I came acquainted with is that of the French Traveller. René Caillié, whose travels were published a few years ago and translated in England, in 2 vols. 8vo[5] 1830—the title of the work is Travels through Central Africa to Timbuctoo. This vocabulary is the more valuable, as it was prepared under the eye and with the assistance of M. Jomard, an able linguist in Paris—it contains about 200 words and phrases. M. Jomard has also compared it with that of Park and some other travellers—and he refers to some other works containing vocabularies. The original French work would be best authority, if to be found.[6] [all emphasis as in original]

[5] Refers to "*octavo*" or "the eighth."

[6] AMA Archives FI 4606, The *Amistad* Research Center, New Orleans, Louisiana, USA.

Along with this linguistic search and the continuous gathering of word lists, the abolitionist's letters reflected how the interpreter's search narrowed to focus on New York City. Urgent tones embedded in the letters mirrored the overall pressing task: "but can you not find a native Mandingo in the city of New York?"[7] Already in the nineteenth century, New York City displayed cosmopolitan traits. Ships sailing from Europe, Africa, the Caribbean and Latin America, and the southern USA facilitated rich, ethnic, political, and linguistic exchanges. Ports open the gates for the ebb and flow of supplies, skilled workers, and immigrant communities that enriched the mix. The English Commission vessels were among the anchored ones. They policed the Atlantic Ocean interrupting the enslaving transatlantic activities that violated signed treaties. On board on one of these liberating brigs, the main *Amistad* interpreter was found.

Finally, the book search yielded positive results. Caillié's book was purchased for $7.50 USD in Washington, D.C., not from New York as expected, and made it to the New Haven-based *Amistad* Committee.[8] A translated English version, not the ideal French one, advanced the cause: "Dear Sir, We have in this office 'Caillié's Travels to Timbuctoo' which shall be at the service of the Committee if desired. It is in English."[9] Caillié's source travelled throughout the northeastern corridor that ended up in Salem, Massachusetts, where thriving African-descended communities resided, many from the Caribbean. Without standardized means to certify an interpreter for his or her linguistic abilities, this book provided a way to "test" the language competency of the interpreter. Pickering wrote to Gibbs to report that Samuel Barney, an African living in Salem and of the "Mandingo" [emphasis in original], spoke his native language along with other African "dialects" [*sic*]. After "trying him with the vocabulary in Caillié's Travels," he surmised that "his services may be useful in communicating with the captured Africans of the schooner *Amistad*."[10]

Barney exemplified one of the many viable and trustworthy candidates who visited the jail in hopes of serving as a linguistic mediator. However, as with the case repeated with several candidates for more than thirty days, he did not possess the required linguistic pair to assist the *Amistad* Africans in telling their story. The vocabulary list compilation continued even after the Mende-fluent interpreters were found. For instance, Professor George Day, who assumed the responsibility for the instruction of the Africans and

7 AMA Archives FI 4606, The *Amistad* Research Center, New Orleans, Louisiana, USA.
8 AMA Archives FI 4671, The *Amistad* Research Center, New Orleans, Louisiana, USA.
9 AMA Archives FI 4620, The *Amistad* Research Center, New Orleans, Louisiana, USA.
10 AMA Archives FI 4625, The *Amistad* Research Center, New Orleans, Louisiana, USA.

for acquiring a deepening knowledge of their language, collaborated in this endeavor with "two or three young men to assist." Together with Gibbs, who was "unworried in his labor to get all the information possible," they worked "day and night." Both were "able to form a considerably copious vocabulary."[11] The *Amistad* movement depended on Day's expertise, time investment, and "warm" dedication toward them.[12] With the use of Sign Language, a disposition to understand the other, and body language, they also gathered a bilingual list of numbers in Mende. This proved, in fact, the most effective recruitment strategy that guaranteed the two Mende interpreters, James Covey and Charles Pratt, after the Kissi interpreter, John Ferry. Josiah Gibbs paced back and forth along the NYC ports reciting the Mende word list,[13] until Covey and Pratt responded with glee. However, facility with number and word lists, or published glossaries, were not the only tests. A selective list enumerated the essential components required of the ideal interpreter.

Job Qualifications for the Mende Interpreter

Unbeknownst to the *Amistad* abolitionists and interpreters, the qualifications attached to the job rapidly expanded in tandem with the anti-slavery movement rationale and objectives. Referring to them as "job qualifications" represents an afterthought. These were compiled after scrutinizing the accomplishments of the interpreters who assisted the *Amistad* Africans from the moment the Africans arrived until after their release from prison while awaiting their return to Africa. These qualifications pertained to the tasks and skills associated within the contexts of each of these settings. Personal correspondence and newspaper articles both implicitly and explicitly alluded to seven main interpreting qualifications that can be categorized into four professional areas: judicial or court interpreting, medical interpreting, community interpreting, and conference interpreting.[14] Court interpreting signifies interpreting that occurs within the legal system; medical interpreting refers to linguistic mediation within the context of health settings; community interpreting represents interpreting that serves those in a wider social context in both public and private settings, which may include schools, governmental offices, the police, and even the previous

[11] AMA Archives FI 4660, The *Amistad* Research Center, New Orleans, Louisiana, USA.

[12] AMA Archives FI 4660, The *Amistad* Research Center, New Orleans, Louisiana, USA.

[13] This exact version has been only corroborated by one historical account in Barber's narrative.

[14] As in the case at hand, the category of court interpreters existed at the time of the *Amistad* trial. The other three categories are borrowed from contemporary usage.

two categories; and conference interpreting mostly identifies interpreting for large audiences, mostly employing the modalities of simultaneous and/or consecutive interpreting with the assistance of interpreting technology not invented during this researched period. Community interpreting settings are often characterized by asymmetrical relationships of power,[15] one party representing a language with more power than the language and positionality of another party. Factors present in the interpreting encounter produce stressors and impact the available options of the interpreter.

The first three job qualifications vital in the *Amistad* case allowed defendants to have their day in court: the ability to interpret in client/attorney conferences to assist in their own defense, in off-the-record and on-the-record proceedings, and in witness testimonies during the trial. These qualifications resemble some of those required for court interpreters in the twenty-first century, for example, client/attorney conferences including defendants' or plaintiffs' confidential information—almost always protected—used in litigation preparation. From day one, *Amistad* lawyers expressed the burning need to open communication via the interpreter. On-the-record interpreting afforded *Amistad* plaintiffs, officers of the court, defendants, and all parties to argue their positions. African plaintiffs in court, and reckoned as defendants by an enslaving society, exerted their agency to participate actively in their defense. Two additional skills, nonetheless, superseded these requirements: "ethnic competency" and a predisposition for "advocacy," which challenged ethical codes and professional standards known then and today.

Historically, the code of ethics and professional standards for court interpreters have excluded ethnic competency and advocacy, although actual professional praxis exhibit applications of these competencies. The medical interpretation codes of ethics have understood the need for both skills, as "cultural competency," that is, cultural awareness or cultural brokering[16] described as one of the areas of proficiency expected for medical interpreters. These terms refer to knowledge of self and others as necessary for deciphering meaning or when an intervention from the interpreter may be suitable to unblock communication affecting delivery of services. Instead

[15] Sylvia Kalina, "Ethical Challenges in Different Interpreting Settings," 72. In MonTI Special Issue 2 / (2015). Catalina Iliescu Gheorghiu and Juan Miguel Ortega Herráez, eds., *Insights in Interpreting. Status and Developments/Reflexiones Sobre La Interpretación. Presente Y Futuro,* https://rua.ua.es/dspace/bitstream/10045/52569/1/MonTI_2015_Special_Issue.pdf.

[16] For more information on these later terms and relevancy to the medical interpreting profession, refer to *The Medical Interpreter: A Foundation Textbook for Medical Interpreting*, ed. Marjory A. Bancroft (Columbia, MD: Cross Cultural Communications, 2016).

of the term "cultural competency," I opted for the term "ethnic competency," because the latter stretches beyond the knowledge of language and cultural traditions, encompassing historical and geographical knowledge, as well as the understandings of heritage and sociopolitical backgrounds.

An interpreter in the health service context may also serve as an advocate, but "only when appropriate and necessary . . . using professional judgment."[17] The International Medical Informatics Association (IMIA) and the National Code of Ethics for Interpreters in Health Care (NCIHC)—the certifying organizations for professional medical interpreting—incorporate "advocacy" as part of their professional medical interpreting standards. This type of intervention is encouraged for a medical interpreter if other actions have not proved useful in response to intercultural mediation, or "when the patient's health, well-being, or dignity is at risk . . . with the intention of supporting good health outcomes."[18] In the realm of court interpreting, thus far, ethical codes lack the inclusion of this component. Conversations and discernment surrounding latitude for advocacy while in the performance among judicial interpreters tend to be addressed apprehensively and rarely welcomed. The development of a universal code of ethics for professional interpreters and translators may pose an alternative code that creates the space to consider and respond actively and intentionally to matters involving human rights, empathy, compassion, and common sense in the delivery and rendition of their services. This type of code opens the door to analyze the ways in which current codes of ethics divorce the professional impact and linguistic performance either advertently or inadvertently, intentionally or not, when attempting to exert neutral, partial, and objective positions.

The ethnic competencies of the African-descent *Amistad* interpreters allowed them to testify in court as to their personal backgrounds and similarities to those of the *Amistad* Africans gathered through interviews. The interpreters' ethnic knowledge constituted the basis to qualify as interpreters and expert witnesses. Their acquired competency grew as a result of their personal experiences that began in freedom, then entangled with enslavement, and ended in liberation. Their ethnic expertise formed the basis for understanding the journey of the Africans that ultimately corroborated the stories narrated by the Africans.

[17] Claudia V. Angelelli, *Healthcare Interpreting Explained* (New York: Routledge, 2019), 161.

[18] A National Code of Ethics for Interpreters in Health Care, 3, Www.Ncihc.Org/Assets/Z2021images/Ncihc%20national%20code%20of%20ethics.Pdf.

As expert witnesses, court interpreters are expected to serve as linguistic experts. As such, their credibility may be questioned on language matters, "the role which the interpreter plays make him/her subject to having his/her interpretation challenged and impeached just like any other expert witness."[19] The *Amistad* interpreters faced this risk. Shortly after meeting the Mende Africans, James Covey was deposed and reported:

> These prisoners speak of the River "*Mwa*", of the place "*Jomboko*," both of which I have seen, in Africa, and they speak no language except native African, and from their language and manners, and appearance, I am sure they are native Africans. I learned to speak English language in Sierra Leone. . . . I was born in the Mandi [*sic*] country, in a place called Gho = noun, [illegible] the Mandi is my native language. I conversed with these Africans separately in the presence of Mr. Gibbs, and they are consistent in their history of the place from which they sailed in Africa, and of their voyage, to the Havanna.[20]

As an expert witness, Covey made available central facts on behalf of the defense of the Mende Africans. Not only was he questioned about their place of birth and the language they spoke, as the excerpted text illustrates, but he was also questioned regarding the false names given by the Spaniards and recorded in the *licencias*. Their authentic names became a key finding in their defense, possible only through linguistic mediation. Attesting to their native language, which was not Spanish, was pivotal to proving that their arrival in Cuba happened as a result of an illegal slave trade transaction months before; they were *Bozales*, not *Ladinos*, as claimed by their captors. Ethnic competency and personal-historical knowledge entwined. The Christian abolitionists were aware of the two distinct roles that the court interpreter for the Mende captives needed to play. Rev. Tappan, Esq. wrote to Baldwin on October 12, 1839, to instruct him of the following: "James Covey is a witness and interpreter. If so, will you have him subpoenaed."[21] His dual role

19 Nancy Schweda-Nicholson, "Court Interpreter Training: A Growing Need," May 1985, 5. ED272024. *ERIC* http://files.eric.ed.gov/fulltext/ED272024.pdf.

20 Baldwin Family Papers (MS 55). Manuscripts and Archives, Yale University Library. This testimony was gathered through the judicial instrument identified as a "deposition," as declared in this document. However, it displays characteristics also common to affidavits. The four-page document, not numbered, is dated October 4, 1839, a day after the arrival of James Covey to the New Haven jail. The document is signed by James Covey and by an administrative judge from the New Haven County Court certifying the document.

21 Baldwin Family Papers (MS 55). Manuscripts and Archives, Yale University Library.

was identified early in the process. Once the abolitionists found their ideal interpreter, they were willing to ensure his presence at trial by any necessary means. Language, culture, ideology, and history, intrinsically braided, supported the evidence in the case.

Lastly, the role of James Covey as an interpreter involved assisting as a historical narrator of the *Amistad*. Abolitionists availed themselves of all sources to disseminate the stories of the *Amistad* Africans and earn the sympathies of the anti-slavery side and those on the fence. Among the thirty-plus pages of his chronicle, Barber published in six pages some basic facts about each of the *Amistad* Africans, accompanied with a profile of each prisoner. The last profile drawing and most extensive bio was reserved for Covey, who served as the interpreter (see Figure 5.1). Printed in May 1840, it included excerpts from newspaper articles, letters, and congressional documents in the hopes of continuing to increase public support for the cause. The brief preface to his compilation reported:

> A correct statement of the facts of this extraordinary case, is deemed desirable, and the compiler has availed himself of the facilities at this command, for the attainment of this object . . . the compiler also had the opportunity of personal conversation with them, by means of James Covey, the Interpreter, and has confined himself to a bare relation of facts.[22]

Barber's pamphlet was anthologized within four months after the successful January 13 date when Judge Judson made his ruling. Judson affirmed that "the *Amistad* captives were "born free" and kidnapped in violation of international law." They had mutinied, he reiterated, out of a "desire of winning their liberty and of returning to their families and kindred." He ordered that the *Amistad* be "delivered to President Van Buren for transport back to Africa."[23] Covey's skills remained necessary after the January trial for such tasks as this one and also while waiting for the appeal. Despite his angst about being away from home, and his love for the Africans, especially the girls, the abolitionists did not authorize his return. He waited until he could return home with his fellow Africans two years later. From his first joyous encounter with the *Amistad* Africans, Covey developed a relationship with them and became a valuable support during their time inside and outside jail. This familiarity and closeness affirmed trust and assured vital disclosure. The

[22] Barber, *A History of the Amistad Captives*, 1.

[23] Douglas O. Linder, *The Amistad Case* (Kansas City, MO: School of Law, 2007), 5.

next section elaborates on additional requirements and qualities of the ideal interpreter, most of them fulfilled by James K. Covey.

Wanted: A Court Interpreter for the *Amistad* Case and a List of Requirements

Terms like "job qualifications" and "requirements" have been used interchangeably. Neither accurately describes the abilities, experiences, or skills sought for the *Amistad* interpreters in the absence of established guidelines set by the judicial bodies, certifying interpreting organizations or interpreting companies. Requirements apply to specific skills or personal characteristics necessary to perform the job as an *Amistad* interpreter. Without established job responsibilities' requirements by US federal or state judicial bodies back in the nineteenth century,[24] officers of the courts did not have guidelines for finding, hiring, or qualifying interpreters. Neither did aspiring professionals in the field have access to a career roadmap to pave the way or for guidance. Nevertheless, the abolitionists and lawyers knew that interpreters made it possible for the Mende Africans to hear the evidence presented in their favor and against them, to consult with lawyers to assist in their own defense, to confront witnesses via their lawyers, to testify on their own behalf, to listen to arguments posed by all parties, and to engage with the court. These basic tasks motivated the abolitionists to find a suitable court interpreter. The racially charged context prodded them to be unconcerned with the issues of invisibility, neutrality, or impartiality, as prescription for the optimal interpreter during recruitment and through the trial period. In interpreting encounters framed with inequality, "it may be appropriate for an interpreter to give up his/her impartiality or neutrality."[25] This was also relevant in the *Amistad* Case for the interpreters of the Africans. Also, in this situation of inequality, neither did the opposing party, represented by the Spaniards, their crown, the prosecutor, and the US executive branch uphold the concepts of invisibility, neutrality, and impartiality. Claiming impartiality in impartial situations increases the power imbalance and hinders the exercise of justice and fairness. Most past and current ethical codes and

[24] Neither did they borrow job descriptions and qualifications from other governmental agencies from parallel empires. As discussed, the Spanish Empire and colonies through Royal Decrees stipulated job requirements and codes of ethics during this period. Similarly, the English–Spanish Commission employed court interpreters to hear cases involving the people captured of slave ships as a result of the transatlantic trade.

[25] Kalina, "Ethical Challenges in Different Interpreting Settings," 76.

professional standards for interpreters fail to consider the power-imbalanced contexts. Partiality and parallel ideological positions have the potential to yield the positive effect of trust and reliability. "Trust in the interpreter and his/her skills is a crucial condition for successful interpreting."[26] While in most instances today, "no one would want a biased interpreter rendering services in a court proceeding," it is important for the interpreter "to establish the rapport with the individuals with whom she is working."[27]

As the correspondence demonstrated in the *Amistad* case, abolitionists looked deliberately for someone who was partial and who could be trusted by the movement, but above all by the captives themselves. In highly charged environments, it may be difficult, perhaps impossible, for an interpreter to maintain a sufficient level of objectivity;[28] for instance, keenly aware of the historical-adversarial dynamics as well as the prophetic opportunities. The abolitionists sought someone trustworthy, meaning someone who did not side with the enslaving narrative and who could further threaten their lives, the lives of the captured Africans, and of the interpreters. In their view, only one committed to the ending of slavery would satisfy the job requirements as an interpreter.

A critical approach to the archival material regarding the interpreter's skills, experiences, characteristics, and traits resulted in thirteen requirements for the *Amistad* court interpreter. I have further grouped them into the following categories: social connection, linguistic skills, agency, embodiment, and activism (refer to Table 4.1).

The quest for the *Amistad* interpreter sought a bilingual person with a high degree of linguistic competency in the pair languages of English, the language of the court—for court-related proceedings and for the litigation team to prepare the case—and Mende, one of the languages spoken by the African defendants and plaintiffs—for court-related proceedings, to tell their stories, to aid in their defense, as well as to interact with their surrounding communities. In addition to the issue of bilingualism, two other constants prevailed in the historical materials.

One, all possible interpreter candidates who were spoken about in the correspondence and who visited the New Haven jail were men. Two, an African who had migrated and lived in the northern USA, or someone bilingual and bicultural who had lived among Africans became the ideal interpreter candidate. The search team assumed that this type of candidate would have preserved his native African languages better than a second-

26 Kalina, "Ethical Challenges in Different Interpreting Settings," 77.
27 Mikkelson, "Evolving Views of the Court Interpreter's Role," 83.
28 Mikkelson, "Evolving Views of the Court Interpreter's Role," 83.

Table 4.1 Qualifications for Interpreters

Social Connections	**Linguistic Skills**
Faithful and trustworthy Known by the inner circle Connected to the community A churchgoer With family ties	Fluent in the African language "Easy" accent and fluency in English A Spanish speaker
Agency and Embodiment	**Activism**
Trusted by "the kidnapped Africans" Chosen by the Mende Africans	Sympathizer of the cause against slavery Able to advocate for the African prisoners A "spy"

generation speaker pressured to adopt the language-at-large and abandon his heritage language. All candidates except one were African born and raised. Bilingualism or multilingualism of European languages, as has already been mentioned, was relatively common among the formally or informally educated in the USA. Curricula incorporated the teaching of these languages, later cemented by cultural immersion in a European country where the language of study was spoken. Interest in acquiring competency in African languages existed, mainly for undertaking imperial and Christian-evangelistic pursuits. Janes, from the beginning, envisioned that the ideal interpreter would be found in New York City. As the search progressed, efforts honed on this cosmopolitan city, place of three of the interpreters ultimately chosen: James Covey, John Ferry, and George Day.

Other factors surfaced during the interpreters' interviews: fluency in the language of the "unfortunate" Africans and in English, but also having an "easy accent" amenable to a court limited in their acceptance of linguistic accents. With life threats being inflicted on the abolitionists and the USA's pro-enslaving society, a stranger, one not known by the trusted immediate circle, someone foreign to the community, or a recent arrival to the vicinity would not have satisfied the job requirements. Reputable social connections ensured physical safety and testimonial reliability. Qualities of affectivity emerged as key factors in selecting the final interpreters in this case. Physical manifestations of trust, joy, and acceptance on the part of the captured Africans alerted the abolitionists that the right interpreter had been found. A spirit of distrust predominated among the Africans after their gruelling seven-month journey of captivity, except for the two months when they steered the *Amistad*. The litigation team were aware from day one that without the fundamental element of trust, the Africans would not share their story. The agency of the *Amistad* Africans selected the optimal interpreter, and the abolitionists honored their decision.

Finally, an uninvolved interpreter, one favoring slavery, or one who "only" performed his interpreting duties would have not been a good fit for this job. Abolitionists and Africans overwhelmingly preferred someone who stood against slavery and who willingly would advocate for the Africans, if needed. And they did.

The "Simple Truth": Many Were Called; Few Were Chosen

From the first court hearing, no one could deny the need for an interpreter for the Africans. A sense of urgency permeated the recruitment correspondence as expectations increased on who could "get'" data to support or disprove their legal hypothesis. Three days after their arrival, on August 29, 1839, Janes wrote to Baldwin and Leavitt, on behalf of the abolitionists in New London, Connecticut, "to request that you will find some old African in your vicinity who can speak the native language, so that you may learn the facts from them."[29] Early in the process, issues of "trust" and "trustworthiness" became apparent (refer to Table 4.1). In a follow-up letter authored by Janes to Baldwin, he recommended that the interpreter should communicate with the imprisoned "that they are among friends or they will be unwilling to say much."[30]

On September 4, 1839, abolitionist Seth P. Staples wrote enthusiastically to counsel Baldwin. He conveyed that "an interpreter goes up this Boat who understands several negro dialects and should be glad to hear what you may learn thro' him."[31] This represents the first documented candidate who visited the jail. References to "an interpreter" equate the bilingual abilities in English and the yet-unknown African language. The archival materials do not reveal whether those identified as "interpreters" had performed previously in this role. For the purpose of this research, the term "interpreter" has been reserved for those who actually conversed with the African captives. All others are designated as "candidates."

The *Amistad* abolitionists organized with speed. The visit of the first candidate did not bear the desired fruits. The search continued with haste. On that same date, September 4, 1839, the "friends of human rights" organized the *Amistad* Committee to appeal to "The Friends of Liberty" in

[29] AMA Archives FI 4593, The *Amistad* Research Center, New Orleans, Louisiana, USA.
[30] AMA Archives FI 4594, The *Amistad* Research Center, New Orleans, Louisiana, USA.
[31] The Baldwin Family Papers (MS 55), Manuscripts and Archives, Yale University Library.

support of the *Amistad* Africans. Letters manifesting that possible candidate were delivered to New Haven in increased numbers. By September 6, Janes also reported that counsel Baldwin "willingly agreed to engage in the defense of these poor injured fellow beings."[32] On September 10, 1839, Mr. Hansen and Mr. Ferry, two African-descent candidates went to the jail to meet the captives. Rev. D. Burguess informed Rev. Joshua Leavitt that "Mr. Hansen went to N. Haven this morning and hope he will be able to converse with the Africans. As he understands several languages."[33] On that same date, Rev. Simeon Jocelyn, one of the friends of human rights who organized the *Amistad* Committee wrote to L. Tappan that "Mr. Ferry will go to Hartford today."[34] Mr. Hansen moved to other roles in the *Amistad* struggle, as an English instructor to the Africans. An affidavit on record signed by him stated that the Africans were not Spanish speakers. John Ferry, however, featured as the first of the three main court interpreters for the Mende Africans in *Amistad*-interpreting history. Summarizing the spoken languages, Prof. Gibbs[35] stated that, in addition to Mende, "another is the Vey, the language of John Ferry[36] our first interpreter. He conversed with Grabbeau in this language."[37] Grabbeau was the second in leadership after Cinque. But Cinque, also a material witness in the case, did not speak Vey. The *Amistad* legal team preferred Cinque as the main spokesperson for the *Amistad* Africans to testify in court. Ferry's contribution was significant, as he unveiled the main aspects of the story that sustained the legal theory. The quest continued. Broadening the circle became necessary to fulfill their recruitment goal. Toward this end, they published an advertisement in the September 19, 1839, issue of *The Emancipator*, a New York City abolitionist newspaper, which ran weekly every Thursday. The main goal consisted of employing "interpreters and able counsel" (refer to Figure 4.2).

Someone known and established was of utmost importance. This letter stressed a desire that the interpreter be born in Africa. It became clear that someone not known by the abolitionists, bilingual though they might be, did not fit the interpreter's profile. The preference resided for "some old African"—one who had arrived recently from Africa or who was freed

[32] AMA Archives FI 4602, The *Amistad* Research Center, New Orleans, Louisiana, USA.
[33] AMA Archives FI 4607, The *Amistad* Research Center, New Orleans, Louisiana, USA.
[34] AMA Archives FI 4628, The *Amistad* Research Center, New Orleans, Louisiana, USA.
[35] Gibbs's involvement in the recruitment process was instrumental in identifying the primary language of the Africans, studying that language, and finding the main interpreter for this case.
[36] Ferry interpreted using relay interpreting. This means from Mende to Vey and then from Vey to English.
[37] AMA Archives FI 4592B, The *Amistad* Research Center, New Orleans, Louisiana, USA.

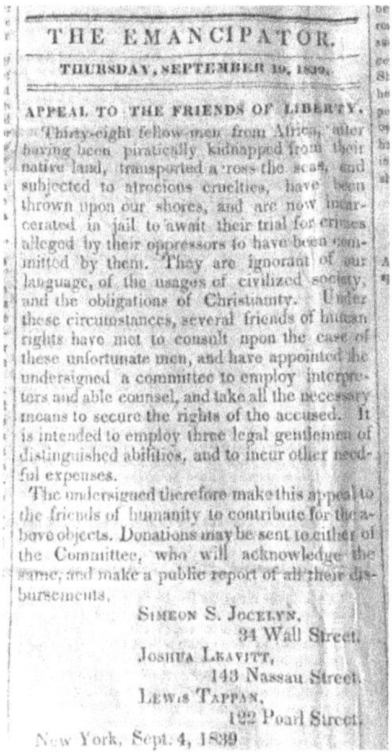

THE EMANCIPATOR.

THURSDAY, SEPTEMBER 19, 1839.

APPEAL TO THE FRIENDS OF LIBERTY.

Thirty-eight fellow-men from Africa, after having been piratically kidnapped from their native land, transported across the seas, and subjected to atrocious cruelties, have been thrown upon our shores, and are now incarcerated in jail to await their trial for crimes alleged by their oppressors to have been committed by them. They are ignorant of our language, of the usages of civilized society, and the obligations of Christianity. Under these circumstances, several friends of human rights have met to consult upon the case of these unfortunate men, and have appointed the undersigned a committee to employ interpreters and able counsel, and take all the necessary means to secure the rights of the accused. It is intended to employ three legal gentlemen of distinguished abilities, and to incur other needful expenses.

The undersigned therefore make this appeal to the friends of humanity to contribute for the above objects. Donations may be sent to either of the Committee, who will acknowledge the same, and make a public report of all their disbursements.

SIMEON S. JOCELYN,
34 Wall Street.
JOSHUA LEAVITT,
143 Nassau Street.
LEWIS TAPPAN,
122 Pearl Street.

New York, Sept. 4, 1839

Figure 4.2 September 19, 1839. *The Emancipator*.

through the Underground Railroad.[38] They hoped to find someone who would be highly competent in the Mende language and who appalled the institution of slavery. As discussed, linguistic erosion menaced those who had spent too much time immersed in another language from losing their own. A letter written on September 10, 1839, mentioned the existence of an African, a "Mandingo [emphasis in original], but has been in this country many years and may have lost his native language."[39] Pickering, corresponding with L. Tappan in the abovementioned letter, commits to writing back, if confirmed, that "he retains his native language."[40] As the date for the trial approached, without a trace of a possible interpreter, this insistence on having an "old African" waned. Issues of trust continued to percolate through the letters. Pickering combined matters of language and trust: "it will be all important

[38] The Underground Railroad built a route from the southern part of the USA that protected and hid fugitive slaves moving through the northern sections of the USA or Canada toward freedom. Letters after October 1839 reveal that Antonio, a creole boy, disappeared from prison into this "railroad" and was taken to Canada after the decision of the court that he should be returned to Spanish territories.

[39] AMA Archives FI 4606, The *Amistad* Research Center, New Orleans, Louisiana, USA.

[40] AMA Archives FI 4606, The *Amistad* Research Center, New Orleans, Louisiana, USA.

to the prisoners to have a faithful [emphasis in original] and trustworthy interpreter."[41] Again, another letter by Rev. Burguess, introducing another possible candidate, touches upon this important reflection: "he was educated in England, but has spent many years in his native land, and is familiar with the languages of the Gold Coast . . . and he is, as I feel assured, perfectly trustworthy."[42]

The historical context of 1839 generated a deep-seated distrust in both captives toward the *Amistad* abolitionists, and of the abolitionists toward the community at large. The repeated worry contained in the letters culminated in an apologetic-style narrative justifying the preference of one candidate over another. This produced unease. The "kidnapped Africans" were accused of a felony; death awaited them if found guilty as charged. This preoccupation shaped most of the job responsibilities for the desired oral translator in this case, of which "faithful and trustworthy" represented one of them.

The abominable experience of enslavement of the Mende Africans and the threats on the abolitionists produced other eligibility requirements that weigh in their careful approach, despite their desperation to find an interpreter. Having ties to the community, being known within the close circle, and being a sympathizer with the cause against slavery all served as a guarantee that pro-slavery infiltrators were kept at bay from the friendlier *Amistad* circle. Pickering tried to recruit Samuel Barney, a father, a man of integrity, whose interpreting could be trusted, and whom he had known for twenty years (refer to Figure 4.3).[43] Barney met all the requirements, except one: he spoke a different African language.

> He should proceed to the place of trial; when you will soon discover [illegible] that the captives recognize him as a country man. I should add that I have known him for more than twenty years. And he had even sustained the character of an honest, industrious, hardworking man; he now has a family of grown up children—and I should place full reliance upon his statements. I hope he may be made useful in this interesting and important case.
>
> I am, Dear Sir,
> With great regard,
> Yours, John Pickering

[41] AMA Archives FI 4606, The *Amistad* Research Center, New Orleans, Louisiana, USA.
[42] AMA Archives FI 4601, The *Amistad* Research Center, New Orleans, Louisiana, USA.
[43] AMA Archives FI 4625, The *Amistad* Research Center, New Orleans, Louisiana, USA.

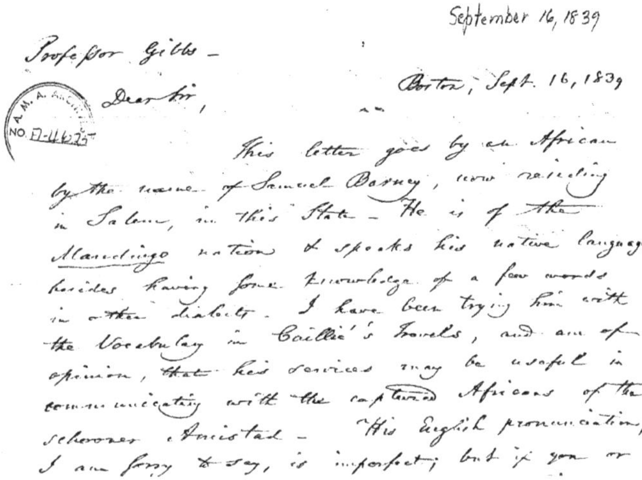
September 16, 1839

Professor Gibbs –

Dear Sir,

Boston, Sept. 16, 1839

This letter goes by an African by the name of Samuel Dorney, now residing in Salem, in this State. He is of the Mandingo nation & speaks his native language, besides having some knowledge of a few words in other dialects. I have been trying him with the Vocabulary in Caillie's Travels, and am of opinion, that his services may be useful in communicating with the captured Africans of the schooner Amistad. His English pronunciation, I am sorry to say, is imperfect; but if you or

Figure 4.3 AMA Archives FI 4625. The *Amistad* Research Center, New Orleans, Louisiana, USA.

All of these filters of authenticity became heightened when John Shain, a European-descent candidate, was found, thus adding some new requirements. Isaac Parish, a Philadelphia-based physician and abolitionist, corresponded with Leavitt in New York, on September 12, 1839, just one day after the formation of the *Amistad* Committee in Philadelphia. Parish felt sure that he could converse "freely with these Africans." He prefaced his letter forewarning Leavitt that Shain was "White" [emphasis in original], as it was not common to interact with a non-African, African-speaking bilingual. Parish dedicated various letters to introduce his trustworthy candidate and report on his encounter with the Africans. Shain acquired his linguistic capabilities in the Sazo and the Mandingo languages and his ethnic competencies when "he was placed on board of slave ship and lived 6 or 7 years amongst the Africans." The correspondence remained unclear as to whether he was stationed as a "cabin boy" or as a child receiving interpreter training. Afterward, he lived in Africa and travelled extensively to the West Indies where he continued to practice languages. Immersion and long-term exposure resulted in language proficiency and fluency, key requirements for an interpreter.[44]

[44] AMA Archives FI 4613, The *Amistad* Research Center, New Orleans, Louisiana, USA.

> I am rejoiced to be able to state that we have found a man who I think will be of immense service as an interpreter. He is a White [emphasis in original] man about middle-age named John Shain. When a child, he was placed on board of slave ship and lived 6 or 7 years amongst the Africans he scarcely saw a white man during this time and obtained an intimate knowledge of the Sazo, and Mandingo languages. He is well acquainted with the customs of the people, the geography of the country! Has since been in Africa and up to the present time [stricken in original] a recent period has been employed in vessels trading with the West Indies. Has conversed with Mandingos in the West Indies within 18 months and still retains an excellent knowledge of their language. And he had no doubt he can converse freely with these Africans.[45]

As a "White" candidate, it was paramount to validate him as someone who befriended "slaves" and who could "empathize" with their suffering. Parish resorts to an apologetic narration in response to hypothetical questions about his acceptability as a candidate. Third-party references from Shain's employer and membership into a place of worship secured his social connections and confirmed reliability. Parish felt the need to describe his character:

> Shain is an intelligent and worthy man and abhors slavery and the slave trade. Says when amongst the Africans he received many acts of kindness from them and has always felt grateful for it. He came forward voluntarily to D P Brown and offered to go and said if he were not a poor man he would willingly engage in the case, without any remuneration—and appears to be entirely disinterested. [word stricken] I am assured by his present employer James Mulford, a respectable grocer of this city, that all he says may be relied on that he is a member of the Baptist denomination and although a seafaring man, he is in every respect a worthy, honest, sober person. He also speaks Spanish.[46]

Shain, aka Shane,[47] gained Parish's trust. But he had to justify his candidacy to the New York and New Haven abolitionist communities. Parish presented him as an intelligent man who was grateful for the way Africans treated him: "when amongst the Africans he received many acts of kindness from them and has always felt grateful for it." Parish failed to report the context of these

[45] AMA Archives FI 4613, The *Amistad* Research Center, New Orleans, Louisiana, USA.
[46] AMA Archives FI 4613, The *Amistad* Research Center, New Orleans, Louisiana, USA.
[47] The spelling of the name of this candidate varies in the letters.

interactions. Whether these acts occurred on an enslaving ship or plantation, along the enslaving African coast, or in liberation activities, these were not specified. A non-African-descent candidate needed to prove positive attitudes toward the African community in the highly adversarial *Amistad* period. Shain as a candidate turned out to be beneficial in other ways. In a subsequent letter, on September 15, 1839, Parish informed L. Tappan that he, along with Shane, visited an "old Mandingo man" with whom Shane spoke the Ausso language.[48] Similarly to the utilization of lists and vocabularies in the recruitment process,[49] other African language speakers served as "language-competency evaluators." Spanish competency was equally sought. A Spanish-fluent interpreter could eavesdrop on the conversations in court between the Spaniards their lawyers, and Antonio's remarks. Letters captured feelings from one to the other spectrum of the pro- to anti-slavery continuum. The search for the Mende interpreter engendered an array of similar and opposing feelings, from anxiety, to anger, to joy, to despair, to hate. The writers expressed their excitement, hope, or despair depending on how close they were to the next trial date:

> I write in haste at 11PM to state that I have just returned from a very interesting visit to an old Mandingo man in company with John Shean [*sic*] F. Coffin V. [word stricken] Shean and he conversed fluently and readily in the Ausoo Language. And it was hard to tell which of them was the most pleased. The old man is nearly 80 years of age speaks several African languages—French—and English the latter very imperfectly—If he should be wanted we will send him on. He is very anxious to go.[50]

Fluency and pronunciation—a common topic of conversations in the letters—constituted another important requirement for this *Amistad* court interpreter. Shain spoke English "very imperfectly."[51] Pickering observed that Samuel Barney's accent, from Salem, Massachusetts, may be of hindrance in a court of law:[52] "His English pronunciation, I am sorry to say, is imperfect; but if you or some other person will sit down with him, your ear will soon get accustomed to it, and you will then find no difficulty in understanding

[48] AMA Archives FI 4624, The *Amistad* Research Center, New Orleans, Louisiana, USA.

[49] Toward the end of this last letter, Parish mentions not only René Caillié's travels, but "Brodchit [*sic*] travel's in Africa," "which contains a number of vocabularies and is in the Philadelphia Library." The first word of the title of this book is hardly legible.

[50] AMA Archives FI 4624 The *Amistad* Research Center, New Orleans, Louisiana, USA.

[51] AMA Archives FI 4624 The *Amistad* Research Center, New Orleans, Louisiana, USA.

[52] AMA Archives FI 4606, The *Amistad* Research Center, New Orleans, Louisiana, USA.

him though it may be difficult, in a public room (like a court house) to follow him."[53]

The abolitionists were aware of the two major contexts in which the interpreter would perform his duties, in the courtroom as legal interpreter and off the record in the prison or holding key client–attorney conferences. Just the voice carried weight, affecting comprehensibility and even credibility, which could sway the judge's opinion or that of the public. In a letter from Harris to Rev. Leavitt, on September 13, 1839, the author analyzed the skills and reached his determination:

> I called upon a Mr. Mosses who has spent some years in Africa who can speak the Sousou well. The Mandingo he knows but little about cannot act as an interpreter in that dialect but the Sousou he understands as well as he does the English.[54] [emphasis in original]

Despite Shain's linguistic abilities and good intentions, he was unable to communicate with the Africans. Parish's last letter informed search team members of another disheartening piece of news. It brings to a close another frustrated attempt to recruit an interpreter for the Africans. The letter read: "[I] was almost as much disappointed as Sheian [*sic*] himself, that he failed to converse with the Prisoners—althou' I cannot doubt from his account that he had the full confidence of Joseph Cinquez."[55] The information contained therein suggests that some communication transpired between Shain and some of the Africans, and, most importantly, that the Africans trusted him. Yet, the language competency desired and needed was not attained. In the end, those "interpreted" judged the effectiveness of the interpreter. Within the prison walls, power, authority, and agency were transferred to the *Amistad* Africans to identify the competency of a trustworthy interpreter through this candidacy process. When oral languages did not match, embodied consent or dissent, alongside body language perceived and respected, corroborated their final candidate. Feelings and affect became an essential component of the *Amistad* recruitment process.

A "spy" became the last-identifiable trait of preference for the ideal. Feelings of distrust, on the one hand, and the fear of re-enslavement construed a form of resistance in both the Mende Africans and the abolitionists. Given the unequal footing of linguistic minorities within the US judicial system, having a double "agent" offered some advantages. A final count of six

[53] AMA Archives FI 4606, The *Amistad* Research Center, New Orleans, Louisiana, USA.
[54] AMA Archives FI 4616, The *Amistad* Research Center, New Orleans, Louisiana, USA.
[55] AMA Archives FI 4634, The *Amistad* Research Center, New Orleans, Louisiana, USA.

languages were employed through the duration of the *Amistad* saga: Mende, English, Spanish, Vey, Sign Language, and Portuguese. Spanish and English commanded similar linguistic-imperial privileges on the power scale. Once the Spaniards returned to Cuba after making bail, however, Spanish and Mende coexisted on a similar plane. Antonio's, the enslaved-Spanish speaking "cabin boy," the *grumete*, interpreting needs were ignored, circumventing his testimony from implicating the Spaniards. The idea of a "spy" envisaged a means to pick up any side conversations in Spanish, to check the testimony of the Spaniards and Antonio, and to discover any problems with the oral translation of the Spanish interpreter, all as part of a litigation strategy to aid the Africans. Regarding the Spanish-speaking abilities of Shain, Parish suggested to L. Tappan:

> He speaks Spanish very well—we have suggested that this knowledge may be of service to our cause in detecting any misrepresentations on the part of the Spaniard, and this African interpreter—if such should be attempted. We have advised him not to let his knowledge be known to the opposite side.[56]

Coffin, another abolitionist from Philadelphia, reiterated the leverage of enlisting a trilingual interpreter: "Mr. Shane can speak the Spanish both classical and creole and [it's] not improper to suggest the propriety of not saying a word about his knowledge of Spanish unless the question is asked [of] him in Hartford."[57] A spy representing the *Amistad* legal team would be someone in solidarity with the anti-slavery cause, an activist.

These thirteen job requirements, grouped into the four categories—social connection, linguistic skills, agency and embodiment, and activism—mapped the way to recruit the *Amistad* court interpreter as the search continued.

Interpreters Found! "Covey and Pratt of Brig *Buzzard*"[58]

The unwavering search bore fruit: Three letters—two dated October 3 and October 5 (by New Haven abolitionist Amos Townsend, one mailed to Rev. Joshua Leavitt and the other to Lewis Tappan, Esq.) and another dated October 4 from Tappan to Baldwin—revealed the joyful news. All efforts

[56] AMA Archives FI 4624, The *Amistad* Research Center, New Orleans, Louisiana, USA.
[57] AMA Archives FI 4626, The *Amistad* Research Center, New Orleans, Louisiana, USA.
[58] AMA Archives FI 4638A, Envelope, The *Amistad* Research Center, New Orleans, Louisiana, USA.

to identify the language spoken by most of the Africans yielded positive results. Prof. Gibbs took an intentional walk up and down the ports, first of New Haven, and later of New York. The recruitment strategies brought forth two interpreters, James Covey and Charles Pratt. Both were sailors working on board the Brig *Buzzard*, an English vessel carrying intercepting enslaving vessels in violation of African-transatlantic trade treaties. These ships depended on African language interpreters to learn the stories of those captured, their ethnicities, and their sailing journey to detail the illegal activities and to decide the course of action.[59] While the *Amistad* archival materials have not confirmed the interpreting roles of Covey and Pratt among this ship, it is very likely that their linguistic background afforded them opportunities to assist as interpreters in the mission of *Buzzard*-like ships. The commander agreed to release them from their duties to go to New Haven. Tappan, beside himself, informed Baldwin on October 4, 1839, that "Capt. Fitzgerald, of the brig *Buzzard*, called on me today, and consented to have both Covey and Pratt remain several days longer. In fact, he would not be displeased to have one of them remain here for months if necessary."[60] Fast-forwarding a few weeks, Pratt continued sailing with the Brig after it was determined that Covey's English-language skills were more developed than Pratt's. Covey became the main court interpreter for the Mende Africans, meeting all but two of the thirteen requirements: he did not speak Spanish and was not known by the abolitionist community, although he had been well rooted in the seafaring community for three years. Covey eventually stayed in New Haven not for months, but for years to come, until his return to Africa in the same vessel with the freed Mendeans.

"The interpreters are found!" read the postscript on the back of the envelope. On October 3, Amos Townsend, Jr., recalled the festive occasion to Rev. Leavitt based in New York detailing the encounter between James K. Covey and the *Amistad* Africans: "Dear Sir, I . . . am most happy to be able to say that two Africans brought by Prof. Gibbs are able to converse fluently with all the prisoners" (refer to Figure 4.4).[61] The abolitionists were relieved to finally have a candidate with whom the Africans could "freely" communicate after all this time. The linguistic tension accumulated during approximately forty days found an escape. Someone now established communication between the imprisoned Africans and the outside world,

[59] Graden, Dale T., "Interpreters, Translators, and the Spoken Word in the Nineteenth-Century Transatlantic Slave Trade to Brazil and Cuba," *Ethnohistory* 58, no. 3 (Summer 2011): 405, doi:10.1215/00141801-1263839. Copyright 2011 by American Society for Ethnohistory.

[60] The Baldwin Family Papers (MS 55), Manuscripts and Archives, Yale University Library.

[61] AMA Archives FI 4660, The *Amistad* Research Center, New Orleans, Louisiana, USA.

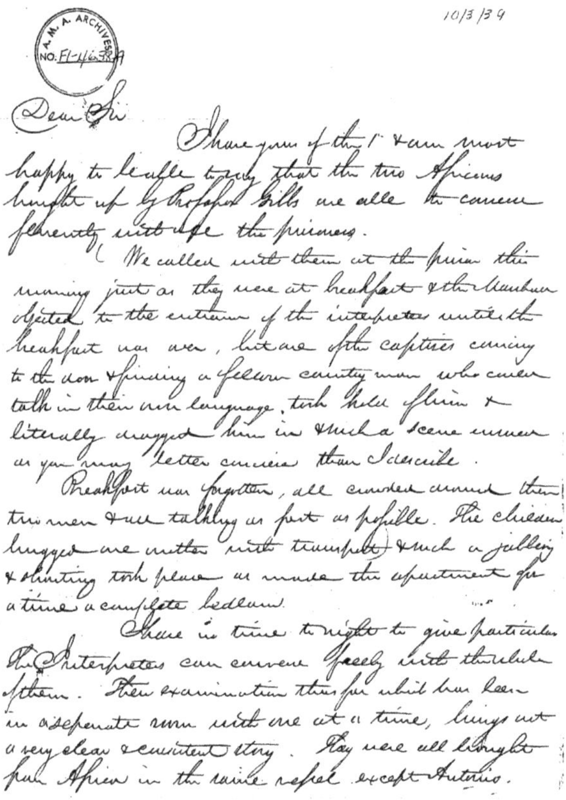
10/3/39

A.M.A. ARCHIVES NO. FI-4638A

Dear Sir

I have yours of the 1st & am most happy to be able to say that the two Africans brought up by Professor Gibbs are able to converse fluently with the prisoners.

We called with them at the prison this morning just as they were at breakfast & the Marshall objected to the entrance of the interpreters until the breakfast was over, but one of the captives coming to the door & finding a fellow countryman who could talk in their own language, took hold of him & literally dragged him in & such a scene ensued as you may better conceive than I describe.

Breakfast was forgotten, all crowded around these two men & all talking as fast as possible. The children hugged one another with transport & such a jabbering & shouting took place as made the apartment for a time a complete bedlam.

I have no time tonight to give particulars. The Interpreters can converse freely with the whole of them. Their examination thus far which has been in a separate room with one at a time, brings out a very clear & consistent story. They were all brought from Africa in the same vessel except Antonio.

Figure 4.4 AMA Archives FI 4638A. The *Amistad* Research Center, New Orleans, Louisiana, USA.

the litigation team in particular. The “examination” that proceeded with the interpreter verified the hypothesis of the *Amistad* abolitionists. Townsend continued narrating:

> I have no time tonight to give particulars. . . . Their examination thus far which has been in a separate room with one at a time, brings out a very clear and consistent story. They were all brought from Africa in the main vessel except Antonio.[62]

[62] AMA Archives FI 4638A, The *Amistad* Research Center, New Orleans, Louisiana, USA.

Townsend's conclusions based on the Africans' testimonials granted crucial information as the basis for a suit filed from the *Amistad* Africans against the Spaniards, for which the Spaniards were arrested in the weeks to follow: "the captives universally complain of the most inhuman treatment from the Spaniards."[63] The interviews continued. Two days after his initial letter, Townsend wrote to Tappan with compelling revelations from these sessions. The only persons mentioned in the letters are the Africans and the interpreters, which underlines the importance of trust and the ethnic connection between them. The *Amistad* African and interpreter combination unleashed the torrent to design the case. Townsend stated that "[the Africans] were cruelly beaten and one of them is now lame, so as hardly able to walk as he declares from blows received on board the *Amistad*."[64]

Writing to Rev. Bacon on October 4, 1839, Tappan underlined the consequential affair of tracking down a suitable court interpreter. He encouraged the *Amistad* abolitionists "to make the most of this Providential occurrence."[65] He reflected on "the convergence of the facts"—an event that would inject passion into the abolition movement—"the simple truth," which referred to the Africans' story of capture, the Atlantic trajectory and enslavement story, one repeated millions of times through the Americas. This convergence afforded them the momentous opportunity to stir "the heart of the nation through the power of sympathy. We calculate to produce discussion that will bring the whole subject matter of slave as well as the slave trade." Bacon urges the abolitionists in New Haven:

> We ought to make the most of this Providential occurrence. The simple truth . . . must produce a lasting effect. I have long thought that the heart of the nation would not be effectively touched except through the power of sympathy . . . but did not anticipate such a mysterious [illegible] as has occurred.[66]

Joy was shared also by the interpreters in this process. Knowing fellow prisoners whom they could assist bred in them a sense of contentment, someone they could share their stories of liberation with, to instill hope, and to shine a light at the end of the judicial tunnel. Their parallel story contributed to the trust, joy, and success of this event. Townsend served as an eyewitness to the interpreting encounter. He commented: "James and

[63] AMA Archives FI 4638A, The *Amistad* Research Center, New Orleans, Louisiana, USA.
[64] AMA Archives FI 4660, The *Amistad* Research Center, New Orleans, Louisiana, USA.
[65] The Baldwin Family Papers (MS 55), Manuscripts and Archives, Yale University Library.
[66] The Baldwin Family Papers (MS 55), Manuscripts and Archives, Yale University Library.

Charles can communicate very freely with all of them, and have acquitted themselves to a perfect interpretation. They have given their whole time to it with great cheerfulness."[67] Linguistic and ethnic competency similarities, excitement, and trust brought recognition and approval to these interpreters. The *Amistad* minors exemplified this exhilarating moment. Africans and attorneys could finally hear each other with the assistance of the interpreter.

The Christian abolitionists proved triumphant in their ardent search and were ready to guard their excellent results. Yet, they worried that they may lose Covey as the trial interpreter. Members of the search team employed repressive measures to secure their search. Archival materials suggests that Covey experienced a type of sequestration. Two letters from Tappan to Baldwin, dated October 4 and 12, 1839, disclosed the readiness of the abolitionists to protect their interests, which involved negotiations with Captain Fitzgerald of the *Buzzard*. Evidence of Covey's subpoenae needed to be presented to the captain "who will want it to exhibit on his return to his station." Referring to Pratt, "the other young African can return to the Brig."[68] Was this only a bureaucratic tactic to ensure that Captain Fitzgerald agreed to the petition and to shield Covey from being deemed incompliant? These suppositions remain unanswered. The letters only record conversations between a captain and the lawyers—Tappan and Baldwin—who ideologically belong to privileged groups in contrast to Covey's status as a sailor and African immigrant.

Nonetheless, one critical opportunity became possible thanks to James Covey; the counter-stories of the Mende Africans could be told in court.

[67] AMA Archives FI 4660, The *Amistad* Research Center, New Orleans, Louisiana, USA.
[68] Baldwin Family Papers (MS 55). Manuscripts and Archives, Yale University Library.

5

The Transatlantic Interpreters in the *Amistad* Case

James K. Covey: The Final Court Interpreter of the *Amistad* Case

James Kaweli Covey En Route to the *Amistad* (refer to Figure 5.1)

In his seminal research on the *Amistad's Orphans*, Benjamin Lawrance explores the lives of the six children in this case, three girls and three boys, four of whom served as interpreters—Antonio, Covey, Kinna and Kale—in different capacities and repercussions throughout the unfolding *Amistad* history. They all shared a parallel enslaving journey from Africa, but of the three, Antonio and Kale sailed aboard the *Amistad* schooner. Lawrance's work brings to the forefront the forgotten lives and journeys of enslaved children during the nineteenth century. As major imperial European nations engaged in human trading, while signing treaties abolishing the African-transatlantic slave trade, covert operations increased, and women and children became the preferred exchangeable commodities.[1] Enslavers operated from the patriarchal view that African women and children were more docile and less prone to rebel, on the one hand, and on the other, their smaller sizes and shapes increased the number of slaves that could be packed into the bellies of ships. Cuban and Brazilian markets demanded a greater number of children; consequently, African minors were estranged from their families of origin, communities, and identity rituals. Their lives were traumatized at a young age as a result of kidnapping, poverty, enslavement, violent acts, the first-hand witnessing of cruelty, and physical, psychological, and emotional violence.

He views the *Amistad* children as orphans. Although Covey was the oldest, his age placed him at the cusp of adulthood, and the archival information about him abounds. Born around 1825, he was kidnapped from

1 Benjamin N. Lawrance, *Amistad's Orphans: An Atlantic Story of Children, Slavery, and Smuggling* (New Haven, CT: Yale University Press, 2015), 35.

James Covey.

JAMES COVEY, the interpreter for the Africans, is apparently about 20 years of age; was born at Benderi, in the Mendi country. His father was of Kon-no descent, and his mother Gissi. Covey was taken by three men, in the evening, from his parents' house, at Go-la-hung, whither they had removed when he was quite young. He was carried to the Bullom country, and sold as a slave to Ba-yi-mi, the king of the Bul-loms, who resided at Mani. He lived there for three years, and was employed to plant rice for the wife of Ba-yi-mi, who treated him with great kindness. He was sold to a Portuguese, living near Mani, who carried him, with 200 or 300 others to Lomboko, for the purpose of being transported to America. After staying in this place about one month, Covey was put on board a Portuguese slave-ship, which, after being out about four days from Lomboko, was captured by a British armed vessel, and carried into Sierra Leone. Covey thus obtained his freedom, and remained in this place five or six years, and was taught to read and write the English language, in the schools of the Church Missionary Society. Covey's original name was *Kaw-we-li*, which signifies, in Mendi, *war road*, i. e., a road dangerous to pass, for fear of being taken captive. His Christian name, James, was given him by Rev. J. W. Weeks, a Church Missionary, at Sierra Leone. In Nov., 1838, he enlisted as a sailor on board the British brig of war Buzzard, commanded by Captain Fitzgerald. It was on board this vessel, when at New York, in Oct., 1839, that James was found, amid some twenty native Africans, and by the kindness of captain Fitzgerald, his services as an interpreter were procured.

Figure 5.1 "James Kaweli Covey." This side profile drawing was taken from John W. Barber's account *A History of the Amistad Captives . . . an Account of the Trials* (1840). In his chronicle, compiled from interviews interpreted by James Covey, the biographical narratives of the *Amistad* captives included profiles taken "by a pentagraph from the wax figures now exhibiting through the country by Pendleton & Curtiss, which are striking and accurate likenesses of the Africans, taken from life by Mr. Moulthrop" (Barber 1840, 8). Barber does not specify whether Covey's pentagraph was modelled after a wax figure. All other side profiles are identified by a number corresponding to the wax figure of the exhibition.

his African home and encountered slavery early in his life.[2] As an enslaved child in Africa, he worked on a rice farm for a few years, before he was "sold" from African hands to a European enslaver and into a transatlantic hold.[3] Violently uprooted from his community, he was coerced into the slave vessel, the *Segunda Socorro*. Shortly after setting sail, the *Segunda Socorro* was intercepted by the Royal Navy West Africa Squadron, operating from Freetown, Sierra Leone. The enslavement process further infantilized children as well as adults by stripping them of decision-making powers and subjecting them to condescending behaviors and attitudes.

The first mention of Covey appears on the ship's papers of the *Segunda Socorro* in 1833, from where he disembarked in Freetown.[4] Archival records from Sierra Leone and the British National Archives give an account of a nine-year-old boy "height of four feet nine inches, named 'Covie,' branded 'B'

[2] Lawrance, *Amistad's Orphans*, 35.
[3] Lawrance, *Amistad's Orphans*, 8.
[4] Lawrance, *Amistad's Orphans*, 37.

on his left arm, as slave number 2709."[5] The Court of the Mixed Commission decided the fate of the enslaved Africans freed from these vessels. Full liberation was not immediate for those "liberated" from enslavement vessels. An emancipation period followed in which the "emancipated" status remained in a limbo between freed and enslaved. A "freed" enslaved spent time "working" inside a few designated places for a period of time before acquiring their Emancipation Letter.[6] After the term completion, the emancipated applied for the letter to obtain their true awaited freedom. In Covey's case, he was mandated to attend school for five years at the Church Missionary Society (CMS) in Bathurst followed by an apprenticeship.[7] This transition pushed Covey from one form of constricting and colonizing environment to another. His "placement" afforded him an unusual opportunity: "he was part of a special and experimental pact with education and training at the core. Covey was one of 103 boys whose education and apprenticeship were contracted by the colonial government to the CMS."[8] The CMS experience coupled with the apprenticeship turned him into an English-bilingual person, as Covey stated during the *Amistad* trial on January 15, 1840. Court files include a transcript from his examination as an expert witness, "I learned to speak English in Sierra Leone. Was put on board a man of war one year and a half" [emphasis in original].[9] The first declaration alluded to his time at CMS; the second to his apprenticeship on board of the *Buzzard* some nine years later. The Royal Navy's fleet mission consisted of intercepting slave vessels engaged in trafficking despite the signed treaties. A similar squadron procured his release; now he was one of them. By the time he arrived in New York City (NYC), Covey was eighteen, nine years of which he had lived as an enslaved child, followed by a forced assimilation and restricted freedom in the CMS. In other words, by the time he became an *Amistad* interpreter, Covey "had just survived a very tumultuous Atlantic crossing."[10]

Captain Fitzgerald commanded the British Brigantine *Buzzard*, built in 1834, that sailed from England to the Gold Coast of Africa in 1838 intercepting illegal trafficking. Her "crew consist[ed] of 20 Blacks and 30 white men and boys."[11] Aboard the *Buzzard,* James Covey and Charles Pratt mediated to liberate other boys, girls, women, and men transported as slaves, circumstances they had also experienced. Interpreting must have been a

5 Lawrance, *Amistad's Orphans*, 185–6.
6 Personal communication with Erika Melek, PhD, April 20, 2023, Havana, Cuba.
7 Lawrance, *Amistad's Orphans*, 189–90.
8 Lawrance, *Amistad's Orphans*, 190.
9 *Thomas R. Gedney Schooner Amistad*, 165.
10 Lawrance, "*La Amistad's* 'Interpreter' Reinterpreted," 194.
11 Lawrance, "*La Amistad's* 'Interpreter' Reinterpreted," 194.

day-to-day activity for the recently released as they tried to make sense of their new status. "The Asylum" received the liberated slaves brought to Sierra Leone and relocated them into different villages. Pratt and Covey lived in the Asylum after their liberation from the slave ship. The CMS induced an English-language immersion convenient for the mission of vessels like the *Buzzard* and the evangelical pursuits of the Asylum teachers. The *Buzzard* recruited six of the African boys raised in the Asylum. Exposure in the CMS-asylum prepared Covey to serve as interpreter for his kindred as they struggled for liberation from enslavement and jail.

Lawrance speculates that in 1838, a contract mediated Covey's transfer from the CMS school to an apprenticeship with the Royal Navy.[12] However, "the experience of apprenticeship often resulted in further exploitation. Apprentices were bought and sold like chattel, and many found themselves a second time on slave ships."[13] Covey's work as an interpreter may have been an upgrade from his previous apprenticeship. Apprenticeship afforded an emancipated state, a partial liberation. The contractual provision examined by Lawrance compounded with evidence found in AMA letters and the Baldwin Family Papers suggest that Covey lacked the self-determination to stay on as interpreter in this anti-slavery case after the trial. Missives from Covey to Tappan exposed his limited decision power to leave the USA for his native Africa when he pleased. Whether a written or verbal agreement mediated from the *Buzzard* to his service as the suitable interpreter in the *Amistad* case remains unclear.

But one thing is undoubtedly true: the abolitionists eagerly safeguarded the *Amistad* interpreter as necessary after such an arduous process. In preparation for the November trial, Tappan sent Baldwin a list of suggested witnesses to be subpoenaed, including the Mende interpreter: "[Covey] will probably be subpoenaed as a witness in the suit to be commenced against Montes and Ruiz."[14] Other letters between counsels, Tappan to Baldwin, demonstrated the abolitionists' readiness to protect their own interests over the rights of the interpreter: "will you have [Covey] subpoenaed, and evidence of it forwarded to me for Capt. Fitzgerald of H. B. M. Brigantine *Buzzard*."[15] Covey was not the only one listed for witnesses to be subpoenaed. He was joined by "John Jay Hyde, the *New London Gazette* editor, Savilion[16] Hayley,

[12] Lawrance, "*La Amistad*'s 'Interpreter' Reinterpreted," 217.

[13] Lawrance, "*La Amistad's* 'Interpreter' Reinterpreted," 217.

[14] "Tappan to Baldwin," November 11, 1839, The Baldwin Family Papers (MS 55), Manuscripts and Archives, Yale University Library.

[15] "Tappan to Baldwin," October 12, 1839, The Baldwin Family Papers (MS 55), Manuscripts and Archives, Yale University Library.

[16] Not sure on the spelling of his first name, unclear graphology, perhaps, "Lavilion."

Dwight P. Janes, R. R. Madden, and Profs. Gibbs and Day."[17] Subpoenaing Covey seemed like a logical strategy to enable him to return to the Brig in the future. At first glance, it seemed to protect Covey and the commander, but it also undermined Covey's agency. In the end, Covey was the only witness subpoenaed by the *Amistad* litigation team, the others appeared in court as witnesses. In case of failure to appear in court, those cited could face incarceration if found in contempt.

Abolitionists employed drastic measures. In the same letter, New York abolitionist Tappan writes, "I suppose it will be necessary to detain James Covey as a witness and interpreter."[18] Use of the word "detain" was reserved only for Covey. Reference in letters to the "arrest" of the Spaniards Montes and Ruiz may be expected for the Africans had filed a suit against them for cruel mistreatment. The same language repeated in another letter from Townsend to Tappan noted the need to "detain"[19] Covey.[20] Although, in the end, Covey was not arrested to secure him as an interpreter, the mere possibility is disturbing. In their fervor to liberate the *Amistad* Africans and to advance the anti-slavery ideal, the Christian abolitionists put in practice oppressive and colonizing actions that limited the freedom of Covey, another African. This racialized experience added to the long list of experiences that infantilized him and denied him of his agency. Newspaper articles covering the January 1840 *Amistad* trial indicated that Covey stayed behind in Connecticut after having been subpoenaed by the US courts.

James Covey, "Interpreter Found!"

By the time Covey encountered the *Amistad* Africans in the New Haven jail, more than a common language and ethnic background solidified their bond. A similar enslaving journey and a need to trust in highly volatile circumstances mediated their communication. After some forty days of mostly nonverbal communication, when the Africans heard a fellow Mendean with whom they could speak and be understood, their joy was uncontainable. The children rejoiced and "breakfast was forgotten" (refer to Figure 4.4). The agency of the Africans prevailed in this encounter. They chose to reduce the physical, social, linguistic, and cultural barriers by "dragging" the interpreter as close as possible to their bodies, context, and experiences. Body language and

17 "Tappan to Baldwin," October 12, 1839, The Baldwin Family Papers (MS 55).
18 "Tappan to Baldwin," October 12, 1839, The Baldwin Family Papers (MS 55).
19 Probably, to be "detained" referred to a less-restrictive definition legally or physically. Research efforts were employed to clarify this possibility without a successful result.
20 Lawrance, "*La Amistad*'s "Interpreter' Reinterpreted," 308.

affectivity confirmed the right candidate. Speaking "as fast as they could" connotes a cacophony of feelings, probing, hope, excitement, and reliable communication. African interpreters and captives communicated flawlessly, a scene that depicted human and ethnic connections cemented with a profound sense of joy and relief. An interaction with interpreters achieved the abolition of noncommunication and sociolinguistic invisibility, opening the gateways for stories to be told and heard. According to this narration, no counsel was yet in sight.

After weeks of anticipation for an interpreter to enable lawyers to conduct their discovery, these first letters omit registering their attendance. Current court interpretation professional protocol prescribes avoiding interpreting scenarios without the presence of a court officer. This happened several times in the months to come. The previously described scene lacks resemblance to contemporary attorney–client meetings. For circumstances like the *Amistad* case in contexts of conflict, racial violence, and war, seldom do prescriptive interpreters' codes of ethics appear entirely applicable. Most codes of ethics do not envision the effect of war, the witnessing of human rights violations, high-level conflict, and enslaving, colonizing, or racialized contexts for the interpreter and for those requiring their help with communication. The codes disregard considerations such as when the interpreter is the only person who speaks the language of the defendants along a 300-mile stretch of coastline, the approximate distance between Boston, Massachusetts, to Philadelphia, Pennsylvania, and thousands of miles removed from their African continent. A contemporary measure envisions similar conflicting situations.

In 2012, three interpreting organizations, Red T, the International Association of Conference Interpreters (AIIC), and the International Federation of Translators (FIT) created a "Conflict Zone Field Guide for Civilian Translators/Interpreters and Users of Their Services."[21] The guide instructs all parties on their rights and responsibilities, including "how to work with T/Is" (Translators and Interpreters) in contexts of strife. The guide advises that "interpreters contracted to work in conflict zones are often nonprofessional linguists, yet [they] play a key role in stressful communications." The guide informs the recruiters that because their services are rendered in high-risk environments that make the interpreters vulnerable, special protection before, during, and after the conflict is required. Slavery

[21] The Red T organized to protect "translators and interpreters Worldwide." Their mission foments a work environment "free from fear of persecution, prosecution, imprisonment, abduction, torture and assassination." The guide may be found in the following websites: https://red-t.org/our-work/safety-guidelines/english-english/?get=s; https://aiic.org/uploaded/web/Basic%20Texts/T-I_Field_Guide_2012_ENG.pdf; https://en.fit-ift.org/ (accessed June 16, 2023).

in the nineteenth-century courts framed the high-risk environment of the *Amistad* story and its interpreters. No guide could project the challenges inherent in this conflictive context.

Nowadays, these twenty-first-century guides remind the nonprofessional of her/his rights, from the wearing of protective gear to clear role definition, and to the right to appropriate remuneration. Parallel to court interpretation codes, impartiality occupies a prominent place in the guides, reiterating how interpreters should refrain from "expressing [their] opinions or sympathies. You cannot be an advocate for any cause and must declare any conflict of interest."[22] Nonetheless, an impartial[23] interpreter, unlike Covey, did not represent the ideal nonprofessional for the case at hand, a concept that shatters once again the notion of optimal partiality or neutrality for professional interpreting. Critical Race Theory offers its own perspective on the notion of objectivity and impartiality: "Neutrality and objectivity are not just unattainable ideals; they are harmful fictions that obscure the normative supremacy of whiteness in America."[24] The judicial environment and the more extensive enslaving society constituted the conflict zones in the *Amistad* case. A partial perspective afforded the interpreter as well as the Africans a communal experience and the connections they needed.

On October 3, Amos Townsend, Jr., abolitionist from New Haven, informed Rev. Leavitt of the jubilation that ensued between the Mende Africans and the interpreters. Townsend also rejoiced at the meeting. His narration encapsulated the unforgettable response of the Africans when they heard someone speak their language:

> We called unto them at the prison this morning just as they were at breakfast and the marshal objected to the entrance of the interpreters until the breakfast was over! But one of the captives coming to the room and finding a fellow country men [*sic*] who could talk in their own language took hold of him and literally dragged him. . . .
>
> Breakfast was forgotten, all crowded around the two men and all talking as fast as possible. The children hugged one another with trumpet and much jolleing [*sic*] and shouting took place as made the apartment for a time a complete bedlam. (refer to Figure 4.4)[25]

[22] Ibid.

[23] The appearance of partiality may also yield similar life-threatening situations as in the case of enslavement. Impartiality does not guarantee for safety.

[24] Francisco Valdes, Jerome McCristal Culp, and Angela P Harris, eds., *Crossroads, Directions, and a New Critical Race Theory* (Philadelphia: Temple University Press: 2002), 1.

[25] AMA Archives FI 4660, The *Amistad* Research Center, New Orleans, Louisiana, USA.

The fortuitous encounter of this diasporic Mende community became the basis for Covey and Pratt to sign sworn affidavits presented at trial as witness testimonies. As officers of the court, interpreters are considered expert witnesses. In the *Amistad* litigation process, in addition to the need for interpreting in client/attorney interviews and interpreting at the witness stand, the linguistic expert testified on the linguistic and ethnic veracity of the Africans' testimonies. James Covey's ethnic competencies and background became crucial to qualifying him as an expert witness. In a double role, the interpreter corroborated the stories narrated by the Africans: "[Covey's] childhood experiences were fundamental in establishing the context of illegality and making his mediation possible."[26] As argued, other roles exercised by James Covey in the *Amistad* case challenge regular standards and ethical codes for the profession, two of which I would like to highlight: the role of remaining "impartial" and "ethnic competency."

Typical professional standards and codes of ethics for court interpreters include clauses advising interpreters to practice impartiality and avoid, at all costs, expressing conflicts of interest: interpreters "must be impartial and unbiased and must refrain from conduct that may give an appearance of bias."[27] The subsequent narrative expounds on what to do if interpreting tasks pose conflicts of interest and the impact of the "appearance of bias" when "other people perceive that you are biased or partial." In both cases, the interpreter should recognize the conflict or bias, and if unable to comply with the professional duties, should consult with the judge or an officer of the court, or even recuse him/herself from the task at hand.[28] In the *Amistad* case, Covey was selected by both Mende Africans and *Amistad* abolitionists because, indeed, he leaned ideological in the direction of the jailed. He sympathized with the anti-slavery cause and established a close connection with the Africans; all of these subjective components would exclude him on the basis of current professional standards and codes. The *Amistad* context evinces the benefit of subjective elements in the recruitment and performance of interpreters in certain contexts.

The currently listed preferred requirements and qualifications deviate from those pursued today by recruitment personnel, yet proved necessary in the *Amistad* case. Subjective elements such as "trust," "advocacy," and "partiality"[29] fail to be considered as positive elements in the exercise of

26 Lawrance, "*La Amistad*'s 'Interpreter' Reinterpreted," 4.
27 "Professional Standards and Ethics for California Court Interpreters," 4th ed., June 2008, 26. http://www.soniamelnikova.com/CodeOfEthics.pdf.
28 "Professional Standards and Ethics for California Court Interpreters," 26.
29 Zaragoza-De León, "The Search for a Mende Court Interpreter."

interpreting professional tasks. Neither do the current code of ethics and professional standards for US court interpreting consider either ethnic or cultural competencies, although a certain level of these competencies is expected of medical or healthcare interpreters. The International Medical Informatics Association (IMIA) Code of Ethics establishes that an interpreter may serve as an intercultural mediator when not doing so would hamper communication, thus affecting the delivery of quality services. In this context, an interpreter mediates as an advocate. The parallel national organization to the IMIA, the National Council on Interpreting in Health Care (NCIHC), further stipulates that "the interpreter continuously strives to develop awareness of his/her own and other (including biomedical) cultures encountered in the performance of their professional duties."[30] Self-awareness and a commitment to grow in these areas should be practices included in guidelines for professional interpreters in other settings.

As court interpreters and linguistic experts, their credibility is continuously at stake. Opposing parties may question them on varied issues to challenge their credibility on behalf of their clients, such as language, statements, and roles. Impeachment represents a real possibility for these trial experts: "the role which the interpreter plays makes him/her subject to having his/her interpretation challenged and impeached just like any other expert witness."[31] Covey experienced exactly this. The January 1840 trial entertained motions and arguments attempting to impeach James Covey on the grounds of off-the-record interpretation, a situation that will be discussed later in this book. His linguistic competencies surpassed the expertise needed in this high-profile case, an inconvenience for the opposing parties. Moreover, uncertain as to whether Covey would be able to stay in Connecticut for subsequent court hearings, the *Amistad* legal team secured his expert opinion. The transcription of this deposition combines the third- and first-person perspectives. Shortly after meeting the Mende Africans, James Covey deposed:

> These prisoners speak of the River "Mwa," [emphasis in original] of the place "*Jomboko*," both of which I have seen, in Africa, and they speak no language except native African, and from their language and manners, and appearance, I am sure they are native Africans. I learned to speak English language in Sierra Leone. . . . I was born in the Mandi [*sic*] country, in a place called Gho = noun, [illegible] the Mandi is my native

30 A National Code of Ethics for Interpreters in Health Care, 4, Www.Ncihc.Org/Assets/Z2021images/Ncihc%20national%20code%20of%20ethics.Pdf.

31 Schweda-Nicholson, "Court Interpreter Training," 5.

> language. I conversed with these Africans separately in the presence of Mr. Gibbs, and they are consistent in their history of the place from which they sailed in Africa, and of their voyage, to the Havanna.[32]

As an expert witness, Covey confirmed central facts for the defense of the Mende Africans. He was examined on their place of birth and native language and corroborated their real African names in contrast with the false ones recorded in the *licencias*. Court testimony further verified their authentic names as a key defense issue, only possible after the interpreter could mediate linguistically. However, *Amistad* court files uncovered show the court was privy to this fact early on in the judicial process. On August 29, 1839, Norris Wilcox, US Marshal, proceeded to arrest the Africans. Later, he attested:

> Then I proceeded to arrest the within-named persons, but found they did not answer to the names set forth in this warrant in being the names given them at Havanna for the purpose of shipment but found them to answer to the following names to wit, Cinque, Burnah . . . and therefore took the above-named persons into custody and then committed to the custody and keeping of the jailor at New Haven in said district.[33]

This arrest constituted one of the first legal violations of the rights of the Africans when they landed in Connecticut shores. The marshal executed this warrant taking into custody people who did not respond to the names therein. Yet, Wilcox's testimony in court also validated their native languages as other than Spanish, a pivotal element in proving that their arrival in Cuba was recent, and did not take place before 1817. Another statement enclosed in Covey's above mentioned deposition[34] demonstrated the crucial implications of being ethnically competent. It read:

> The above mentioned colored persons with whom he can converse, speak the Mandi language, which is a native African language, and was taught me [*sic*] by my father and mother, and the words of the above mentioned colored persons are the words which I use and as well understand each

[32] Baldwin Family Papers (MS 55). Manuscripts and Archives, Yale University Library. The four-page document, not numbered in the reel, is dated October 4, 1839, apparently a day after the arrival of James Covey at the New Haven jail. The document is signed by "James Covey" and certified by a judge from the New Haven County Court (*United States v. Cinque and Others*).

[33] *Thomas R. Gedney v. Schooner Amistad* [September 1839 Term], US District Court in Connecticut, Record Group 021.

[34] Baldwin Family Papers (MS 55). Manuscripts and Archives, Yale University Library.

> other when speaking the Mandi. The names of the Africans who are now in said jail have meanings, the name "Fulch" means "the sun". The name "Grabaung" means "God save us." [All emphasis in original][35]

Ethnic competency and personal-historical knowledge interlinked in his declarations. Language, ethnicity, and ideology aligned to win this case.

Antonio Ferrer aka "Antonio, the cabin boy"

Antonio Ferrer apparently survived the revolt for his ability to serve as a linguistic conduit between the Africans and the Spaniards.[36] He was featured early in the historical narratives, letters, and newspaper articles. Born in Sierra Leone between 1825 and 1826, he arrived in Cuba *c.* 1835–6 as a result of the slave trade.[37] Before the night of the revolt, he had served for three years as a "cabin boy," a form of enslavement, for Captain Ferrer, the owner of the *Amistad* schooner. Antonio declared in court how the cook, using signs, communicated to the Africans that they would be killed and eaten by the crew.[38] Whether it was a bad joke on the cook's part (who himself was an enslaved person), an act of gross insensitivity, or a reflection of the effects of internalized oppression, after several months of transatlantic agony the slight possibility of this becoming true ignited the fire in the Africans to pursue their dignity and right to live—a revolt was inevitable.[39] Antonio witnessed the *Amistad* revolt and the dealings of this vessel. In his testimony, interpreted by Lieut. Meade, Antonio reported that as a member of the *Amistad* crew, he witnessed the active role of the *Amistad* in enslavement activities. In addition to affirming that Ramón Ferrer was his master,[40] he declared that "the Scho' *Amistad* had carried slaves before, every two months made trip. Ruiz had before carried slaves."[41] This assertion provided a serious challenge to the Spaniards' claims of the inculturation process of the *Amistad* Africans. Ruiz and Montes, regularly, transported the enslaved.

35 Baldwin Family Papers (MS 55). Manuscripts and Archives, Yale University Library.
36 Barber, "A History of the *Amistad* Captives," 7.
37 Lawrance, "*La Amistad*'s 'Interpreter' Reinterpreted," 9.
38 The *Amistad* Case, US District Court for the District of Connecticut, *Thomas R. Gedney v. Amistad Schooner*, 172. www.Fold 3.com.
39 Enslaving ships operated by creating a hierarchy among enslaved people, a system that was efficient at attempting to privilege some over others and for the enslaved to carry out the orders of the enslavers.
40 U.S. Dist. Court Conn., *Thomas R. Gedney et al. v. Amistad Schooner*, 172.
41 U.S. Dist. Court Conn., *Thomas R. Gedney et al. v. Amistad Schooner*, 173.

The night of the revolt, four days after *La Amistad* left Havana, Cuba, the Africans considered killing the young boy Antonio. But according to Barber's account, Antonio's skills were valuable, as he functioned as an interpreter. Barber recorded Ruiz's sworn testimony in English, during the first judicial proceeding in this case,[42] regarding the role of Antonio:

> The slaves told [Ruiz and Montes the] next day that they had killed all; but the cabin boy said they had killed only the captain and cook. The other two he said had escaped in the canoe—a small boat. The cabin boy is an African by birth but has lived a long time in Cuba. His name is Antonio and belonged to the Captain. . . . Antonio is yet alive. They would have killed him, but he acted as interpreter between us, as he understood both languages.[43]

On the record, Don José Ruiz testified about Antonio's role as interpreter aboard the *Amistad*. No record exists of this observation being seconded by Antonio. The account provided a sketch of the slave trade and the horrors of the Middle Passage, including the proceedings on board the "Long, Low, Black Schooner, *Amistad*." The account delineated Antonio's role as linguistic mediator between the Spaniards and the Africans on the journey between Cuba and the Northeastern Island coast:

> When any vessel came alongside, Jingua would stand by Ruiz, the only man who could speak English, and watch him with fearful intensity.
>
> The organ of communication between Señor Ruiz and the Congolese was Antonio, the captain's slave. He is by birth an African but has lived in Cuba eight or ten years. He speaks both Congolese and Spanish. He had been employed as a cabin boy.[44]

If Antonio was an African by birth, he, too, arrived in Cuba illegally in violation of the international treaties abolishing the transatlantic-African trade. Although the *New York Sun*, on August 31, 1839, reported that "Joseph," aka Cinque, addressed his fellow compatriots in "Congolese," it was later found that most of them spoke Mende. Other archival information

[42] On August 29, 1839.

[43] Barber, "A History of the *Amistad* Captives," 7.

[44] *A True History of the African Chief Jingua and His Comrades: With a Description of the Kingdom of Mandingo, and the Manners and Customs of the Inhabitants—An Account of King Sharka, of Gallinas. A Sketch of the Slave Trade and Horrors of the Middle Passage: With the Proceedings on Board the "Long, Low, Black Schooner," Amistad* (Yale University Library, Beinecke Rare Book and Manuscript Library, 1839), 14.

contradicts the notion that Antonio had been born in Africa, and was kidnapped at an early age. As a growing child he acquired some fair linguistic Mende and intracultural skills that facilitated Antonio's communication with the Africans. Having lived in Cuba for eight to ten years created a cultural and linguistic immersion where he gained the ability to communicate mainly in Spanish. At this young age being under a forced assimilation, away from his motherland and under the stress of racism and colonialism, hampered his ability to foster his African linguistic skills. The association between the Africans and their "Congolese" speaking abilities remains an interesting supposition. The kidnapping of people from this African region to the Caribbean region resulted in a common practice, while other times, generalization practices of this vast geographical, political, and ethnic expansion of the African continent became the norm, which depicted an inaccurate monolinguistic characterization of the African's reality in which multilingualism reigned. Imperial discourse often pivots toward reductionistic principles and polarizing views in order to simplify and decontextualize reality to dominate through their expansive actions.

Antonio's ability to speak Congolese or any other African language with enough competence dissipated shortly after the beginning of the judicial proceedings, despite the claims of the article published in the *New York Sun*. The editor of the *New York Sun* travelled to New Haven to conduct the interview. Though printed in English for its readership, the article claims that Antonio narrated his Spanish version of the story with the assistance of John Jay Hyde, another interpreter. Mr. Hyde, Esq., editor of the *New London Gazette* newspaper, mediated linguistically between Antonio and the *New York Sun* editor. As the story unfolded, the lengthy narration written in third person steered imaginative readers to conclude that Antonio was well versed in both Spanish and "the language" of the Africans. Most probable, counsel Hyde, acting as a Spanish and English interpreter, "manipulated" Antonio's interview to improve understanding and credibility among the readership. An excerpt from this article memorialized an alleged speech given by "the African chief" interpreted by Antonio and relay-interpreted by Hyde:

> According to the interpretation of Antonio to Spanish, and from Spanish to English by John Jay Hyde, Esq . . . [it] was as follows—My brothers, I am once more among you, having deceived the enemy of our race. . . . I come to tell you that you have only one chance for death, and none for liberty. I am sure you prefer death, as I do. . . . It is better for you to do

> this, and then you will not only avert bondage yourselves, but prevent the entailment of unnumbered wrongs on your children.[45]

A back translation into Spanish from these "translated" phrases, for example, "having deceived the enemy of our race," "will not only avert bondage," or "the entailment of unnumbered wrongs" point toward an embellished technique. Unlike Covey, who attended a CMS school, Antonio, approximately fifteen in 1839, did not have the opportunity to be schooled. No sworn declaration or affidavits exist by Antonio in the court files, with or without his affixed signature, attesting to his linguistic competency, a document which characterized the main interpreters of this case. Hyde's conceivable adornment of Antonio's interview exalted the heroic leadership of Sengbe to influence public sentiments in favor of the Africans and to continue to inform the anti-slavery supporters of the real-life experiences of the enslaved.

Another inexplicable interpretation event turned into news when the US officers intercepted the *Amistad* ship. The Africans interacted with Captain Green, who apparently told them that they were to return to the schooner the following day. The surprised reporter added, "how this conversation could have occurred, when not one of the negroes can speak a word of English, is a mystery to us, unless Capt. Green, or his friend, speak Congolese."[46] The bewildered reporter concluded, "we only tell the story as he told it to us."[47] Did "signing" assist the communication, or did someone interpret body clues, or did memory play a role in narrating these events? These linger as unanswered questions.

During the first judicial investigation on the *Amistad* hearing, after being sworn in, Antonio testified using the interpreting services of Lieut. Meade. Meade, who was not sworn, together with Green and Gedney had vested interests in the outcome of this case. They also filed a suit against the Schooner *Amistad*, excluding themselves from being partial in this case, and seeking a reward for the salvage. Barber's account follows a summary format. The questions and corresponding answers are missing from his narration, a constant in these primary sources. Meade only interpreted in court on behalf of Antonio at this time, never to be repeated. Legal counsel may have noted the conflict of interest, withdrawing Meade from this task.

45 "The whole of the particulars concerning the piracy, mutiny, and murders, on board the Spanish schooner Amistaed [*sic*], which was captured on Monday last, and carried into New London, CONN," *New York Sun*, August 31, 1839.

46 Ibid.

47 Ibid.

It was a constant. The judicial system failed to protect speakers of languages other than English, and children of other ethnic heritages targeted for subjection and domination. In the September 1839 proceeding, Judge Thompson delivered his decision: "The three girls and Antonio, the cabin boy, are ordered to give bonds in the sum of $100 each to appear before the said court and give evidence in the aforesaid case, and for want of such bonds to be committed to the county jail in the city of New Haven."[48] The judicial system expected orphaned children to pay for their own bond as no legal guardian was appointed. Without a family or connections to the community, the court failed to assign them legal guardians, another alarming decision. Instead, the court resolved to remand them to jail, another very disturbing legal remedy to ensure their appearance in court. While Meade, Ruiz, and Montes were also charged "$100" to appear and provide "evidence" in their case, their adult privileged bodies were not committed to jail, since they possessed the means to submit payment.

Antonio remained in jail until at least November of that year, the time when Don Antonio G. Vega pleaded to the court for his release. This is evidenced in the documents gathered for the appeal before the Supreme Court of the USA. Mr. Antonio Vega, vice consul of Spain, who resided in Boston, interceded by requesting the release of Antonio as the "lawful property" of the legal representatives of Captain Ramón Ferrer. Vega argued that Antonio wished to return to Cuba, and, therefore, he should be released from custody into his care so that he may be returned to his lawful owner in Cuba, the wife of Captain Ferrer (refer to Figure 5.2).[49] No other resource corroborated Antonio's alleged desire to return to Cuba. But as the case progressed, and he became acquainted with the abolitionists and the Africans in the neighboring cell, his desire to stay increased, while his loyalties as a servant decreased. As Lawrance observes: "Antonio's encounters with courts were particularly complicated because his allegiances to different parties in the suits changed over time."[50]

At the Grand Jury hearing, all realized that Antonio spoke only Spanish. *The Emancipator* published, "Antonio, the Creole lad, who was servant to the Spanish captain, and who can speak no other language than the Spanish, has been before the grand jury, and they have applied for the interpreter."[51] An assertion that he only spoke Spanish generated some key unanswered

[48] Barber, *A History of the Amistad Captives*, 8.

[49] The United States, Appellants v. The Libellant and Claimants of the Schooner *Amistad*. "No. 42" (March 1841).

[50] Lawrance, "*La Amistad*'s 'Interpreter' Reinterpreted," 194.

[51] November 21, 1839. Records of this judicial proceeding have not been found to date.

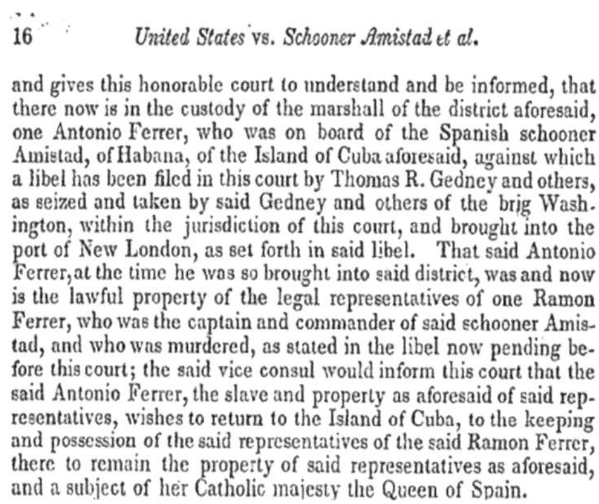

16 *United States vs. Schooner Amistad et al.*

and gives this honorable court to understand and be informed, that there now is in the custody of the marshall of the district aforesaid, one Antonio Ferrer, who was on board of the Spanish schooner Amistad, of Habana, of the Island of Cuba aforesaid, against which a libel has been filed in this court by Thomas R. Gedney and others, as seized and taken by said Gedney and others of the brig Washington, within the jurisdiction of this court, and brought into the port of New London, as set forth in said libel. That said Antonio Ferrer, at the time he was so brought into said district, was and now is the lawful property of the legal representatives of one Ramon Ferrer, who was the captain and commander of said schooner Amistad, and who was murdered, as stated in the libel now pending before this court; the said vice consul would inform this court that the said Antonio Ferrer, the slave and property as aforesaid of said representatives, wishes to return to the Island of Cuba, to the keeping and possession of the said representatives of the said Ramon Ferrer, there to remain the property of said representatives as aforesaid, and a subject of her Catholic majesty the Queen of Spain.

Figure 5.2 "Re Antonio's return to Cuba."

questions: If he only spoke Spanish, and not any African language, how was he able to serve as a linguistic mediator on board the *Amistad*? Second, who interpreted for him while testifying for the Grand Jury? The indicting court identified the need for a Spanish-language interpreter for Antonio and, apparently, did apply for one. The Grand Jury recognized the importance of having Antonio's testimony on the record. But there is no confirmation that the court responded positively to this application. Except for Lieut. Meade, the court did not produce another interpreter for Antonio.

On September 19, Antonio testified in court through the assistance of Lieut. Meade, after application to the court by counsel for the Spaniards. Though the article does not reveal who made the application, "John B. Purroy, Esq., a Spanish lawyer of the city of New York, well known there, and William Hungerford, Esq., of this city, appeared with Mr. Ingersoll as counsel for the Spaniards."[52] In the "September Term, 1839" publication, a forty-seven-page pamphlet, on the "Trial of the Prisoners of The *Amistad* on the Writ of Habeas Corpus before the Circuit Court of the United States, for the District of Connecticut, at Hartford, Judges Thompson and Judson"[53] broadcasted in great detail the use of interpreters in the case. Regarding Antonio and his testimony, it recorded:

[52] Ibid.

[53] To date, this seems to be the most complete source of the judicial hearing transcripts on the *Amistad* case between August and November of 1839. The equivalent was not published for the January 1840 trial, and no other official transcripts have been found, except for the reporters' accounts on the newspapers of the time.

> The counsel for the Spaniards, brought in Antonio, the slave of Captain of the *Amistad*, to invalidate the affidavit of Baboo.[54] Antonio being able to speak only Spanish, Lieutenant Meade, of the United States Navy, was introduced as interpreter, Lieut. Meade was first sworn; after which he explained and interpreted the oath to Antonio; and was then again sworn as interpreter. He was then directed what questions to ask, which he did, and interpreted Antonio's answers.[55]

Another newspaper article published by *The Emancipator* on September 12, 1839, seconded the idea that Antonio only spoke Spanish. It mentioned another interpreter, "an African interpreter," most likely Ferry, who also spoke Spanish. "Antonio[56] who can speak only in the Spanish language, which the African interpreter[57] well understands, said he was rather over fourteen years of age, that he was born at Havana, and had been a servant to the captain of the *Amistad*. He had been attached to the vessel three years."[58]

While acting as interpreter may have assured his life prior to landing in the USA, during the US trials Antonio was not employed as an interpreter. His role as a witness became more prominent. As a material witness, Antonio's declarations in court were crucial to the position argued by counsel for the *Amistad* Africans. Mr. Baldwin, cross-examining Antonio, with the assistance of Lieut. Meade as interpreter, testified under oath that the Africans "came in a vessel from Africa, under the Portuguese flag. They could not speak Spanish."[59] Albeit this interpretation and testimony failed to support the Spaniards' claims that the Mende Africans had lived in Cuba before 1820, this testimonial continued to support what the abolitionists already knew: the Africans had landed in Cuba recently, in violation of the

[54] Baboo is one of the *Amistad* Africans whose deposition was possible with the interpreting services of John Ferry.

[55] Trial of the *Amistad* Prisoners of the *Amistad*, 29.

[56] The exact origins of where Antonio was born and raised have not been confirmed. Lawrance, "*La Amistad*'s 'Interpreter' Reinterpreted," 135.

[57] Given its publication date, "the African interpreter" mentioned was John Ferry. A newspaper article published in *The Emancipator* explained, "John Ferry, the African interpreter, was called, and said he had explained to Baboo, the nature of an oath" (September 26, 1839). While the term "African interpreter" may refer to another unknown interpreter of an African language, to date, John Ferry is the only African interpreter whose presence coincides with the dates in question. The article dated September 12, 1839, written by Lewis Tappan, makes known a private examination with the *Amistad* prisoners. Their counsel, Marshal Wilcox, Esq., professors Olmstead and Gibbs, and Revs. Bacon and Ludlow cited "Anthony, the black boy, who speaks only the Spanish language, the native African interpreter, and myself [Tappan]."

[58] *The Emancipator*, September 12, 1839.

[59] Barber, *A History of the Amistad Captives*, 29.

treaties signed by England and Spain. Further manipulation in his testimony seemed apparent. Lieut. Meade, Antonio's interpreter, vested his interest in supporting the Spaniards as a way of guaranteeing his salvage. In the same transcription document, Antonio affirmed under oath that the *Amistad* was not used to carrying slaves. Instead, it was "always employed in carrying sugar."[60] This stood in direct contradiction to his earlier affidavit stating that "the Schooner *Amistad* had carried slaves before—every two months made trip. Ruiz had before carried slaves."[61] Antonio's different version came in response to fear of reprisal from the other side.

Mr. Hungerford, Esq., counsel for the Spaniards, worried as Antonio's testimony in court began to implicate the Spaniards. Consequently, Hungerford attempted "reinterpreting" Antonio's statements to avoid detrimental effects for his clients. Regarding Antonio's observation that the Africans did not speak Spanish, he rebuked, "again, that they were unable to speak the Spanish language, is not strange . . . they are put on a plantation and remain there for years, entirely ignorant of a language except their own."[62] Mr. Staples, an ordained minister and abolitionist, and a member of the legal team defending the Africans, addressed the court after a long exposition by Hungerford discrediting the defense's argument on the fact that the Africans spoke a language other than Spanish. The *Amistad* team was not advocating for Antonio early in the case. Staples vehemently tried discrediting Antonio's testimony in this September 20 proceeding. Regarding Antonio's testimony, Staples argued:

> Who is that boy? A poor miserable slave that belonged to the master of the vessel which bought these persons here. Is that the source we are to look to for the truth? . . . if he is to be regarded at all. . . . He says they knew no Spanish; and he must have known, for he knows that language. So far, then, from contradicting our testimony, the boy supports it. But they say this boy contradicts the affidavit of Baboo. . . . It is against the facts and probabilities. Here is a boy, the first time he "found himself," very young, speaking Spanish. That shows that those that are born there, begin very early to speak the Spanish language.[63]

Staples used Antonio's primary language as proof that African descendants living in Cuba for a long time assimilated the Spanish language. If they

[60] Barber, *A History of the Amistad Captives*, 30.
[61] National Archives, *Amistad Schooner*, 173, fold 3.
[62] Baber, *A History of the Amistad Captives*, 34.
[63] Barber, *A History of the Amistad Captives*, 35.

were *Ladinos/Ladinas*, as claimed in the *licencias*, this would have been true. Antonio's testimony was "translated by Lieutenant Meade" in court, apparently during the court proceedings from August to November of 1839. By the January trial, Meade became a libellant, not an interpreter. Conveniently, the court failed to provide a Spanish interpreter for Antonio in the trial. Two Portuguese interpreters attempted to serve Antonio to no avail. The African legal team resorted to innovative strategies to resolve this impediment—an *Amistad* legal representative. This will be discussed in detail in the *Amistad* trial chapter.

After the January 1840 trial, Judge Judson ruled that Antonio be returned to Cuba, a decision upheld by the Supreme Court. But he never made it to Cuba. A letter dated February 16, 1858, from Mr. Sherman, Esq., writing to Simeon E. Baldwin, recalled Antonio stopping by his house on his way to Canada:

> When I was about seven years of age, my father, Elias B. Sherman, resided in Enosburg, Vermont. He was one of the original abolitionists and was a "conductor" and "station agent" of "The Underground Railroad." One morning I found that a handsome young negro had mysteriously arrived during the preceding night; it was Antonio, the cook of the *Amistad*,[64] who had escaped. . . . A night or two afterwards, he disappeared as mysteriously as he had come—my father had taken him to Canada. . . . The occurrence made a very vivid impression upon my mind, and I recall the circumstances, as though but yesterday.[65]

After Antonio left for Montreal, Dougall wrote to Leavitt, "I am happy to inform that the boy Antonio of the *Amistad* celebrity came in here safely two or three days ago and is consequently beyond the reach of all the slave holders in the world."[66] As the case progressed beyond the January 1840 trial, the abolitionists held private conversations with Antonio not accounted for in the archival materials, which convinced him to abandon the idea of returning to Cuba.

[64] The cook of the *Amistad* was Celestino, killed on the night of the rebellion.

[65] "Baldwin to Sherman," February 16, 1858, Baldwin Family Papers (MS 55). Manuscripts and Archives, Yale University Library.

[66] "John Dougall to Joshua Leavitt," April 26, 1841, AMA FI 4983, The *Amistad* Research Center, New Orleans, Louisiana, USA.

John Ferry, the First African Interpreter in the *Amistad* Case

After September 1839

After a two-week letter-writing campaign within the abolitionists' inner network coupled with a week of running ads, the African-interpreter recruitment efforts bore the first fruit. John Ferry became the second interpreter of African descent in the *Amistad* story, and the third following Antonio and Lieut. Meade. Simeon Jocelyn, living in New Haven, recorded the first mention of Ferry in this *Amistad* saga. In a letter dated September 16, 1839, from New York City, he announced: "Mr. Ferry will go to Hartford today."[67] There, he interpreted at the second judicial *Amistad* investigation set for September 17. The Africans arrived in Hartford "by the way of the canal . . . from Farmington they probably crossed the country to Hartford . . . in wagons."[68] An entourage of abolitionists, including Leavitt and Mr. Norton, also travelled to this city for the trial. Prior to going to Hartford, Ferry met various times with the Africans and the litigation team. Ferry headed north confident of the effective communication between the defendants, the legal team, and himself.

The *Amistad* Committee found Ferry in the city "after repeated trials and much inquiry." Years before his collaboration in the *Amistad* case, Ferry had lost his African-given name for an English one, as happened to thousands in the Atlantic violent linguistic crossover. In contrast to Covey, who received a new name as pupil in the established missionary schools, Ferry lost his in Latin America. His US enslaving master "took" him from Suriname in the Caribbean to Baltimore, Maryland. Behind the veil of an English name, he carried his knowledge of African languages corresponding to those needed in the *Amistad* case; he spoke some Mende, and "Vey," also known as "Kissi." His multilingualism proved helpful to give voice to another one of the Africans, Grabbeau, as the litigation team earnestly continued to draw a more complete picture of the journey of the Africans from Africa to Cuba to the northern USA. Reminiscing two years after the Africans' arrival in the USA, some of the *Amistad* abolitionists recalled that "John Ferry [was] our first interpreter. He conversed with Grabbeau in this language."[69] Ferry's actual recruitment can only be approximated. In an article dated September 12, 1839 in *The Emancipator*, the author reported that three interpreter

67 AMA Archives FI 4628, The *Amistad* Research Center, New Orleans, Louisiana, USA.
68 AMA Archives FI 4628, The *Amistad* Research Center, New Orleans, Louisiana, USA.
69 AMA Archives FI 4592B, The *Amistad* Research Center, New Orleans, Louisiana, USA.

candidates visited the prison to test their language skills with the Africans: "the next morning, we found, to our great disappointment, that only one of the [three], J.F., was able to converse with the prisoners."[70] Although only one of them, Ferry, is described by name, dates strongly suggest that Augustus W. Hanson, of African birth, joined the group of candidates that came from New York City to New Haven to apply his linguistic skills. Rev. D. Burguess[71] wrote to Rev. Joshua Leavitt in a postscript expressing high hopes that "Mr. Hanson . . . will be able to converse with the Africans. As he understands several languages."[72] Although his linguistic expertise did not match the Africans', his contribution in this case was appreciated. An affidavit signed in his name, found in the case files, was submitted in court reiterating that the "girls" only spoke African languages and not Spanish, an important observation to sustain the overall claim in favor of the Africans.

Although finding Ferry did not pause the search for an interpreter, his interactions with the Africans moved the liberation compass closer to Africa:

> he [was] able to converse a little in the Mandingo dialect. . . . Most of the prisoners can understand him, although none of them can speak his Kissi dialect. You may imagine the joy manifested by these poor Africans, when they heard one of their own color addresse them in a friendly manner, and in a language, they could comprehend![73] (refer to Figure 5.3)

For the Africans, Ferry offered a necessitous relief. Ferry brought joy to the imprisoned Africans. Someone they could lean on. As court interpreter, "J.F." delivered the main points of the African's story at the September 17 trial in Hartford. As a medical interpreter, he mediated linguistically between the captives and the physician in receiving adequate medical treatment. An article entitled "Private Examination of Cinquez, alias Jingua" described Tappan's visit to the "hospital department of the prison," where he spoke with Dr. Charles Hooker. Tappan recorded that, thanks to the interpreter, the doctor was able to converse with the Africans:

> Five or six are sick with white flux, or diarrhea, peculiar to warm climates—one or two of them dangerously, as the physician thinks, who,

[70] *The Emancipator*, September 12, 1839.

[71] I have kept the prefix "Rev" when affixed to the name to illustrate the religious interconnectedness to the *Amistad* movement.

[72] AMA Archives FI 4607, The *Amistad* Research Center, New Orleans, Louisiana, USA.

[73] *The Emancipator*, September 12, 1839.

To the Committee on behalf of the African Prisoners:

I arrived here last Friday evening, with three men who are natives of Africa, and who were joined the next day by two others, to act as interpreters in conversing with Cinquez, or as it is pronounced by himself, Jingua, and his comrades. He said he knew nothing of the name of Joseph. On going to the jail, the next morning, we found, to our great disappointment, that only one of the men, J. F., was able to converse with the prisoners. He is about 30 years of age, a native of Kissi, which is about 100 or 150 miles from the mouth of the river Gallinas, in the interior, which is about a day's journey south of Sierra Leon. He was kidnapped when about 12 years old, and was liberated in Columbia, by Bolivar. He is able to converse a little in the Mandingo dialect, but understands better that of Gallinas, which some of the prisoners can speak. Most of the prisoners can understand him, although none of them can speak his Kissi dialect. You may imagine the joy manifested by these poor Africans, when they heard one of their own color address them in a friendly manner, and in a language they could comprehend!

Figure 5.3 "John Ferry meets the *Amistad* Africans."

> through the interpreter, conversed, for the first time, with his patients.... Some of the sick are convalescing. The doctor says he has seldom had patients who showed so much gratitude when relieved by medicines. One of the sick men, named Jooah, writes in some unknown language, which does not appear to be the Arabic. They said they were forced to drink a great deal of salt water on "board the slaver", and that had made them sick.[74]

The physician's observations transcended the Africans' health conditions. Dr. Hooker commented on their physical attributes, which correlated to their geographical-African origins. The doctor observed that most of the prisoners were circumcised: "and it is well known that many pagan [*sic*] nations perform this rite."[75] Dr. Hooker's surprised reaction suggests that male circumcision was uncommon during that period in the USA, at least among Christians. This ethnic characteristic further championed the cause of their origins.

After the medical examination, counsels for the captives continued with the judicial one. Baldwin and Staples interviewed Sengbe and Bowle. Many attended this proceeding: Mr. Wilcox, Esq., acting as court marshal; Profs. Gibbs, Olmstead; Rev. Messrs. Bacon and Ludlow; Antonio, "the black boy, who speaks only Spanish"; Tappan; and John Ferry, "the interpreter." In this judicial proceeding, Ferry's knowledge of the Spanish language proved useful

[74] *The Emancipator*, September 12, 1839.
[75] *The Emancipator*, September 12, 1839.

in assisting Antonio in his declarations.[76] Ferry did not speak Mende well enough to serve as the main interpreter for Cinque and the other Africans. Jingua's[77] leadership and commanding spirit generated credibility in a court of law; the abolitionists knew this. While it was important for all Africans to converse and be understood by the interpreters, exquisite communication with Jingua proved that the ideal interpreter had been found.

Ferry's knowledge of "*Gallina*," "Galena," aka "Vey," the language spoken in the Gallina region, alleviated, momentarily, their interpreting needs. In what is referred today as "relay interpreting," Sengbe, aka Jingua, speaking Mende to Bowle and Bowle speaking Vey to Ferry, allowed Ferry to convey Sengbe's message in English for the record. The same article in *The Emancipator* described:

> Cinquez (or rather Jingua) and Bowle are natives of the same tribe, the Mandingo, but as the latter can speak the Gallinas dialect better than the former, the interpreter, who, though neither a Mandingo nor a Gallina, but a Kissi (which was spelled incorrectly in previous communication Gheeshee), found it easier to communicate with Jingua by the aid of Bowle, who translated the Gallinas to him in Mandingo.[78]

Abolitionists used newspaper articles to augment the support for their cause by humanizing them and honoring their ethnic traditions. Their cultural ways helped the Africans to survive the colder weather and political discord. A lengthy article, published by *The Daily Herald* in New Haven and dated September 16, 1839, was entitled "List and Description of the Captured Africans," written by Prof. Josiah W. Gibbs, Yale Hebrew scholar. The article developed a comprehensive list of all the languages spoken by the captives and the numbers from one to ten in each of their native languages. Many possible language combinations existed among the Africans. "We found, during the investigation, that the prisoners speak at least six dialects [sic],

[76] In his August 29 letter, Janes suggested the possibility of Antonio serving as interpreter to the captives, if he communicated to them that they were "among friends." This may explain why Antonio was part of this interview process, of which his testimony is not solicited, or at least not included as part of Tappan's narration. It is possible that a linguistic exchange between Antonio and John Ferry led Tappan to conclude that Ferry understood Spanish "well." If this were the case, an unanswered question remains as to why Ferry was not used as "Spanish interpreter" for Antonio, during the remainder of the judicial proceedings.

[77] In most newspaper articles, the Africans' leader name appeared as "Jingua." Spelling of his name varies. Jingua, as spelled from Covey's pronunciation, "sounded" closer to the original African name, instead of Cinque, Cinquez, or José, as the *licencias* misconstrued.

[78] *The Emancipator*, September 12, 1839.

that the Gallina dialect is the Vey and Tey, and that one or more speak the Susoo."[79] This list included Ferry's working languages and identified Ferry as an interpreter. The first section of this article listed all the Africans including those who had died, some physical characteristics, such as height, and a phonetic listing of the numerals. Personality traits such as "very intelligent," or particular events in their lives, for instance, "spoke over the corpse of Tûa, after Rev. Mr. Bacon's prayer" characterized these descriptions. Another article recorded how the African girls, when given shawls, turned them "into turbans," as they shielded from the cold, celebrated their identity, and sought cultural-comfort."[80] Their mourning practices also reinforced their native origins. Abolitionists invested resources and time to comprehend and shorten the cultural distance between them and the Africans to mount their defense. They portrayed the Africans and people of African descent in a human light in their earnest belief of their human rights. For their anti-slavery movement to grow, they needed to eradicate the inhumane and inhuman images brewed in southern USA and partnered with northern racist attitudes in the north.

Gibbs's ethnographical and linguistic study of the Africans also concluded that the captives communicated in no other language than their native languages. Most of the thirty prisoners spoke "Mandingo." It was not until Covey that the term "Mende" was introduced as a synonym for "Mandingo." Ferry helped Gibbs identify the main six languages spoken by the Africans through summarizing and interpreting, and by sharing his own expertise: (1) Mandingo, (2) Fai—the Mandingo Fai, (3) Congo, (4) Timmani, and (5) Bullom.[81] The sixth language identified was the one also spoken by John Ferry. When referring to "Gabaung," self-identified as a "Mandingo Fai," Gibbs remarked: "He counts in Fai or Gallina, like the Fai or Fallina of John Ferry, the interpreter, from New York . . . [Grabaung] counts also in Gissi (Kissi of Prichard),[82] the native tongue of John Ferry, the interpreter."[83] Ferry's linguistic expertise did not match Cinque's language pair or that of the rest of the African natives, but it proved sufficient at the time. Ferry unveiled in detail the ethnic background of the Africans, crucial information to undergird the defense's claim—they lived in Africa shortly before being taken to Cuba. Ferry's interpreting furnished a cornerstone for the pursuit of evidence to feed the legal strategy.

79 *The Emancipator*, September 12, 1839.
80 *The Emancipator*, September 12, 1839.
81 *The Emancipator*, September 12, 1839.
82 Prichard, only known by his last name in these primary sources, authored the book *Physical History of Mankind*. His full name, James Cowles Prichard, offered a more holistic view of race, language, and ethnic identification.
83 *The Daily Herald*, September 16, 1839.

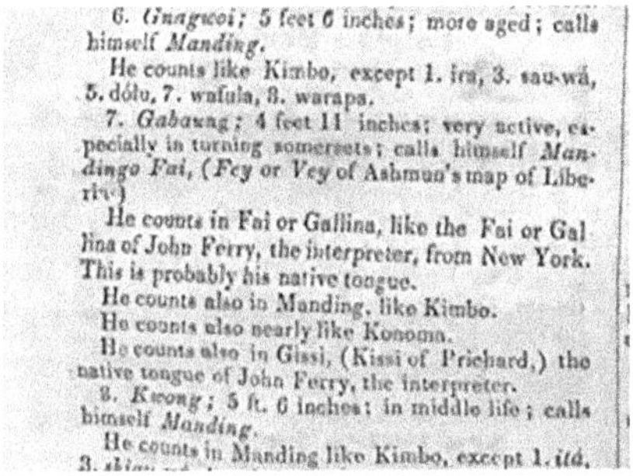

6. *Gnagwoi*; 5 feet 6 inches; more aged; calls himself *Manding*.

He counts like Kimbo, except 1. ira, 3. sau-wá, 5. dólo, 7. wafula, 8. waraps.

7. *Gabaung*; 4 feet 11 inches; very active, especially in turning somersets; calls himself *Mandingo Fai*, (*Fey* or *Vey* of Ashmun's map of Liberia.)

He counts in Fai or Gallina, like the Fai or Gallina of John Ferry, the interpreter, from New York. This is probably his native tongue.

He counts also in Manding, like Kimbo.

He counts also nearly like Konoma.

He counts also in Gissi, (Kissi of Prichard,) the native tongue of John Ferry, the interpreter.

8. *Kwong*; 5 ft. 6 inches; in middle life; calls himself *Manding*.

He counts in Manding like Kimbo, except 1. *ita*,

Figure 5.4 "Ferry and the languages of the Africans." *The Daily Herald*, September 16, 1839.

Interpreting storytelling scenarios posed interesting protocols. Newsprints of on-the-record and off-the-record linguistic mediations often prefaced the information solicited from the Africans with phrases such as "through the interpreter" or "via the interpreter" which featured the impossibility of obtaining the information without the assistance of a linguistic mediator. On other occasions, the editors described the interaction by saying the "prisoners told the interpreter." The recorders or the legal team that narrated the linguistic questions witnessed the interpreters in action, but not at all times. The African prisoners also shared with interpreters in meetings without the presence of legal representation. "The prisoners told the interpreter" suggested that Ferry and others conversed with the Africans without the occurrence of an interpreted dialogue. In these situations, interpreters later relayed the information to the legal team which included summarization mixed in with their own expertise and opinions. A preamble to ethnic-historical disclosure from the Africans noted that the Africans "told the interpreter" that "they were Mandingoes," from "the district of Mandingo, in the Senegambia country . . . by the Atlantic Ocean, and is directly north of Liberia."[84] The Africans continued telling the interpreter that the three other men and three of the girls were Congolese from the coast and south of the equator.[85] Further conversations with the interpreter revealed more details about the geographical area of the *Amistad* Africans, their neighboring tribal nations, and the richness of their languages (refer to Figure 5.4):

Within two weeks of the schooner's arrival in New London, Connecticut, the abolitionists learned a few lessons: "the tribes in Africa are very numerous, almost every tribe having a distinct language, and it often varies, it is said,

[84] "The Captured Africans," *The Emancipator*, September 12, 1839.
[85] "The Captured Africans," *The Emancipator*, September 12, 1839.

from village to village."[86] In the process of finding Covey, a few languages mediated between the captives and the outside world. The abolitionists experienced the exhaustive and exhausting technique of relay interpreting. The linguistic interaction among the interpreter, the Africans, and the rest required fluidity and competency. Despite all the information gathered with the assistance of John Ferry, the abolitionists continued to search to find another who could best suit the role. Without the right interpreter, "no person will be able to converse with them well until they can speak the dialect of Mandingo . . . yet it is difficult to find an interpreter who can converse with them readily and intelligently."[87] The search concentrated its efforts in New York City, where a large African-descent community lived, and from where Ferry travelled to New Haven.

The language match was only one of the elements to ensure communication that would enable the story to be told. As discussed previously, trust was necessary. Trust played a crucial role through the *Amistad* story. The presence or absence of trust eased or hampered the willingness of the Africans to speak, or encouraged them to fake not understanding spoken speech. Janes's letter recorded what happened when Ferry attempted to establish communication with Jingua in prison, providing another marking event in the *Amistad* linguistic saga. The eventful untrusting dialogue made its way to a newspaper:

> At first [Jingua] seemed averse to answering the questions of the interpreter, and made the impression that he could not speak the Mandingo dialect. But after the interpreter had told him that they had conversed freely with his comrades, he conversed very freely, and with much energy of expression and action, R.S. Baldwin, Esq., of counsel for the prisoners, and Prof. Gibbs, having accompanied the interpreter.[88]

Trust led this dialogue. In a situation of life and death, trust was earned, not guaranteed. Distrust was so prevalent that the Africans faked not speaking and understanding their native languages. Trusting represented a precursor to the possibility of an interpreted dialogue. The *Amistad* highlights the role of trust in interpreting settings where tangible signs of discomfort or ease are expressed. The interpreter's role kept expanding to involve reassuring the Africans that it was safe to disclose information. Ferry and the rest of the interpreters arrived at this conclusion themselves—the abolitionists were trustworthy. The African captives took a risk on behalf of their lives and

[86] "The Captured Africans," *The Emancipator*, September 12, 1839.
[87] "The Captured Africans," *The Emancipator*, September 12, 1839.
[88] "The Captured Africans," *The Emancipator*, September 12, 1839.

entered the interpretation scenario while the *Amistad* litigation team prayed they did so that they could defend their lives. Trust opened the door for the Africans to express their fears of being killed. What words could not express, signs and body language communicated. Tappan reported that "the prisoners appeared to be under much apprehension and asked the interpreter if they were to have their throats cut, passing their hands across their necks when they made the inquiry. He replied no and endeavored to quiet their fears."[89]

In the face of life and death, distrust was to be expected. Trust unfolded in both directions: Africans to US abolitionists, US abolitionists to Africans. A newspaper article described how the communities at large perceived the African chief now captured. They compared Sengbe to Othello, a seventeenth-century Shakespearean character, and with Osceola, a Seminole-tribal leader from the US southern state of Florida.[90] The first extended a cultural reference that inspired trust in those who were educated in European literature and promoted European ideals. The second inspired trust through recent stories of land struggle and ethnic resistance parallel to those of the Africans. Other signs of trust manifested during the interpreting encounter between the Africans and Ferry. During the examination "occasionally, [Sengbe] would shake hands with the interpreter, and laugh very heartily."[91] Physical closeness showed a connection of trust between the interpreter and the Africans. Trust was not a byproduct of the interaction but, instead, a requirement for effective communication. For the Africans to tell their story in court and to participate in their own defense, they needed to trust their immediate environment and to feel that the interpreter was on their side.

Such a display of closeness validated the ability of Ferry to provide service. This display of affection opposes current court professional standards for interpreting, but perhaps not the reality. Nowadays, most professionals in the field as well as court officers would resist this level of physical proximity for safety and/or other reasons. Although this physical gesture may have been initiated by the person receiving interpreting services, this would

[89] *The Emancipator*, September 26, 1839.

[90] Sengbe's commanding spirit characterized this African-born captive in his struggle for freedom. His leadership inspired various portraits and paintings, some conserved to this day. Newspapers attested to how he addressed English audiences in Mende for lengthy periods of time without an interpreter, even when interpreters were present. During these events, he enjoyed the full attention of his audience. An article in the September 12, 1839, *The Emancipator*, reported that "his general deportment is free from levity, and many white men might take a lesson in dignity and forbearance from the African Chieftain, who, although in bondage, appears to have been the Osceala of this race." Osceola, a Seminole Tribe leader in Florida, USA, led a resistance movement, dying in jail in 1838.

[91] *The Emancipator*, September 26, 1839.

compromise two of the most venerated professional standards for court interpreting: not to give the appearance of impropriety and not to convey the perception that the court interpreter has taken sides.[92] "Shaking hands," in the middle of an interpreting dialogue would question the integrity and impartiality of the interpreter, compromising the trust comfort of the other parties within the power spectrum.

In the *Amistad* case, no objection was recorded on either side. "Shaking hands" demonstrated that trust existed among all parties. Current tendencies in our application of the code of ethics and professional standards for court interpreting dismiss an important question raised in this research and present in all communication spaces—how trust facilitates, or lack thereof, interferes in linguistically mediated dialogues. With Ferry as interpreter, the Africans began telling their stories and "counter-stories." It opened the gates for painting a fuller picture of the truthful journey and to design related strategies accordingly. A larger number of advocates and adversaries began to connect the dots as disclosure and comprehension evolved. As a result of the information interpreted or told to the interpreter, Tappan published a second advertisement to narrow down the search for the *Amistad* interpreter. This advertisement provided specific geographic information and identified the language pairs sought and the national origin of the ideal interpreter:

> If there are native Africans in this city,[93] or elsewhere in this country, who were born near the sources of the river Niger, or in Mandigo, or who can converse readily in this Susso, Kissi, Mandingo, Banbarra, or Gallinas dialects, they will confer a great favor by calling, or sending word to the undersigned, for the Committee, at No. 143 Nassau Street, New York City. A native Mandingo would be the best interpreter.[94]

Ferry's interpreting services facilitated Baboo's deposition, which was followed by his own. Baboo's affidavit reiterated that two of the girls and "the little boy, Carle [Ka'le]" were known to him. Baboo stated that he knew "these children" that they "are the same that came over from Africa." Each on opposite sides of the prison bars shared a common enslaving background, after surviving the Atlantic passage. Both interpreter and the African he interpreted for signed judicial declarations with "a cross," signifiying that the

[92] The revised 2016 Canon 4 on "Unobtrusiveness" reiterates that a court interpreter "should not interject or reveal their own feelings, moods, attitudes, or beliefs while performing their professional duties." See https://njcourts.gov/public/assets/langSrvcs/codeconduct.pdf?cacheID=yLRNEv1.

[93] This refers to New York City of publication for *The Emancipator*.

[94] *The Emancipator*, September 12, 1839.

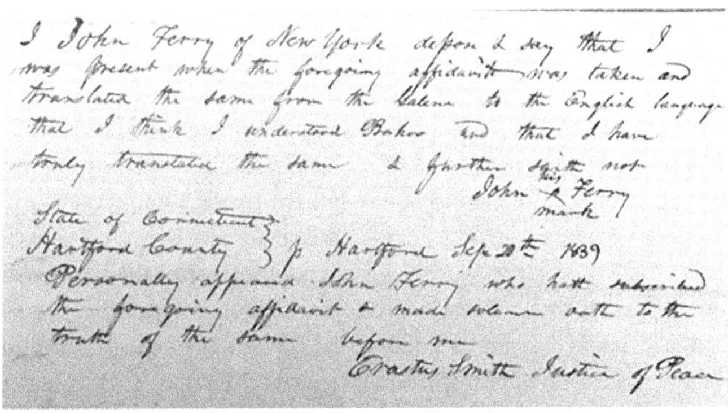
I John Ferry of New York depose & say that I was present when the foregoing affidavit was taken and translated the same from the Galena to the English language that I think I understood Baboo and that I have truly translated the same & further deposeth not

John his x Ferry mark

State of Connecticut }
Hartford County } ss Hartford Sep 20th 1839

Personally appeared John Ferry who hath subscribed the foregoing affidavit & made solemn oath to the truth of the same before me

Erastus Smith Justice of Peace

Figure 5.5 "John Ferry's Affidavit," September 20, 1839, National Archives in Boston.

person did not know how to write their name using the English or Spanish alphabet. Nonetheless, they both saw the writing on the wall of distrustful systems. In the September 17 proceeding, counsel for the Africans introduced Baboo's affidavit (aka Bowle). Unfortunately, Bowle passed away before the November proceeding. Thankfully, Ferry's accompanying affidavit of Baboo's affidavit confirmed that he swore having "translated" from the Galena—the Gallina language—into "the English language." Ferry was not able to ascertain how well he understood his deponent. In an affidavit, transcribed by Erasmus Smith and signed by Ferry with a cross, Ferry affirmed "that [he] think[s] that [he] understood Baboo"[95] (refer to Figure 5.5).

The abolitionist newspaper detailed how "the African interpreter," John Ferry, "explained to the deponent the nature of the oath, and that he appeared to comprehend it, and that he truly translated his testimony."[96] Ferry "explained" the nature of the oath, beyond interpretation. It involved expounding with one's own words. Constantly in this case, additional steps on the record were taken to ensure that the oath was thoroughly understood by the Africans. In the next sentence, Mr. Thomas Gallaudet, a Sign Language (SL) interpreter, entered the scene reporting the following: "Mr. Gallaudet, which was present, informed the prisoner's counsel that he had conversed with him [Baboo] by sign, and he appeared to have intelligent idea of a Supreme Being, and of the penalties incurred for telling a falsehood."[97]

95 *The Emancipator*, September 26, 1839.
96 *The Emancipator*, September 26, 1839.
97 *The Emancipator*, September 26, 1839.

This unorthodox religious cross-examination would also be repeated by Mr. Gallaudet in the *Amistad* trial in January 1840.

Baboo received an explanation on "who God was," one of the main trinitarian aspects of the Christian God, and how penalties may be imposed if his testimony lacked veracity. Not all oath structures include the phrase "so help you God," or "and nothing else but the truth." Other court customs involved court marshals strongly urging witnesses to place their right hand on a Bible, the Koran, or the Hebrew Bible as a mirror of the witness's faith preference. Taking "an oath" stems from the Christian tradition.[98] Nonfaith-professing witnesses may prefer not to swear under oath. For them, the courts offer the alternative to affirm, *afirmar*, or protest *protestar*. "Protesting" grew from those opposed to being asked to take an oath involving a divinity or religious belief. Reviewing oath practices in the context of the *Amistad* case outlined a fact to be proven via translated documents and interpreted testimonies: the Africans did not spend enough time in Cuba to acculturate religiously. The nature of the oath needed to be explained, along with its religious implications to the judicial proceedings. This also proved how culturally foreign these entire religious allusions were, though common for those living for decades in Spanish- or English-speaking countries exposed to parallel judicial settings. In contradiction with their own testimony, this explained why the Spaniards doubted that the Africans would be aware of the meaning behind such an oath. In doubting their faithfulness to this practice, the Spaniards also implicitly acknowledged that the Africans had only recently arrived from the African continent.

Before September 1839

The *Amistad* abolitionists wanted the community to ascertain the background of Ferry to garner wider financial and movement support. Regarding the interpreter's place of birth, another newspaper article written by Lewis Tappan, included "the river on whose banks the interpreter was born is called Moan. It runs through the district where Jingua—was born

[98] This practice dates to the ninth century when citizens gathered by the altar to finalize certain transactions, swearing on the Christian Gospels. The judicial system integrated this tradition three centuries later, with witnesses kissing the Bible as they took the oath. According to Helen Rosenfield, "by placing a hand on the book and then kissing it, the oath-taker is acknowledging that, should [the person] lie under oath, neither the words in the Bible nor [the person's] good deeds nor [the person's] prayers will bring [the person] any earthly or spiritual profit." With time, this swearing practice made its way into the USA's legal system. https://www.newyorker.com/books/page-turner/a-brief-history-of-oaths-and-books.

to sea. It is sometimes very deep."[99] Other articles expounded that he was "a native from Kissi, which is about 100 or 150 miles from the mouth of the river Gallinas, in the interior, which is about a day's journey south of Sierra Leone."[100] Affidavits submitted in court by Ferry and Hanson indicated that Ferry was "a seaman."[101] Ferry shared with the *Amistad* orphans a truncated childhood, kidnapping from the interior of the African continent, being juggled between different sets of enslaving hands, and forced into a vessel across the Atlantic. Differently from Covey, Antonio, and the other children liberated by the mission activities of the Joint Commission or by the *Amistad* rebellion, Ferry's transatlantic journey took him at around twelve years of age to southern Latin American colonies:

> He is about 30 years of age, a native of Kissi, which is about 100–150 miles from the mouth of the river Gallinas, in the interior, which is about a day's journey south of Sierra Leone. He was kidnapped when about 12 years old, and was liberated in [Gran] Colombia, by Bolívar. . . . You may imagine the joy manifested by these poor Africans, when they heard one of their own color address them in a friendly manner, and in a language they could comprehend!

Tappan referred to *El Gran Libertador* of the Americas. Alluding to him by his last name only signals to his influential persona and his international leadership. It also pointed to the transatlantic trait of the abolitionist movement.[102] US abolitionists were cognizant of the successful movements in Latin America and the interconnectedness of justice-led efforts. Simón Bolívar became a leader people aspire to. Bolívar led the newly decreed Republic of "*Gran Colombia*" to liberation in 1821. Nine years afterward, in 1830, he died. In 1839, he was quoted in a US newspaper as having freed an enslaved, an *Amistad* interpreter. Ferry, born circa 1809, was about thirty years old when recruited by the *Amistad* Committee. Similar to Covey and Antonio, they all shared the journey of African childhood enslavement, orphanhood, and liberation. Covey said in his deposition that he was liberated by a British brig at sea from an enslaving vessel, while Ferry attributed his liberation from slavery directly, "by Bolívar" (refer to Figure 5.3). At first glance, his journey from capture to enslavement and from enslavement to liberation traces the development of his African and Spanish linguistic competency, respectively.

[99] *The Emancipator*, September 26, 1839.
[100] *The Emancipator*, September 26, 1839.
[101] *The Emancipator*, September 26, 1839.
[102] *The Emancipator*, September 26, 1839.

He must have spent at least three years or more in a Spanish-speaking, newly formed country in order "to understand Spanish very well." It was not until the next *Amistad* proceeding in court that we learn more details about Ferry's background and the connection to Bolívar, but not before SL took a center role in the case.

Sign Language Interpreting in the *Amistad* Case

Sign Language occupied a prominent place in the *Amistad* thread of events. George Day[103] and Thomas Hopkins Gallaudet acted as SL interpreters from the onset of this case until the January trial. "Mr. G.," aka the Rev. Thomas Hopkins Gallaudet, graduated from Yale College and Andover Theological Seminary. Gallaudet was known for being the founder of the first school for the deaf in North America, established in Hartford, Connecticut in 1817, later known as the American School for the Deaf. Much later, Gallaudet University would carry his name. Gallaudet and Day both served as instructors to the Africans while they were in jail and once liberated.

Additionally, Gallaudet served as a teaching language consultant for the Africans. Responding to Gallaudet's advice on guidelines, on October 19, 1839, George Day requested that Lewis Tappan purchase more materials to be used in English-language instruction of the Africans. Day reported on their educational progress: "in accordance with the advice of Mr. Gallaudet, we have procured pictures of single objects & commenced by teaching them the name of these objects."[104] Day commented on the Africans' intelligence and fast learning skills, "they manifest as much intelligence, as any promiscuous collection of white men [*sic*]."[105] Equating their intelligence to those identified as "men" and of European descent, as standards of intelligence, matched the limited beliefs of many abolitionists at the time, instead of exalting them for "displaying high levels of intelligence," period. The Africans quickly mastered the first "20 to 30" vocabulary cards. More primary sources and picture books were needed from which to create educational materials. Day requested: "will

[103] George Day, also a Hebrew scholar at Yale College and professor at the New York Institute for the Deaf and Dumb [*sic*], was also invited to form part of the committee. He assisted in many ways, including the English language and religious instruction of the captives in jail.

[104] AMA Archives FI 4648, The *Amistad* Research Center, New Orleans, Louisiana, USA.

[105] AMA Archives FI 4648, The *Amistad* Research Center, New Orleans, Louisiana, USA.

you have the kindness, sir, to send us up as great [a] variety of pictures suited to our object as you can find?"[106]

Instructors of the "Deaf and Dumb," as they were referred erroneously in the nineteenth century, were called upon to communicate with the Africans and to act as interpreters. Rather quickly, they passed the trust test of the African captives. SL instructors[107] belonged to a linguistic minority in a society that gives preference to oral languages. This experience equipped them with greater cultural and political sensitivities and skills in the second-language acquisition. As Kim A. Silva, SL historian, surmises: "where the *Amistad* Committee's African-language translators [*sic*] failed, the signs used by the deaf succeeded. Deaf educators Thomas H. Gallaudet and George E. Day relayed riveting stories of the captives to the newspapers and helped to identify the elusive Mende language."[108] Although US culture, then and today, privileges oral languages and tends to be unwelcoming to non-English speakers from the global south, the nineteenth-century ethnic composition of the USA demonstrated a growing representation of speakers of other languages and other countries. Gallaudet and Day served as bridges. Gallaudet authored a source to assist missionaries in communicating with non-English-speaking individuals in *Literary and Theological Review* used in the instruction of the Africans.[109]

The *Amistad* case prompted anonymity and discretion issues among its informants, especially around language matters. In the same letter, Day diplomatically asked Tappan not to make the "note [the letter] become public." As the story progressed, more letters authored by or received by Tappan appeared in newspapers. In his letter to Tappan, Day[110] requested

[106] AMA Archives FI 4648, The *Amistad* Research Center, New Orleans, Louisiana, USA.

[107] Day invited Tappan to ask two instructors from the same institute to help in the selection and preparation of these instructional materials, Mr. Bartlett and Mr. Cary. However, his letters attributed the "burden of the instructions" to two "gentleman." One is Griswold and the other one's name is illegible. Griswold received numerous invitations to accompany the Africans on their journey back to Africa, but he declined the invitation.

[108] Kim A. Silva, "Signs of Freedom: Deaf Connections in the *Amistad* Story," in *Telling Deaf Lives: Agents of Change*, ed. Kristin Snoddon (Washington DC: Gallaudet University Press, 2014), 136.

[109] Silva, "Signs of Freedom," 141.

[110] Other sources reinforced Day's involvement as an instructor for the Africans. A forty-seven-page document printed by abolitionists, titled "The African Captives. Trial of the Prisoners of the *Amistad* on the Writ of Habeas Corpus, Before the Circuit Court of the United States, for the District of Connecticut, at Hartford: Judged Thompson and Judson. September Term, 1839," provided a transcription of the September proceeding, including articles and information provided by George Day. Contrary to "Doc. 185" published by the US Congress and reprinted by the Anti-Slavery Society, "The African Captives," published as an "anti-slavery" publication, remained the most complete "official" transcript of the September 17, 1839, proceeding.

that the first person be changed to the "3rd" person, or rephrase the message: "should you deem it desirable to send to the papers any of the facts . . . I should not object to it. In that case, however, they should be stated in your own language or, at least, in 3rd person."[111] Not only was knowledge of the Spanish language something to be hidden from the public, but so too SL knowledge and instruction, and those involved in the *Amistad* movement fearful of reprisals.

The SL community has recognized the connection between the *Amistad* case and interpreting issues. As Kim A. Silva recounts, "oral history from the American School for the Deaf (ASD) affirms that the founders of the school, Laurent Clerc and Thomas H. Gallaudet were the first interpreters for Cinque, the leader of the *Amistad* revolt . . . it was easy for the Africans and the Deaf students to communicate because both used sign language and gesture."[112] Clerc became one of the key instructors for the Africans. Laurent Clerc's diary mentions how the *Amistad* Africans impacted his theological journey as a divinity student at Yale, though the archival material lacks the support of his role as an interpreter. English and Sunday School instructors for the Africans needed interpreting skills to communicate with their African pupils. To date, this research has not revealed a direct interpreting role for Clerc, Griswold, or other instructors in off-the-record or on-the-record interpreting during trial hearings or preparations.

Applying Gilbert J. Garraghan's method of corroborating oral historical veracity, Silva affirms how the signing community appropriated the contribution of this freedom story to their own interpreting history. Silva explicates the richness of the Mende culture, dance, storytelling, and mime, which facilitated the interactions of the Mende Africans and the surrounding community.[113] She indicates how, during their stay in Connecticut, Christian abolitionists in Farmington continued "to sign" with the Africans. The Norton family hosted Sengbe and Grabbeau at their house, and while "the *Amistad* leaders were not fluent in spoken English . . . the Norton family could sign."[114] *Amistad* abolitionists and SL instructors collaborated. Gallaudet, Day, and other instructors participated in anti-slavery actions

[111] Silva, "Signs of Freedom," 141.

[112] Silva, "Signs of Freedom," 137. Knowledge of this connection seems to form part of the universal history of SL. While lecturing at the University of Warsaw, Poland, in 2017, Dr. Aleksandra Kalata-Zawlocka, Polish SL professor and president of the Association of Polish Sign Language Interpreters, commented on how the *Amistad* story is known within the Polish SL community as part of the universal SL history.

[113] Silva, "Signs of Freedom," 141.

[114] Silva, "Signs of Freedom," 143.

sharing a political agenda supported by theological foundations.[115] Perhaps the discrimination experienced by the SL community helped them to relate to the abolitionist movement. The SL community found a home with the abolitionists committed to serve those on the margins of society.

Newspapers memorialized the contribution of the SL community. *The Emancipator* reported a letter from Tappan revealing how SL interpreting assisted in communicating with the Africans during the official court proceeding of September 17: "Mr. Gallaudet, who was present, informed the prisoner's counsel that they had conversed with him by signs, and he appeared to have an intelligent idea of a Supreme Being, and of the penalties incurred for telling a falsehood."[116] Linguistic differences in court, *Mende v. English*, also marked religious differences. Testimony credibility is based on taking a Christian–judicial oath. Court officers ensured that all Africans, whether defendants or interpreters, understood the implications of telling the truth. Those interpreting the oath carried the responsibility of explaining.

Explanations require additions to original renditions—another interethnic aspect of the *Amistad* case. Unrequested "additions" to or "explanations" may be unwelcomed in professional conversations, but more common in practice. In health settings, medical interpreters may interject comments or suggestions to interlocutors, if deemed beneficial to achieve effective communication among the involved parties. Court-interpreting standards dissuade professionals from initiating either practice, although, professionals may be more prone to apply them in off-the-record proceedings. In the *Amistad* case, additions and explanations proved indispensable as they bridged an ethnic gap to provide legal accessibility to the defendants and credibility to their "Word."[117] The Spaniards[118] put into question the Africans' credibility on the basis of their unfamiliarity with Christian symbols, such as the symbol of the "cross" signed at the bottom of their affidavits in court. Yet, the Spaniards were apparently not concerned with their unchristian actions, fabricating documents and lying in open court—in order to support the unchristian institution of slavery[119] and colonialism.

With the additions, explanations, truths, lies, and the cohort of the *Amistad* interpreters, the *Amistad* hearings, during the September 1839 term and the trial postponed for January 1840, could be heard.

[115] Silva, "Signs of Freedom," 140–1.
[116] "Interesting Scene in Prison," *The Emancipator*, September 26, 1839.
[117] Practices adopted by both sign and oral languages interpreters in this legal case.
[118] Elaborated upon further in the chapter on translation.
[119] Refer to Chapter 1 on the theology and scripture reading of the Christian abolitionists.

6

The *Amistad* Hearings

September 19, 1839: The Second Court Hearing

The introductory pages of *The African Captives: Trial of the Prisoners of the Amistad on the Writ of Habeas Corpus* summarized the before-and-after story of the *Amistad* Africans since arriving on US shores (refer to Figure 6.1). It presented an overview of the organized efforts the *Amistad* Committee mounted on both legal and social fronts. Interpreters gathered the information contained therein, which revealed the known truth: that the Africans were born and raised on their native continent. Although the pro-abolition compiler and/or narrator remained anonymous, George Day features as narrator of a segment therein from an article originally published in the *Journal of Commerce*. The introduction briefs the reader on the "examination" of the Africans with the assistance of the interpreters James Covey and Charles Pratt.[1] It recounts how "the next thing," after engaging the services of able counsel, was "to open a communication with the Africans, through an interpreter."[2] Once the main Mende oral interpreter was found, George Day, who was familiar "with the language of signs, and the other peculiar methods of conveying instruction employed at the New York Institution for the Deaf and Dumb [*sic*]," collaborated by offering "intellectual and religious instruction to these benighted pagans [*sic*]."[3]

This narrative recalled the previous *Amistad* case interpreter, John Ferry, and the newly found interpreters, Covey and Pratt. Ferry effectively facilitated communication between the outside world and the *Amistad* Africans. He conversed "freely with one or two of them, and imperfectly with others."[4] Covey and Pratt seconded the information gathered by Ferry, because "they [could] speak and write English very well, having been brought up at Sierra Leone."[5] After a vigorous and pressing search, finding Covey and Pratt

[1] The front cover listed 1839 as the year of publication, while the anonymous writer dated his introduction "New York, October 15, 1839." "The African Captives," 1839, vi.

[2] *The African Captives: Trial*, ii.

[3] *The African Captives: Trial*, iv.

[4] *The African Captives: Trial*, iv.

[5] *The African Captives: Trial*, iv.

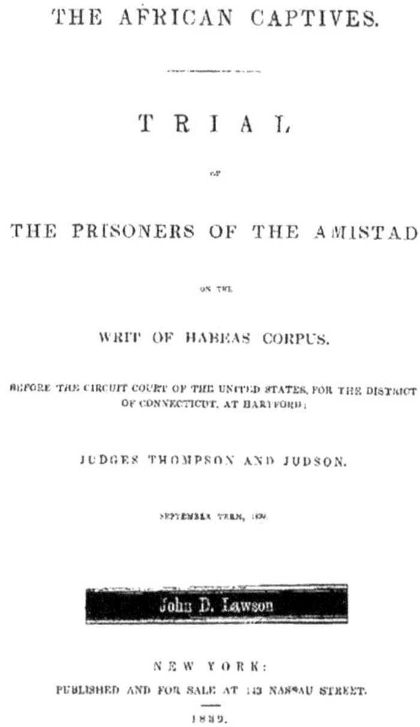
THE AFRICAN CAPTIVES.

TRIAL

OF

THE PRISONERS OF THE AMISTAD

ON THE

WRIT OF HABEAS CORPUS.

BEFORE THE CIRCUIT COURT OF THE UNITED STATES, FOR THE DISTRICT OF CONNECTICUT, AT HARTFORD;

JUDGES THOMPSON AND JUDSON.

SEPTEMBER TERM, 1839.

John D. Lawson

NEW YORK:
PUBLISHED AND FOR SALE AT 143 NASSAU STREET.

1839.

Figure 6.1 "*The African Captives: Trial of the Prisoners of the Amistad.*" U.S. Circuit Court (Connecticut), Thomas R. Gedney, Smith Thompson, and Andrew T. Judson, *The African Captives: Trial of the Prisoners of the Amistad on the Writ of Habeas Corpus, Before the Circuit Court of the United States, for the District of Connecticut, at Hartford* (New York, 1839), Rare and Manuscripts Room, Yale Law Library.

prompted all to use their services nonstop. There was much to learn about the captives' stories, pasts, and needs in preparation of the litigation strategy, particularly of Grabbeau and Kimbo, who supplied key information. After four straight days in New Haven, the interpreters worked without a break. On the afternoon of October 7, they took a brief recess from interpreting attorney–client conferences. The narrator expressed with compassion that it was because Covey and Pratt "were exhausted" (refer to Figure 6.2).

The long-awaited interpreters held the portal to pivotal information, working nonstop for weeks consistently since October 3, 1839, once they had been found. Even if the interpreters were allowed to employ the "team interpreting" skill of switching every twenty minutes precisely to reduce exhaustion, the task at hand would have left them fatigued. Considering that they "were allowed" to summarize signals, they maintained rapid, long, and fast dialogues for long hours. Interpreting nonstop for weeks must have been a draining activity. They came with some background in the field. Their

GEORGE E. DAY.

MONDAY, Oct. 7.

This afternoon, almost the first time in which the two interpreters, Covey and Pratt, have not been engaged with special reference to the trial to take place in November, one of the captives named Grabaung was requested to give a narrative of himself since leaving Africa, for publication in the papers. The interpreters, who are considerably exhausted by the examinations which have already taken place, only gave the substance of what he said, without going into details, and it was not thought advisable to press the matter. Grabaung first gave an account of the passage from Africa to Havana. On board the vessel there was a large number of men, but the women and children were far the most numerous. They were fastened together in couples by the wrists and legs, and kept in that situation day and night. Here Grabaung and another of the Africans named Kimbo, lay down upon the floor to show the painful position in which they were obliged to sleep. By day it was no better. The space between decks was so small—according to their account not exceeding four feet—that they were obliged, if they attempted to stand, to keep a crouching posture. The decks, fore and

Figure 6.2 "*The African Captives: Trial of the Prisoners of the Amistad.*" *The African Captives: Trial*, iv.

experience as seamen granted them interpreting practice, patrolling in vessels searching for ships in violation of the transatlantic treaties. Once the slaves were captured, bilingual sailors like them announced to non-English-speaking captives the good news about their "liberation" bridging linguistic gaps. The *Amistad* case widened their skills during intensive weeks of interpreting.

The second court hearing set for September 17 was postponed to September 19 and then continued until September 20. Counsel for the three African girls—Teme, alias Juana; Ka-gue, alias Josefa; Margu alias Francisca (refer to Figure 6.3)—"moved for a writ of habeas corpus." The litigation team began their on-the-record arguments as they advocated for the three girls. Of all the African captives, the young, orphaned girls were the most vulnerable, without parents or legal guardians. The case of the *Amistad* girls afforded the fastest way to contradict the claims by the Spaniards that their transfer was licit. Moreover, kidnapping children away from their parents and homeland evoked sympathy from parents, court officers, newspaper articles, and those inclined to historical gossip in order to sway public opinion in favor of the Africans and the anti-slavery cause. Given their visibly smaller sizes in contrast with adult bodies, the court would be inclined to understand that the Spaniards contravened international law by smuggling children directly from Africa. Abolitionists remarked on the physical development of the *Amistad* children compared to those of US white northern children: "they are larger than boys and girls of that age usually in this country."[6]

The abolitionists began their day in court with the "least of these" to contrast the cruelty of the institution of slavery. Their adversaries resorted

[6] *The Emancipator*, September 26, 1839.

Figure 6.3 "Margu." William H. Townsend, "Sketches of the *Amistad* Captives," General Collection, Beinecke Rare Book and Manuscript Library, Yale University.

to any possible means to keep the case out of state courts even if it meant using children as pawns for their enslaving ideology. *Amistad* children were remanded to jail throughout the duration of the trial period. As pointed out, during the nineteenth century's stage of the second slavery, children and women overwhelmingly filled the horrific holds of ships. The children of the *Amistad* represented some of these.

The counter-stories of the non-Spanish-speaking *Amistad* girls reiterated how as slaves they were also forced to migrate to Cuba after the 1820 treaty went into effect, under the auspices of slavery. Their bodies evidenced this truth. But the hearing was adjourned until September 19, after a habeas corpus motion from defending counsel requested to bring the girls to court, but their testimony was unsolicited. No on-the-record words were needed. Their childlike Black bodies served as concrete testimony of the illegal slave trade in Spanish/Cuban territory. Counsels argued on the basis of their inability to speak Spanish. To sustain their position, the defense often referred to the linguistic and ethnic expertise of interpreters and candidates. Mr. Sedgwick, one of the three *Amistad* lawyers, proffered the affidavits of Augustus William Hanson[7] and John Ferry "stating . . . that they had seen and

[7] Although there are no records to substantiate that Hanson acted in an official capacity as a court interpreter, counsel named him as "an interpreter" for his ability to converse with the children. The bestowed title of interpreter gave Hanson greater esteem and credibility to his observations in a court of law. William Hanson was also a leader in the abolitionist movement.

conversed with the African girls imprisoned in the jail in Hartford; and that they were native Africans, the eldest about nine years old and the youngest about seven; and that they can speak neither the Spanish nor Portuguese languages."[8] Lawyers availed themselves of the *Amistad* interpreters to narrow the communication gap between them, the Court, and the Africans. Language found a way to establish the place of origin of the *Amistad* minors and adults and their ethnicities in hopes of their freedom. Counsel for the Africans argued in court:

> Here are three children . . . who are proved to be native Africans, who cannot speak our own language or the Spanish language, or any other but the language of their nativity. . . . Does not this honorable Court see they cannot be slaves? They were not born slaves, and they were born in Africa. . . . They have no knowledge of any other language than that spoken on the coast of Africa. . . . And yet this Don Pedro Montez has the hardihood to come into this Court—a man who has been confederating with pirates; for he must at least have purchased these persons of the pirates who kidnapped them. He knew they did not speak the Spanish language—he knew, from their tender age, that they must have been brought to the Island of Cuba in violation of the laws of Spain. He knew all this, and yet he had the hardihood to say he had legally purchased them?[9]

Instead of deposing the *Amistad* girls, the court authorized the deposition of Baboo "who came in the same vessel with the girls, about 25 years of age."[10] The court resorted not to Ferry but to Rev. Gallaudet, present in court to explain the oath by signs to this African. After the satisfaction from the court that Baboo understood the oath, the court admitted the deposition. An annexed affidavit corroborated that Ferry interpreted the content of Baboo's affidavit submitted at a much later date in a court proceeding.

Gallaudet's theological background earned him the task of interpreting and explaining the oath. Christian principles exude credibility in a court of law. Pages dedicated in this primary source to the interpreters' contributions in the proceeding are scant; nonetheless, they were decisive to the outcome of the case. Knowledge obtained by the interpreters became "their best evidence." Without the possibility of birth certificates—direct evidence—interpreters' testimonies, circumstantial evidence bolstered the hypothesis posed by the *Amistad* litigation team. Reiteration on who were these girls

8 *The African Captives: Trial*, 8.
9 *The African Captives: Trial*, 11–14.
10 *The African Captives: Trial*, 11–14.

and what was their place of birth constituted paramount facts confirmed by the interpreters:

> On this subject, we have an African, a colored man, an interpreter, who has been with these children and examined them; and he says they are native Africans. He gives their ages; and the reason for believing them to be native Africans is, their whole language is a dialect of Mandingo. They have no knowledge of the Spanish language. This, at their tender age, is decisive—it is the best evidence we could have.
>
> Well, if these children were born in Africa, they are not old enough to have been brought into the island of Cuba before the law abolishing the slave trade. If the African question is settled, they must have been brought to Cuba since the treaty of [1817]. There is also the testimony of another African interpreter. He gives the same facts, he says they are of the African race—they speak a language spoken nowhere else but in Mandingo. . . . We have the highest possible evidence, not direct, that these children were born and bred in Africa."[11]

The interpreter they are referring to is John Ferry. Ferry communicated the best possible evidence. The children were old enough to speak only Mende. If brought before 1820, their bodies and languages would have visibly been those of young women, not children.

An integral strategy to this proceeding incorporated the submission of the interpreters' affidavits in court as indirect, circumstantial evidence. The other interpreter corroborated the information interpreted by Ferry. Large segments of the content of the affidavits were bracketed. Bracketed information also enclosed annotations and summaries by the drafter of the "unofficial transcript":[12] "[Here the affidavit of John Perry[13] was introduced, to authenticate that of Baboo in the taking of which, Perry [*sic*] acted as interpreter]." A total of forty-seven lines were placed in brackets of this chronicle. Bracketed information selected essential data on the life of the interpreter declared on the record not admitted in court. His personal declarations qualified him to interpret linguistically and culturally for the now-imprisoned Africans. Despite the crucial data revealed via the interpreter, an acting court reporter ordered by the judge determined the key information extracted by the interpreter to be inadmissible. The bracketed

11 *The African Captives: Trial*, 23–4.

12 Throughout the document, information related to interpreting issues was often bracketed.

13 Meaning "Ferry."

information attempted to divorce the intrinsic connection between the personal and professional aspects that equipped Ferry to interpret "faithfully" for the captured Africans.

The third-person subject as the preferred voice suggested a summary of the most relevant content appraised by the writer. Of all factual testimonies given in court, only these remained. The facts enclosed in brackets responded to many inquiries stemming from the newspaper article published on September 19 on the "Examination of the Africans." Mr. Ingersoll, counsel for the opposing party, petitioned to cross-examine John Ferry, the interpreter, and this was granted by the Court. As it may be recalled, Ferry's affidavit stated that he was "almost sure" that he understood Baboo—an admission that raised suspicions among opposing counsel about the certainty of the interpreted information. However, opposing counsel chose to be blind to the ideology supporting the institution of slavery in their interjections and in their petitions in favor of their clients.

Further testimony by Ferry disclosed that, although Baboo spoke Mandingo, he was also versed in Gallinas. Since his liberation by Bolívar, Ferry had practiced speaking this language a few times per week when visiting West Indies plantations and with Africans he met in the USA. Ingersoll examined Ferry on how well Baboo understood the oath, the concept of the Christian God, the importance of "telling the whole truth," and the punishable consequences for not speaking the truth, a common procedure at the beginning of interpretation instances in the case at hand. Theological principles used as tools of information and reprisal to hide the truth.

To justify why the three *Amistad* girls should not be released, Ingersoll tried to discredit Ferry's testimony. He argued that "the affidavit of Perry [*sic*] is an additional reason why this matter [release of the three girls] should be investigated."[14] As normative in the *Amistad* case, interpreters were in the crosshairs of court litigations and social debates by adversaries. Not being able to discredit declarations by English-speaking witnesses on the stand, the opposing party resorted to the next best possibility: to discredit testimonials from African interpreters whose ethnic origins and competency challenged their contentions. In this judicial case, pro-enslavement parties attempted to disprove tactics with those closest to the truth: the interpreters. This signals to the importance, yet precarity, of interpreters in the *Amistad* case. Ferry possessed the best linguistic and ethnic competency to duly voice the stories of the African girls. This is why.

[14] *The African Captives: Trial*, 29.

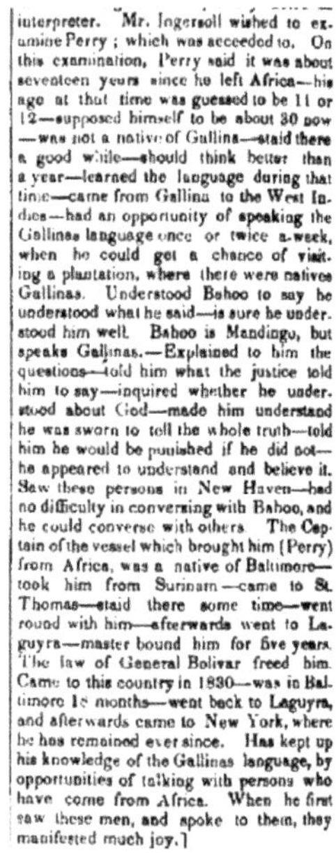

interpreter. Mr. Ingersoll wished to examine Perry; which was acceded to. On this examination, Perry said it was about seventeen years since he left Africa—his age at that time was guessed to be 11 or 12—supposed himself to be about 30 now—was not a native of Gallina—staid there a good while—should think better than a year—learned the language during that time—came from Gallina to the West Indies—had an opportunity of speaking the Gallinas language once or twice a-week, when he could get a chance of visiting a plantation, where there were natives Gallinas. Understood Bahoo to say he understood what he said—is sure he understood him well. Bahoo is Mandingo, but speaks Gallinas.—Explained to him the questions—told him what the justice told him to say—inquired whether he understood about God—made him understand he was sworn to tell the whole truth—told him he would be punished if he did not—he appeared to understand and believe it. Saw these persons in New Haven—had no difficulty in conversing with Bahoo, and he could converse with others. The Captain of the vessel which brought him (Perry) from Africa, was a native of Baltimore—took him from Surinam—came to St. Thomas—staid there some time—went round with him—afterwards went to Laguyra—master bound him for five years. The law of General Bolivar freed him. Came to this country in 1830—was in Baltimore 18 months—went back to Laguyra, and afterwards came to New York, where he has remained ever since. Has kept up his knowledge of the Gallinas language, by opportunities of talking with persons who have come from Africa. When he first saw these men, and spoke to them, they manifested much joy.]

Figure 6.4 "Ferry's testimony in court." *The African Captives: Trial,* 28. The paper misspelled Ferry's name as "Perry."

According to his own testimony in court, Ferry was "brought" from Africa by a captain from Baltimore, Maryland, USA, to the southern hemisphere. Ferry was enslaved in Suriname, St. Thomas, and La Güaira—"Laguyra" as referred to in this nineteenth-century document—a northern Caribbean port of today's Caracas, Venezuela. He testified that in La Güaira, his captain enslaved him for five years, before "the law of General Bolívar freed him."[15] Nine years after Bolívar's demise, Ferry honored this well-known Latin American leader as part of his counter-story of liberation. Ferry stated that afterward he came to the USA and lived in Baltimore for eighteen months, returning to La Güaira for a while before coming to New York City, "where he has remained ever since"[16] (refer to Figure 6.4).

On Monday, September 23, Judge Thompson delivered his decision. He denied the motion to discharge the Africans based on the original application made to the court regarding jurisdictional matters of the District Court of Connecticut versus New York. The judge allowed the prisoners to

[15] *The African Captives: Trial,* 28.
[16] *The African Captives: Trial,* 28.

be discharged if counsel deposited appropriate bail, "but as it must be on an appraisement, their counsel would not consent to it."[17] For the abolitionists, appraising implied acquiescing to the idea that the Africans were slaves; certainly, implicit in the judge's rendered decree. The litigation team, all abolitionists, refused to purchase their freedom with a bail set at the cost of the slave trade. Yet their refusal accomplished three things: kept the captives inappropriately in jail cells, continued to appeal to public opinion toward a growing abolitionist movement, and exemplified how they exercised their privilege. As a direct consequence of their decision, the captives spent over two years in jail while their supporters ambulated in the "free society." The judge added his regrets to his decision. Judge Thompson explained that "he could not be insensible to the fact, that the feelings of the community were deeply involved in the question, and he feared there might be misapprehensions of the real questions to be disposed of by the Court."[18]

He closed his rendition by announcing the intention to further investigate the jurisdictional matter of the seizure of the *Amistad* schooner by doing a field inspection. The narration of *The African Captives: Trial of the Prisoners of the Amistad on the Writ of Habeas Corpus*" came to an end, and so did the printed public transcripts on the *Amistad* case. Despite the narrator broadcasting under new business ("N.B."), that "this pamphlet will be followed by another, containing a full Report of the Trial at the next term,"[19] this never came to pass. To date, similar pamphlets for the November 1839 or the January 1840 term are missing from the annals of history. Instead, handwritten letters and newspaper articles serve as needles to continue to piece together the interpreting and translation issues in this case.[20]

Interpreter's Depositions Support Cultural and Language Identification

As previously argued, language identification was entwined with ethnic identification. Validating the origins of the Africans confirmed that they

[17] *The African Captives: Trial*, 47.
[18] *The African Captives: Trial*, 44.
[19] *The African Captives: Trial*, vi.
[20] The Spaniards selected not to attend the September proceeding without placing a reason on the record; their legal counsel represented them. By the January 1840 trial, the Spaniards were incarcerated in New York, after being accused of abuse and mistreatment by the *Amistad* Africans. During this period, the *Noticioso* continued to advocate for their kin.

were taken to Cuba illegally. Written affidavits by Covey and Pratt served as "linguistic and ethnic depositions." Interpreter candidates, Mr. Hanson, Dr. Madden, and Prof. Gibbs also signed documents swearing to the places of birth and languages spoken by the *Amistad* children and adults. *Amistad* case files contain Ferry's own deposition[21] taken in Hartford and stating in third person:

> That he has seen & conversed with the children . . . and this deponent further saiths that the same children are all Africans by birth. . . . Teme is of the Congo nation, and that Kagne and Margu are of the Mandingo tribe or nation . . . he can judge that the eldest of them is about nine years old and the youngest about seven years of age. [22]

With depositions such as this one, the Spaniards' lies continued to crumble. The young Africans were seven- to nine-year-old children, not natural-born Cubans. The bodies of the three African girls and boy visibly substantiated their age to disqualify the claim of Pedro Montes as their legal "owner." Without any clear timeline on when a suitable interpreter would be found, the abolitionists secured affidavits from those who could provide expert knowledge regarding the ethnic background of the *Amistad* Africans. In the event that the interpreters or deponents did not appear in court, sworn documents were submitted as evidence.

Not all candidates or expert linguists signed affidavits. Those candidates, linguistic experts, and interpreters who signed sworn statements, established the connection between the Africans' ethnicity and their spoken languages. Handwritten letters, as discussed earlier, explicated how the candidates like Samuel Barney and Levi Gauges drew this connection, even though their language proficiency thwarted effective communication for recruitment. Newspaper articles published the opinions of Madden, Day, and Gibbs, corroborating the undeniable truth that the jailed captives were not Spanish speakers and had spent less than a month on Cuban soil. As time drew nearer to the first court proceeding, scheduled for September 17, the interviews corroborated that none of the candidates could serve as a court interpreter.

The *Amistad* Committee became cognizant of the fact that the African's inability to express themselves resulted in an aching reality. A September 26 article, titled "An Interesting Scene in Prison", described a religious service

[21] *Amistad* case files also contain Charles Pratt's and William Hanson's deposition. James Covey's deposition, in contrast, a document submitted as evidence in this case, can be found in The Family Baldwin Papers, at Yale University.

[22] "John Ferry's deposition," National Archives in Boston.

conducted in jail.[23] Despite not having an interpreter, their poised demeanor demonstrated respect for the English-speaking preacher they could not understand. Tappan, who authored this article, noted, "it was interesting, and painful too, to see these pagans [*sic*], from a far distant land, gazing at the speaker, and listening to this discourse which was in a language wholly unknown to them."[24] They sat, disciplined, in the same room throughout the duration of the service until someone requested that the preacher "try to explain to the Africans, through the interpreter."[25] John Ferry, present at the service, along with Grabbeau, interpreted the summary offered by the preacher, Mr. G. The article recorded how Ferry and Grabbeau also employed the method of relay interpretation to convey the sermonic message by Mr. Gallaudet:

> Mr. G. with Mr. Ferry, the African Interpreter, and one of the prisoners named Grah-bah-wah, who is from Gallinas, stood on his right and left to communicate his thoughts to his attentive audience. This man speaks the Kissi dialect better even than Bowle or rather Baboo. Mr. G. expressed his thoughts to Mr. Ferry, he translated them into the Kissi dialect to the man above named, who made them known in the Mandingo tongue, in a very animated manner, to his comrade. (refer to Figure 6.5)[26]

The complication of not finding an interpreter for the Mende Africans called for creative means to facilitate communication. From English, Ferry transferred the message into Kissi, one of the languages spoken by a few of the Africans. From Kissi, Grabbeau converted the message into Mende, the most common language among the *Amistad* captives. Ferry and Grabbeau applied their linguistic skills within a religious–conference interpreting scenario. This relay interpreting episode was conducted at a slow pace. Tappan shifted his narrative style from paragraph to sentence by sentence when describing the interpreted message. The sentences separated by a hard return and quotations strongly suggest the rhythm of the relay interpretation scene. The time that elapsed during the interpreted oration allowed Tappan

[23] Unfortunately, abolitionists invested an equal amount of time to find interpreters for the Africans as to organize evangelistic and proselyting activities with the objective of enculturating them into protestant religiosity, English language, and Anglo culture. Abolitionists referred to the Africans as "pagans" and "savages," racist and condescending terms. Their efforts stand in contradiction to their efforts to liberate the Africans, undermining the Africans' God-given cultural heritage and ethnic diversity.

[24] "Interesting Scene in Prison," *The Emancipator*, September 26, 1839.

[25] "Interesting Scene in Prison," *The Emancipator*, September 26, 1839.

[26] "Interesting Scene in Prison," *The Emancipator*, September 26, 1839.

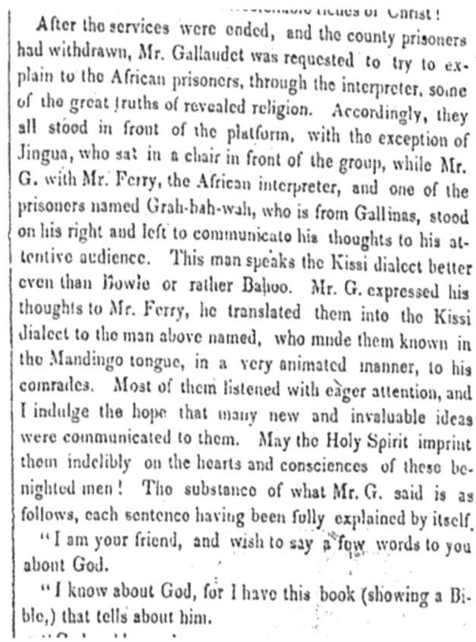

After the services were ended, and the county prisoners had withdrawn, Mr. Gallaudet was requested to try to explain to the African prisoners, through the interpreter, some of the great truths of revealed religion. Accordingly, they all stood in front of the platform, with the exception of Jingua, who sat in a chair in front of the group, while Mr. G. with Mr. Ferry, the African interpreter, and one of the prisoners named Grah-bah-wah, who is from Gallinas, stood on his right and left to communicate his thoughts to his attentive audience. This man speaks the Kissi dialect better even than Bowle or rather Bahoo. Mr. G. expressed his thoughts to Mr. Ferry, he translated them into the Kissi dialect to the man above named, who made them known in the Mandingo tongue, in a very animated manner, to his comrades. Most of them listened with eager attention, and I indulge the hope that many new and invaluable ideas were communicated to them. May the Holy Spirit imprint them indelibly on the hearts and consciences of these benighted men! The substance of what Mr. G. said is as follows, each sentence having been fully explained by itself.

"I am your friend, and wish to say a few words to you about God.

"I know about God, for I have this book (showing a Bible,) that tells about him.

Figure 6.5 "Interesting Scene in Prison." *The Emancipator*, September 26, 1839.

to complete writing the original source, reported in the newspaper "sentence-by-sentence."

The scene displayed represented a nonjudicial scene, a worship service in jail. Alongside their incessant search for an interpreter, unfortunately, the abolitionists thrusted the Africans into religious indoctrination, in an attempt to strip them of their cultural and religious heritage and in substitution for a Christian religion that had forced them to cross the Atlantic.

The Postponement of the November 19, 1839, Trial: James Covey at Fault

The November trial did not happen as planned. Racialized articles blamed James Covey, the interpreter, with scorn. Covey fell ill. This pushed the adjournment of the trial date to January 9, 1840, two months after the expected date. The November 23, 1839 issue of the Spanish newspaper the *Noticioso de Ambos Mundos* promptly opined on this unfortunate situation. Published in the column reserved for matters about the USA, "*Estados Unidos*," the Spanish community anxiously waited for the conclusion of this political nightmare (refer to Figure 6.6).

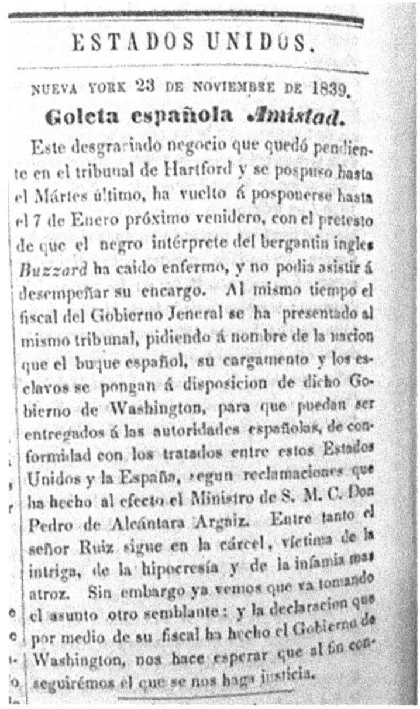
ESTADOS UNIDOS.

NUEVA YORK 23 DE NOVIEMBRE DE 1839.

Goleta española *Amistad*.

Este desgraciado negocio que quedó pendiente en el tribunal de Hartford y se pospuso hasta el Mártes último, ha vuelto á posponerse hasta el 7 de Enero próximo venidero, con el pretesto de que el negro intérprete del bergantin ingles *Buzzard* ha caido enfermo, y no podia asistir á desempeñar su encargo. Al mismo tiempo el fiscal del Gobierno Jeneral se ha presentado al mismo tribunal, pidiendo á nombre de la nacion que el buque español, su cargamento y los esclavos se pongan á disposicion de dicho Gobierno de Washington, para que puedan ser entregados á las autoridades españolas, de conformidad con los tratados entre estos Estados Unidos y la España, segun reclamaciones que ha hecho al efecto el Ministro de S. M. C. Don Pedro de Alcántara Argaiz. Entre tanto el señor Ruiz sigue en la cárcel, víctima de la intriga, de la hipocresía y de la infamia mas atroz. Sin embargo ya vemos que va tomando el asunto otro semblante; y la declaracion que por medio de su fiscal ha hecho el Gobierno de Washington, nos hace esperar que al fin conseguirémos el que se nos haga justicia.

Figure 6.6 "Goleta Española *Amistad*," *Noticioso de Ambos Mundos*, 23 de noviembre de 1839.

> *Este desgraciado negocio que quedó pendiente en el tribunal de Hartford y se pospuso hasta el Mártes último, ha vuelto á posponerse hasta el 7 de Enero próximo venidero, con el pretesto de que el negro intérprete del bergantín ingles Buzzard ha caído enfermo. . . . Sin embargo ya vemos que va tomando el asunto otro semblante; y la declaración que por medio de su fiscal ha hecho el Gobierno de Washington, nos hace esperar que al fin conseguiremos el que se nos haga justicia.*[27,28]

With racist overtones, the frustrated editor referred to the interpreter as "*el negro intérprete*." The editor criticized both the fact that the "interpreter" was "black," and that this "black" person was the "interpreter," undermining and discriminating both identities. While the word "*negro/a*" can often be

[27] "Goleta Española *Amistad*," *Noticioso de Ambos Mundos*, 23 de noviembre de 1839.

[28] Eng. Trans.: This unfortunate matter pending in the Hartford Court, postponed for last Tuesday, has been adjourned again until January 7th with the excuse that the Black interpreter of the Brig Buzzard fell ill. . . . However, we can see that things are shaping up; and the petition made by the prosecutor to the government in Washington makes us believe that, in the end, we will see justice in our favor.

used as an endearment term in Caribbean lingo, this newspaper divulged a different intended meaning. Throughout the course of the *Amistad* case, Spanish proclivities constantly endorsed pro-slavery ideologies. The editor questioned the illness of the interpreter as a reason for postponing the trial: "*con el pretesto de que el negro intérprete del bergantín ingles Buzzard ha caído enfermo*" (Trans.: with the excuse that the Black interpreter of the Brig *Buzzard* fell ill).[29] The *Amistad* Spaniards knew that now, with Covey, the truths of the Africans stood in direct opposition to their colonizing and enslaving objectives inside the hull of their unfriendly vessel. This contradicted the hopes placed by the editor on the US governmental actions and prosecutor to return the schooner, slaves, and property to the Spaniards. An African interpreter delayed their hopes.

As explored in the chapter on translation matters, during the fall of 1839, extensive diplomatic correspondence from the Executive branch revealed a strong inclination on the part of the USA to respond readily to the concerns voiced on behalf of the *Amistad* Spaniards. Based on this correspondence, the newspaper editor expected justice to tilt in their favor, "*nos ace esperar que al fin conseguiremos el que se nos haga justicia*" (Trans.: we are hopeful that in the end justice will be served).[30] The US-based Spanish minister in Washington, D.C., kept the Cuban authorities abreast of the judicial developments and the agreements behind closed doors with the US Department of State and the Executive branch. Their hopes in the judiciary were high. Appalled, they wrote extensively on the lack of jurisdiction of the US courts to decide on property and slaves of another nation, citing international treaties and jurisprudence. As the case progressed, feelings heightened, especially with the arrest of "*los señores Ruiz y Montes*," and on motions filed by the *Amistad* Africans against them for abuse and torture.

Filing these motions represented a byproduct after the African defense team interviewed the captives with the assistance of the interpreters. Covey and Pratt contributed to dismantle slavery and institutionalized racism. The *Amistad* case was unique in this way. The US judicial system rarely holds people enjoying "white privilege" accountable, especially those violating the human rights of the marginalized, the poor, the non-English speakers, and African descendants. While the *Amistad* Spaniards did not serve time in jail as a consequence of a guilty verdict or decision by a judge,

[29] "Goleta Española *Amistad*," *Noticioso de Ambos Mundos*, 23 de noviembre de 1839.

[30] "Goleta Española *Amistad*," *Noticioso de Ambos Mundos*, 23 de noviembre de 1839.

they were imprisoned for several months in jail because of their inability to make bail. In a country divided along ideological postures of slavery, pressing charges on slaveholders for their mistreatment of "their property" represented a symbol of resistance and a slight victory in this case for the anti-slavery cause.[31]

Spanish newspapers maintained that the real victims in this case were the imprisoned *Amistad* Spaniards. The *Noticioso de Ambos Mundos* referred to the Spaniards, "*los blancos*" (the whites), as the "*parte mas débil*" (the victims), not the Africans. As seen earlier, doubt and contempt accompanied the notion of the interpreters' ability to perform their jobs with excellence. With feigned elegance, another article in the same issue condemned the retention of this case in US courts, affirming the ability of the Spanish courts to provide Mende-qualified interpreters, equally or better prepared than those utilized in Hartford. The lengthy article entitled, "*¡Todavía mas [sic] acerca de la goleta Amistad!*" (Still more on the *Amistad* schooner!) was written to buttress the plea of the Spaniards and to communicate their outrage after their arrest. The article, hypothetically, referenced interpreters provided to the Africans if the case was tried in Cuba: "*y los intérpretes que se les dén serán tan legales ó mas que los que aquí han tenido.*"[32] After centuries of multilingual colonizing activities, the Spanish colonial structure was better prepared to provide interpreting and translation services to defendants and plaintiffs in their courts. Yet, linguistic competency and the professional experience of the interpreters within the Spanish colonial system could not outweigh the violent reprisals against the successful rebellions of the African enslaved population.

The *Noticioso de Ambos Mundos* accurately informed its subscribers that the November 1839 trial was postponed. The reported judicial reasons behind the adjournment varied on Spanish and English newsstands. The Spanish newspaper attributed the action to an interpreter fallen ill, not the whole story, while *The Daily Herald*[33] informed its readers of other reasons. Various English newspapers covered the arguments presented in the hearing and the reasons for the new trial date. For instance, Mr. Isham, counsel for libellants Gedney and others, petitioned the court for compensation

[31] Future research seeks to find other cases where similar judicial practices were employed during the nineteenth century in the USA and in Spanish colonies.

[32] "Goleta Española *Amistad*," 23 de noviembre de 1839, *Noticioso de Ambos Mundos*. Trans.: And the interpreters provided would be as lawful or more so than those they have had here.

[33] *The Daily Herald*, November 21, 1839.

"for their services in preserving the property of these Spaniards,"[34] leaving the court to decide on a "reasonable" amount. On the other hand, Mr. Baldwin, on behalf of the Africans, argued the importance for them to be allowed to testify in court, otherwise, "their most important rights would be sacrificed."[35] His arguments emphasized that the court could not consider them as property and that only the "inanimate" portion of the cargo aboard *La Amistad* should be contemplated as compensation to the "salvors." The judge deviated from the arguments of counsels to jurisdictional issues, whether the seizure occurred in New York or Connecticut. For the remainder of the proceeding, the discussion centered on "the examination of witnesses upon this point."

After a few days of court proceedings, a newspaper article summarized:

> Wednesday—The court assembled this morning at the City Court Room; seven of the slaves were brought into court. A great portion of the morning was occupied in discussing a question of adjournment, for a day or two, in order to give time for one or two important witnesses to arrive. P.S.—The Court have just agreed to adjourn, to meet at New Haven, on Tuesday, the 7th of January next, "The Law's delay."[36]

One of two "important witnesses" was the Spanish minister in the USA to testify in favor of libellants.

The phrase "The Law's delay" echoed the words of Hamlet's soliloquy, the second reference to Shakespeare in the *Amistad* saga. The first one compared Sengbe Pieh to Othello. This Shakespearean phrase encapsulated the frustration at the adjournment postponing the case until months later. Thomas Hargis explores the connection of this phrase with the US suffrage movement of the nineteenth century. He explains:

> Before and since Hamlet's soliloquy was written, the law's delay has been a by-word and reproach, a source of anxiety and unhappiness . . . the principal source of the law's delay is the law's defects, originating immediately in the venality, neglect, or incapacity of legislators, which springs from their election by the ignorance, corruption, or partisanship.[37]

[34] *The Daily Herald*, November 21, 1839.
[35] *The Daily Herald*, November 21, 1839.
[36] *The Daily Herald*, November 21, 1839.
[37] Thomas F. Hargis, "The Law's Delay Author(s)." *The North American Review* 140, no. 341 (April 1885): 1.

Justice would not serve either side: the libellants, Ruiz and Montes, or the Africans.[38] From both sides of the slavery issue, Spanish and English newspapers equally echoed their frustrations about the trial being delayed until January 7, 1840. Other witnesses were ready to testify on the original trial date of November. Dr. Madden of the Joint Commission sailed from Cuba. Although James Covey and Charles Pratt were considered expert witnesses, the article failed to explicate their presence or absence as crucial to the defense case. With the negative public image of the interpreter being presented in pro-slavery newspapers, ideologically opposite newspapers attempted to balance that image of the interpreter, adding other reasons for the adjournment without mentioning the health status of the interpreter.

As part of their goal to win this case, abolitionists continued to defend their interpreters in English and Spanish newspapers. A translated letter from Lewis Tappan published in the *Noticioso de Ambos Mundos* read: "*dos hombres, naturales del África, pertenecientes a la tripulación del bergantín de guerra inglés Buzzard, que está ahora en este puerto, están obrando como intérpretes, y entienden bien la lengua nativa de los negros de la Amistad*" (Trans.: two men from Africa, crew members of the *Buzzard,* the brig of war, presently anchored in this port, are serving as interpreters and understand well the native language of the *Amistad* Africans).[39] A postscript to the published letter affirmed the intention of the newspaper to voice contrary opinions. Although no information validated the submission of the letter in English, the usage of the word "*negro*" (black) signals the Spanish translation by the *Noticioso* newspaper. Most English articles redacted by Tappan demonstrated a preference for the term "Africans" versus "Black." Tappan defended the linguistic competency of Covey and Pratt, who also offered a compatible and ideologically trustworthy match for this very controversial case. On the other hand, for the Spaniards, a Mende interpreter portended a different version of their sworn version, even if this had to wait until January 1840.

An editorial from Joshua Leavitt, published by another New York newspaper, the *Zion's Watchman*, summarized the November 19 proceedings and documented the reasons for the postponement. On his way to Hartford to attend the trial, Leavitt stopped in New Haven to converse with Dr. Madden, an "esteemed friend." Madden, a material witness on behalf of the

[38] Articles from *The North American Review* eventually favored the Africans, although during the first week after the arrival of the schooner in New London, they referred to them as "pirates" before the editor's conversion in support of their liberties and freedom.

[39] Back translation by author. This technique describes a translation into the original language when the original is not available.

Amistad Africans, travelled to continue his mission against the illegal African slaving trade. Leavitt's lengthy column began noting the health condition of the "African interpreter" who was "quite unwell, and not able to go up in the evening boat." Leavitt was "grieved" to find out about this situation. He left a note to Mr. Townsend asking his permission to send Covey to Hartford in the morning, although he ascertained that already "Mr. T. urged his attendance as far as a due regard to humanity would allow." Leavitt's explication sounded conflicted. A judicial and justice-related urgency required the presence of the interpreter at the first open court proceeding after being recruited. The timing of Covey's sickness seemed inopportune.

This particular case grabbed the attention of many, especially of Madden. The Africans, the abolitionists, the pro-slavery side, the Executive branch, the Spanish community, and diplomats all waited for the finale of this case. Covey's sickness prevented him from the final act of performing his duties on behalf of his fellow Africans. The archival materials failed to mention the name of his illness, which was treated by a doctor. Leavitt defended the doctor's general opinion that Covey should stay in New Haven. He noted "that the very respectable physician who was in attendance, remained of the opinion that he could not safely take its journey." [40] None of the prior interpreters in this case before Covey replaced him at the November hearing.

Leavitt elaborated on decisions made in court and the reasons for moving the trial. Both venue and date were changed to Hartford on January 7, 1840. Both sides had worthy reasons to defer that proceeding. A sickness detained a material witness in New Haven, James Covey, "on the part of the Africans." When it came to the *Amistad* trial, Covey's role was two-fold, as expert and as material witness. An expert witness is that one who has "special knowledge, skill or experience in the subject about which he is to testify."[41] His expertise involved expert knowledge of the language spoken by the Africans and the language of the court, allowing him to interpret for them and for the Africans to engage with their surroundings. A material witness is "one who can give testimony that might have a bearing upon the outcome of a cause and that no one else is able to give."[42] As the trial date approached, Covey's contribution to the trial evolved from an expert to a

40 Joshua Leavitt, "To the Committee on behalf of the African Captives," *Zion's Watchman,* November 30, 1839.

41 Steven H. Gifis, "Expert Witness," in *Dictionary of Legal Terms: Definitions and Explanations for Non-Lawyers*, 5th ed. (Hauppauge, NY: Barron's Educational Series, 2016), https://search.credoreference.com/content/entry/barronsgkwm/expertwitness/0?institutionid= 1032.

42 Ibid.

material witness, along with Pratt and Ferry. Covey's "materiality" became essential in his geographical knowledge of the West African coast, the African nations of the *Amistad* Africans, their ages, and their spoken languages. As a material witness testifying in court, Covey was subject to interrogation, cross-examination, and even impeachment. Courts accommodate parties' needs for adjournment. Contrary to biased positions by pro-slavery parties in this case, Covey was not solo in causing a postponement of the case. The schedules of Navy lieutenants conflicted with the trial date. Leavitt informed that "to accommodate Messrs. Isham and Brainard, counsel for the libellants, whose engagements rendered it impossible for them to remain in the city after Thursday."[43]

Other pro-slavery voices joined the Spaniards in blaming Covey for the trial postponement. Editorials in English newspapers replicated the bigotry spewed against the Africans and their supporters. The *New York Herald*, aka, *Morning Herald*, diagnosed and opined on the interpreter's illness, three days after the adjournment:

> The *Amistad* case has got the go by, and the parties will have to commence again *de novo*, on the 7th of January. James Covey, the Buzzard interpreter, has an attack of the Gout, or some similar disorder, contracted under the luxurious feed of the New Haven theological students, and the court has adjourned in order to give the *savans* a nurse up the N-. Covey is wanted to help the Africans swear as to the position of the *Amistad*, and the number of N-s on shore at the time of the capture . . . the more the abolitionists have of it the worse they will be off. . . . Leavitt, who is here reporting for the New York penny N-paper. (refer to Figure 6.7)[44]

Covey's supporters received the blame for his contracted illness. The theological students at Yale, Sign Language interpreters, and abolitionists became the culprits for being too close together in physical, theological, and political proximity to the interpreter. While the editor praised Lieutenant Meade's testimony, certain that it would carry the necessary weight to win the case, the others were discredited publicly for their "skin color" and affiliations. The *New York Herald* resented Leavitt's direct involvement in the *Amistad* case. As editor of *The Emancipator*, a newspaper that vouched for the *Amistad* case, committed to anti-slavery ideals, Leavitt reported constantly on the development of this important case, avowing for a greater cause for

43 Leavitt, "To the Committee on Behalf of the African Captives," 191.
44 *New York Herald*, November 22, 1839.

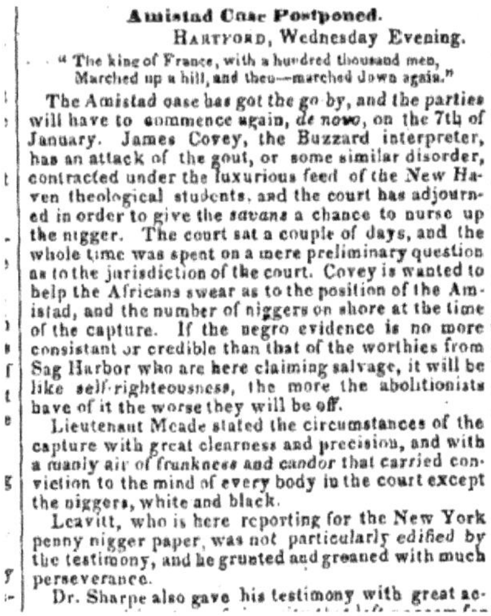

Amistad Case Postponed.

HARTFORD, Wednesday Evening.

"The king of France, with a hundred thousand men,
Marched up a hill, and then—marched down again."

The Amistad case has got the *go by*, and the parties will have to commence again, *de novo*, on the 7th of January. James Covey, the Buzzard interpreter, has an attack of the gout, or some similar disorder, contracted under the luxurious feed of the New Haven theological students, and the court has adjourned in order to give the *savans* a chance to nurse up the nigger. The court sat a couple of days, and the whole time was spent on a mere preliminary question as to the jurisdiction of the court. Covey is wanted to help the Africans swear as to the position of the Amistad, and the number of niggers on shore at the time of the capture. If the negro evidence is no more consistant or credible than that of the worthies from Sag Harbor who are here claiming salvage, it will be like self-righteousness, the more the abolitionists have of it the worse they will be off.

Lieutenant Meade stated the circumstances of the capture with great clearness and precision, and with a manly air of frankness and candor that carried conviction to the mind of every body in the court except the niggers, white and black.

Leavitt, who is here reporting for the New York penny nigger paper, was not particularly *edified* by the testimony, and he grunted and groaned with much perseverance.

Dr. Sharpe also gave his testimony with great ac-

Figure 6.7 "Amistad Case Postponed." *New York Herald*, November 22, 1839.

humanity. Of European descent, Leavitt—one of the three founders of the *Amistad* Committee—stood firmly on the opposite pole of the pro-slavery spectrum. In 1839, he was known to the general public in New York City, even to the pro-slavery proponents of his active participation in such causes. Racial epithets attacked Leavitt and Covey for their choices. Covey was racially scorned for being Black and for his active involvement in assisting the Africans to tell their truth in court. His illness, in part, delayed the trial and angered the anxious pro-slavery Spanish and US diplomatic side.

This article diagnosed Covey with "an attack of the Gout, or something similar." Gout, kings, luxury, privilege, Africans, abolitionists, and interpreter were linked together in this newspaper. A nursery rhyme of kings in the battlefield opened the brief article. The quote alluded to the futile hopes of a "king"—Leavitt and the abolitionists—of winning a battle with his soldiers—the battle of slavery with Covey, the interpreter. Gout, a worthy disease believed to afflict those living in opulence, was attributed a "disease of kings, and the king of diseases."[45] "The luxurious feed of the New Haven theological students" supported Covey, whose illness had the illusive power to have intervened to force the adjournment. Ascribing gout to Covey intentionally

[45] Sydney C. W. Tang, "Gout: A Disease of Kings," in *Uric Acid in Chronic Kidney Disease,* ed. Alejandro Trevino-Becerra and Kunitoshi Iseki (Basel, Switzerland: Karger, 2018), https://www.ncbi.nlm.nih.gov/pubmed/29393108.

portrayed a bigoted perspective. The multiple uses of the N-word[46] and the underlined hateful feeling confirmed this intent. Language, interpreting, and translation issues were racialized in the *Amistad* case when these interrupted the English- and Spanish hegemonic power through its respective imperial pursuits in both legal and public setting. The author of the article imputed Covey et al. for membership in an exclusive army going to battle against slavery. In the end, all efforts and excuses would be ineffective in impacting the unavoidable guilty projection of a pro-slavery populace. The interpreting issues divided along slavery contentions, with Covey, the interpreter, in the middle of the battle. Praised and wanted on the one side made him ethnically funeralized by the other.

Covey's absence did not deter the court in carrying on its judicial business. Dr. R. R. Madden had lived in Havana for over three years and held the office of Superintendent of Liberated Africans, and for a year served as Commissioner of the Mixed Court of Justice. His testimony was not taken in an official courtroom setting, but at the judge's chambers at a local hotel. The *New York Herald* confirmed this unusual meeting place: "the evidence of Dr. Madden, a member of the mixed commission at Havana, was taken at the judge's room at the City Hotel."[47] Court files and other newspapers described how Madden connected the concept of the terms "*Bozales*" and "*Ladinos*" to the fabrication of the *licencias* discussed earlier in the chapter on translation. He testified as to the rampant Spanish–Cuban illegal slave trade through the *barracón Misericordia* of Pedro Martínez, where he affirmed seeing the *Amistad* Africans. Furthermore, Madden stated that none of them spoke Spanish, only African languages.

Covey was not the only one sick. Burna, the eldest of the Africans, stayed in prison while the others went to Hartford "being too unwell to accompany them." Written by an unknown contributor and taken from the *New Haven Record* and published in *The Emancipator* newspaper on November 23, 1839, the narrator spoke of a self-identified "we," as two people "being employed in teaching deaf mutes." Names such as Day and Gallaudet surface as possible participants of this visit. Along with another unidentified friend, they interviewed Burna in order "to obtain information from him through the medium of signs." The Sign Language visitors brought with them pictures, maps, paper, and pencils to facilitate the communication via signage. At first,

46 It is a common practice not to spell or pronounce the two syllable "N-word" in English for those not identifying as African descent people from the USA as a sign of respect, to oppose the derogatory ways in which it has been used historically, and to avoid racialized reinjuring.

47 *New York Herald*, November 22, 1839.

they describe Burna as having "little notion of this way of talking," and that "he did not seem to enter at once into the idea of conducting a narration by signs." However, signs, gestures, marks, objects, and a lot of willingness to understand each other led to further information on the continent of Africa and the places they were from. At the January 7, 1840, *Amistad* trial, Sign Language speakers were present to testify and more.

With James Covey as the "chief interpreter," the abolitionists found someone whose "means of communication [was] good as can be desired heretofore."[48] With Covey's health restored, the trial date was maintained in due course.

Prelude to the November Trial: Knives and the Interpreters for Liberation

Before the November 1839 trial, Covey and Pratt assisted the Africans off the record in other non-linguistic matters. In a letter dated October 23, 1839, from George Day to Lewis Tappan, Day conveyed to him that *The Daily Herald*[49] reported that the interpreters, James Covey and Charles Pratt, bought "knives" for the imprisoned Africans. Day regretted both incidents: the purchasing of these "weapons" and the printing of the story in a public forum. With racist overtones, Day contradicted the reasoning of the interpreters that providing these bladed weapons had anything to do with self-defense or violent resistance. He was convinced that the Africans had good intentions, and, therefore, he attempted to dissuade further public or internal criticism. He concluded: "as I can learn, they wanted the knives to amuse themselves with, like children and savages."[50] A few months earlier, cane knives served as instruments of freedom off the Cuban coast. Now, weeks before the impending November trial, the *Amistad* Africans were being armed in case justice did not side in their favor. For months, unwanted visitors paid 12.5 cents to the jailor to see them as if they were in a reality show taking place in prison. The abolitionists did not interrupt this practice. Instead, they relied on this exposure to mount support in favor of the Africans despite its inhumane practice. Their stories and lives were subjected to unwarranted visibility.

[48] *The Emancipator*, October 10, 1839.
[49] A New Haven newspaper.
[50] AMA Archives FI 4650, The *Amistad* Research Center, New Orleans, Louisiana, USA.

Necessary off-the-record dialogue between the Africans and the interpreters and between the interpreters and the *Amistad* abolitionists occurred as preamble to smuggling knives to the incarcerated. The logistics were planned. The abolitionists had envisioned an alternative escape for the captives if the judge ruled against their case or, in the event that the opposite side planned to re-sequester the Africans. This was a remedy that somehow was implemented for Antonio, the cabin boy who was ordered to return to Cuba. The Africans, suspicious of their surroundings, acquiesced to the plan, as did the interpreters. Abolitionists devised a plan with the interpreters' assistance to carry out the initial steps as part of a larger strategy involving their lawyers. The US judicial system could not be trusted to impart justice. And yet, it is possible that the Africans wanted just simply to feel more comfortable. Or both? Day's handwritten letter manifested one sole purpose for the knives: "self-defense" and "to amuse themselves."

Day criticized how the interpreters responded positively to the request of their incarcerated fellows. He justified their actions, undermining their understanding of the consequences of providing weapons to those in jail. He argued that "the interpreters are too little accustomed to reflection, to think of the impropriety of furnishing men who are under restraint with dangerous weapons."[51] In a condescending and patronizing manner, Day questioned the decision-making capacity of the interpreters to gauge the impact of furnishing the knives in a highly tense situation. Following this negative portrayal of the interpreters, Day quickly interjected to justify their actions, "perhaps, the majority of our own people would have acted as they did."[52] "Our own people," referring to non-African abolitionists, supporting newspaper readers, or the Sign Language community cajoled in similar circumstances in an oral-language privileging country that would have resorted to procuring knives for their fellows.

Surprisingly, no primary source recorded any consequences for their behavior. For an interpreter or officer of the court to agree to furnish weapons for an inmate would grossly violate the court code of ethics and professional standards. Typically, if the court finds any interpreter or an officer of the court responsible for such an act, consequences for them may range from losing her standing in a court, losing their certification, or being charged with conspiracy or another criminal charge. At the next hearing, this incident was not pondered, nor was it used to motion the court to exclude Covey from serving as interpreter. On the contrary, the interpreting skills of Covey and Pratt received praise and acclamation. Pratt eventually returned

[51] AMA Archives FI 4650, The *Amistad* Research Center, New Orleans, Louisiana, USA.
[52] AMA Archives FI 4650, The *Amistad* Research Center, New Orleans, Louisiana, USA.

to the Brig to continue journeying in the Mid-Atlantic, and Covey became the main interpreter in the *Amistad* case. The mysterious knives story entered the *Amistad* scene as a part of a larger plot toward the liberation of the Africans. Notwithstanding, letters from the US government revealed that the *Grampus*, a US Navy ship, waited in the New Haven harbor ready to transport the Africans to Cuba, certain of the court favoring the enslaving perspective. The USA gave its word to the Spanish authorities to bring them back "home," to Cuba. The knives from within would have assisted the abolitionists from the outside to transport the *Amistad* Africans to safety via the Underground Railroad, which included a stop in Farmington, Connecticut.

The *Grampus* was not the only vessel in the harbor. The abolitionists planned a similar strategy with a vessel sailing northbound. Handing knives to the Africans constituted an early step in this plan. Orchestration of a liberating strategy "by-any-means necessary" occupied the anti-slavery movement in case the trial judge ruled against them. The interpreters were part of this plan. Simeon Baldwin, son of Roger Baldwin, reminiscing in 1884:

> The *Grampus* was not the only ship in New Haven harbor under secret orders during these exciting days. The members of the *Amistad* committee, or some of them, in connection with Nathaniel Jocelyn, a brother of Rev. S.S. Jocelyn of the committee, had another vessel here ready to receive the Africans, in case of an adverse decision, and run them off to some more friendly shore. Plans had been laid for their rescue from the jail, for this purpose, if necessary, by force.[53]

Presence of another vessel suggested that the interpreters did not act in isolation. The freedom vessel and the knives were related. The plan responded to a liberating strategy from within and outside the prison. All acted in harmony—Africans, interpreters, *Amistad* lawyers, and the abolitionist community at large—to send them to the Underground Railroad via northward tracks. The interpreters gladly accepted their noninterpreting role in this scheme, having known slavery in their recent past. They knew too well about feeling powerless before judicial, political, and societal structures that supported slavery and colonialism. In those days, without metal detectors and using as a pretext that they were "too little accustomed to reflection," strategists selected interpreters to carry out this task and to take the blame. The abolitionist lawyers who enabled their clients with weapons

[53] Simeon E. Baldwin, "The Captives of the *Amistad*: A Paper Read Before the New Haven Colony Historical Society," May 17, 1886.

could not attribute their actions to being "too little accustomed to reflection." Interpreters offered the right cover for bringing knives to prison.

Covey and Pratt's "knives" intervention exposes various important aspects about trust, closeness, and activism in this case which displays the deep level of trust developed between Africans and the interpreters in less than three weeks since their first meeting. Africans and interpreters exchanged dialogues and visits without the presence of the litigation team. The Africans' linguistic needs extended beyond the limited court-related interpretations. In a short time, they developed a bond of friendship in the process of rendering a linguistic service. In the *Amistad* context, forging a meaningful connection and trust by any means possible was more valuable than following expected court protocol. Africans in the *Amistad* period living outside of the prison spoke English, and Africans behind bars spoke African languages. Both shared a common story. Knives were purchased three weeks after the interpreters arrived and a month before the November trial date. Interpreters proved to have a double function: one, as linguistic mediators; and second, as weapons' concealers. Both were utilized by the *Amistad* Committee as liberating tools.

7

"The *Amistad* Trial" from January 7 to January 11, 1840

Colloquial narrations attribute the term "The *Amistad* Trial" to the January 1840 proceedings in which the trial judge ruled in the Africans' favor. Since their arrival on Connecticut shores, however, multiple "hearings" or "trials" took place. The term "the *Amistad* case" denotes cases appealed to the Supreme Court and is sometimes confused with the January trials. Eight *Amistad*-related cases live at the National Archives in Boston, five of which took place between September 1839 and January 1840:

Thomas R. Gedney v. Schooner Amistad [September 1839 Term]
Thomas R. Gedney v. Schooner Amistad [September 1840 Term]
Thomas R. Gedney v. Schooner Amistad [April 1841 Term]
Thomas R. Gedney v. Schooner Amistad [April 1845 Term]
Pedro Montes and Jose Ruiz v. Merchandise [January 1840 Term]
U.S. v. Cinque and The Africans [September 1839 Term]
U.S. v. Fagnannah and Others [September 1839 Term]
Pedro Montes and Jose Ruiz v. Schooner Amistad [September 1839 Term]

As indicated earlier, the archiving of official judicial transcripts in the 1840 trials did not represent a customary practice of the time. Therefore, they are missing from the federal records. The files contain filed motions, court decisions, depositions, evidentiary documents (for instance, the *licencias*), and some court testimonies. Thanks to public recorders, journalists, and newspaper editors who took copious notes of the hearings, we can piece together what transpired on the record. Newspapers covered the proceedings related to this case, and without pamphlets and newspaper articles on the *Amistad* proceedings, the translation and interpreting stories and counter-stories would have faded into oblivion.

January 7, 1840: First Day of Trial, Language at Trial

According to Lewis Tappan, "the court room was crowded."[1] The *Amistad* litigation team had three attorneys-of-record: Messrs. Staples, Baldwin, and Sedgwick. Lieut. Gedney, who previously acted as the Spanish interpreter, was represented in his claim for salvage by two counsels, Gen. Isham and Mr. Brainard of New London. Captain Green was represented by Governor Ellsworth. Mr. Cleveland, of New London, represented the Spanish owners of the property on board the Schooner *Amistad*, and the US District Attorney represented the Spanish minister and the US Executive branch and international-political interests.

The Emancipator and *The Daily Herald* elaborated on the key jurisdictional and property matters. As we know, the Africans aboard the *Amistad* Schooner were intercepted in the State of New York. However, under the excuse of distance and the poor condition of the Schooner, Lieuts. Meade and Gedney towed the *Amistad* to New London, Connecticut. Anti-slavery advocates believed that another motivation led them to a Connecticut port: "the Africans filed their answer, claiming that having been taken within the jurisdiction of the State of New York, they are free by the laws of that State, which recognizes slavery only in cases of fugitives from service, from other states."[2] Although both sides agreed that the vessel was found within a mile from shore, the pro-slavery side argued that those should be considered international waters. The defense argued the contrary but did not prevail, keeping the trial in Connecticut. The court, promptly, moved to consider other matters. The *Amistad* litigation team acquiesced to the ruling. This proved convenient. The *Amistad* support garnered through Connecticut advanced the organizational aspects of the case.

The first issue regarding interpreters occurred when Mr. Baldwin proffered the deposition of Charles Pratt. On October 4, 1839, Pratt was sworn in and deposed, a day after he successfully conversed with the imprisoned Africans (refer to Figure 7.1). Written in the third person, Pratt, identified as a "colored African," signed with a "mark." He affirmed that he "was born in Sierra Leone," and acquainted with the Mende language, which he learned with his father when trading in the "Mende country." He further deposed that he knew the Bandi language spoken by one of the Africans; and that he "truly interpreted" the questions and answers between that African and Josiah W. Gibbs. Pratt was "the captain's cook on board the British

[1] *The Emancipator*, January 16, 1840.
[2] *The Daily Herald*, Wed., January 8, 1840.

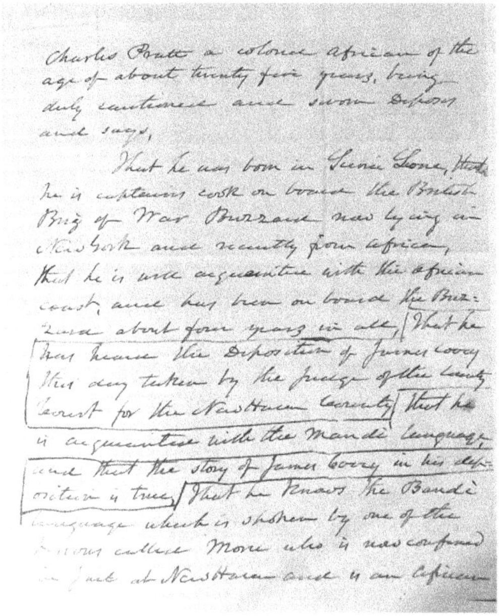
Charles Pratt a coloured african of the
age of about twenty five years, being
duly cautioned and sworn deposes
and says,
That he was born in Sierra Leone, that
he is captain's cook on board the British
Brig of War Buzzard now lying in
New York and recently from africa,
That he is well acquainted with the african
coast, and has been on board the Buz-
zard about four years in all, That he
has heard the Deposition of James Covey
this day taken by the Judge of the County
Court for the New Haven County, That he
is acquainted with the Mandi language,
and that the story of James Covey in his dep-
osition is true, That he knows the Bandi
language which is spoken by one of the
persons called More who is now confined
in jail at New Haven and is an African

Figure 7.1 "Pratt's affidavit." "Charles Pratt," RG 021, USCC CT. "The Matter of the Habeas Corpus for the Three African Girls," September 1839 Term National Archives at Boston. Later in the trial, Judge Judson drew lines indicating the admissible sections.

Brig of War *Buzzard*" where he had worked for approximately four years. During his deposition, he was questioned as to the truthfulness of James Covey's deposition. Pratt confirmed "that he had heard the deposition of James Covey . . . that the story of James Covey in his deposition [was] true." Interpreters used to confirm the veracity of the statements or observations of other interpreters became a common verification practice in the *Amistad* case. The high stakes of this case left no stone unturned, anticipating possible objections and questions of admissibility. Affidavits were quickly secured from interpreters and other linguistic experts in case they would not be available to appear at the trial.

Despite all measures to prove the credibility of these interpreters, Charles Pratt's deposition was inadmissible on the first trial day. A newspaper article expounded: "the deposition was rejected, among other reasons, on the ground that the parties were not duly notified." The "other reasons" were not explicated. Pratt and Madden's depositions (affidavits) shared in common that their statements were not prepared by them or written in the first person.

Instead, these were redacted by an officer of the court. Pratt and Madden's life experiences, social positioning, educational, and racial background constituted their differences. These hampered Pratt's deposition and added to his role as interpreter.

After the admission of Madden's deposition, the Court called "Mr. S. Haley of New London." He testified to José Ruiz's answers to questions posed by Mr. Janes about the Africans' language and their place of origin. According to the summary provided by Tappan and printed in *The Emancipator*, Haley heard Ruiz describe the following: "only one of the slaves could speak English, and he only knew a few words, which he must have learned on the coast of Africa; that, with the exception of Antonio, the Captain's boy, none of them could speak Spanish, as they were just from Africa."[3] Mr. Isham, counsel for the Spaniards, interrupted Haley's testimony. When Haley observed that Ruiz "spoke good English," Isham abruptly added, "did you not know that he was educated in Connecticut?"[4] Baldwin replied in open court, "he ought to have known better, if he was educated in Connecticut."[5] Baldwin presupposed that his educational period in Connecticut would have assuaged him from anti-slavery practices. Dwight P. Janes's testimony followed and corroborated Haley's recollection of the dialogue between Janes and Ruiz aboard the *US Washington* brig. The defense was laying down the linguistic foundation in favor of the Africans using Ruiz's own admission that the Africans were recently brought from Africa after the 1817 treaty. Tappan's summary contained scant narrations about the other side's intervention. The next witness was James Covey.

Tappan recalled that "James Covey underwent a long and interesting examination."[6] Covey's examination on the first day of trial was the longest, not as interpreter but as a material and expert witness. Covey's testimony began mapping his story. Born, raised, kidnapped, enslaved, and liberated, he returned to Africa where "he went to school, learned to read and write, and speak the English language with considerable facility."[7] He testified under oath confirming the consistency of the Africans' version, their "Mende names," and how "they all sailed from *Jomboko*, in Africa, to Havana." Able to speak Mende, Covey was qualified as interpreter in this case. Tappan pointed out a legal resource that prevented Covey from sailing with his brig. More than persuasion and his love for his kinship kept Covey behind as interpreter.

3 *The Daily Herald*, January 8, 1840.
4 *The Daily Herald*, January 8, 1840.
5 *The Daily Herald*, January 8, 1840.
6 *The Daily Herald*, January 8, 1840.
7 *The Daily Herald*, January 8, 1840.

Tappan recalled that "being subpoenaed by the U. States, [he] was left here."[8] Covey's experiences on the witness stand were taxing as he "underwent a … severe cross-examination."[9] Ethnic and linguistic issues proved everything in the case against the Spaniards and toward the freedom of the Africans. Corroboration and re-corroboration built the case of the defense.

Counsel for the non-Africans expressed concern when Josiah W. Gibbs followed Covey at the witness stand. Isham and Brainard raised their objections of Gibbs as expert witness, "an eminent linguist." *The Daily Herald* recorded the objection by the opposing parties. Gibbs's testimony, "merely corroborative of that of Covey, who was himself in court, and had not been impeached, and his testimony therefore did not require support from that of the learned Professor."[10] Counsel for the Africans aimed at reinforcing Covey's on-the-record declarations: "that James and the Africans [spoke] the same language, the Mende dialect."[11] Baldwin "argued with great ingenuity and power" the importance of Gibbs's expertise in court, because "a person skilled in different languages, could judge from their language itself, whether it was pure or whether it was an admixture of foreign words,—whether these Africans used a native language or a dialect formed by the mingling of the Spanish language with their own."[12] The controversial matter of whether to allow Gibbs to testify was not settled at the end of that day. The court adjourned for "9 o'clock tomorrow."

January 8, 1840: Second Day of Trial, the Interpreter at Trial

The Africans' power of communication could be protected by securing James Covey as court interpreter. As the abolitionists set out to challenge the institution of slavery in the *Amistad* case, defending the right of their witnesses to testify became paramount to their litigation strategy. At the beginning of the second day, neither the judge nor opposing counsel was ready to settle the matter of whether to allow Gibbs to testify on ethnic and linguistic issues. Eight hours of arguments, and the judge's indecision amounted to further trial delays. At the end, "the Judge ruled that the testimony was admissible."[13]

8 *The Daily Herald*, January 8, 1840.
9 *The Daily Herald*, January 8, 1840.
10 *The Daily Herald*, January 9, 1840.
11 *The Daily Herald*, January 9, 1840.
12 *The Daily Herald*, January 9, 1840.
13 *The Emancipator*, January 16, 1840.

To convince the judge, Baldwin argued that Gibbs had gathered essential information on the spoken languages and the geographical knowledge of African rivers. In applying this information, Gibbs recruited James Covey, a crewmember "on board the *Buzzard*" docked at the New York City harbor.[14] Gibbs testified that Covey "spoke the same dialect, mentioned the same rivers . . . and that the maps corroborated his statements; also, Covey stated that he was a Mende, and on coming to New Haven and seeing his countrymen in jail, he found nearly all of them were from the same district or county."[15] The linguist professor reiterated Dr. Madden's avowal on the meaning of the terms *Ladino* and *Bozal*, terms that directly pointed "to the power of communication."[16]

The Africans' agency resided in their ability to speak Mende in the courtroom, their native language. Spanish lacked empowering possibilities. Securing their linguistic power required proving that *español* was not their vernacular. In Mende, they could testify their version of the facts and exert their power. Gibbs credited the interpreters for their linguistic knowledge. Tappan chronicled how the "witness had spent much time in investigating the language of these captured Africans [and that] he acquired the knowledge of the Mende language from Covey and Pratt." The intervention of the interpreters generated historical narration and veracity that empowered other witnesses in court, such as Gibbs and Madden. The accumulation of testimonies proved compelling, which led the judge to assert "that he was fully convinced that the men were recently from Africa, and it would be idle to deny it." Covey's linguistic expertise surpassed his ability to interpret for the Africans.

His first intervention in court represented a dual role as an expert and as a material witness, not as an interpreter. He was one of the first witnesses from the defense to testify on the first day of the trial about his knowledge regarding the Mende language and region. From the information that he provided in off-the-record meetings, Covey assisted in preparing other witnesses, like Gibbs, to support the plea in favor of the Africans, around the diametrically opposed reality of *Ladinos*. After winning this small battle, "Jingua, Grabbeau, and Fuliwa" testified on the witness stand, assisted by him, the court interpreter.

Jingua, aka Sengbe, Cinqué, was called first to testify in court "as a witness." As expected, "Covey was sworn to interpret the oath to Jingua, and then to interpret correctly his testimony" (refer to Figure 7.2). Swearing

[14] *The Emancipator*, January 16, 1840.
[15] *The Emancipator*, January 16, 1840.
[16] *The Emancipator*, January 16, 1840.

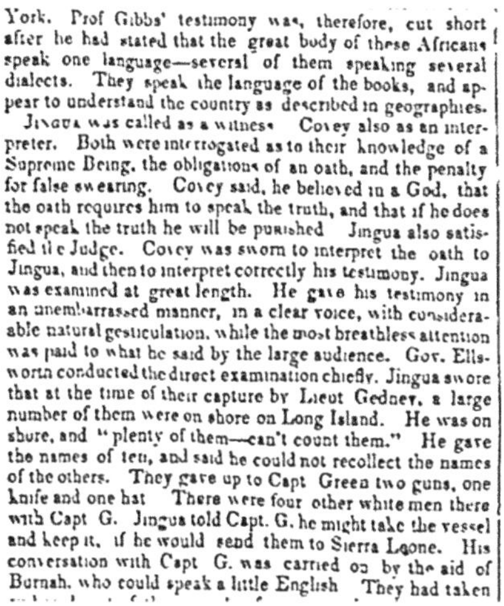

York. Prof Gibbs' testimony was, therefore, cut short after he had stated that the great body of these Africans speak one language—several of them speaking several dialects. They speak the language of the books, and appear to understand the country as described in geographies.

JINGUA was called as a witness. Covey also as an interpreter. Both were interrogated as to their knowledge of a Supreme Being, the obligations of an oath, and the penalty for false swearing. Covey said, he believed in a God, that the oath requires him to speak the truth, and that if he does not speak the truth he will be punished. Jingua also satisfied the Judge. Covey was sworn to interpret the oath to Jingua, and then to interpret correctly his testimony. Jingua was examined at great length. He gave his testimony in an unembarrassed manner, in a clear voice, with considerable natural gesticulation, while the most breathless attention was paid to what he said by the large audience. Gov. Ellsworth conducted the direct examination chiefly. Jingua swore that at the time of their capture by Lieut Gedney, a large number of them were on shore on Long Island. He was on shore, and "plenty of them—can't count them." He gave the names of ten, and said he could not recollect the names of the others. They gave up to Capt Green two guns, one knife and one hat. There were four other white men there with Capt G. Jingua told Capt. G. he might take the vessel and keep it, if he would send them to Sierra Leone. His conversation with Capt G. was carried on by the aid of Burnah, who could speak a little English. They had taken

Figure 7.2 "Jingua as witness; Covey as interpreter." *The Emancipator*, January 16, 1840.

in the interpreter and asking him to interpret accurately the witness's testimony represent normative court-interpreting protocol. However, interrogating the interpreter and witnesses as "to their knowledge of a Supreme Being" constituted a rarity. The court relied on the belief that lying to the divinity would supersede not telling the truth in a court of law. This unusual practice in the case signalled the ethnic and religious differences between the two groups: Africans and non-Africans. Taking an oath as a prelude to one's testimony responded to a judicial culture. But examining the interpreter or the witnesses on their religious knowledge posed more questions and problems than solutions around religious preponderance and racist attitudes. This line of interrogation called into question the Africans' proclivity for telling the truth in conjunction with their theological understandings. Witnesses raised as Christians were exempt from this approach, even when some forgot to tell the truth after being sworn. The court repeated this protocol with all Africans who were "examined on oath similarly to the preceding."

Sengbe was interrogated and cross-examined also "at great length." Counsel for the Africans previously proved to the court that they came from Africa. Their testimony was proffered to "ascertain which of them were on shore when taken in the District of New York." It was in Montauk that the Africans tried to convince Meade and Gedney to take them back home to Sierra Leone. Instead, they ended up in Connecticut jails.

Testimonies of the three Africans in court were not confined to their stories from August 26 when the *Amistad* vessel, Africans, and Spaniards were seized by the US Navy. Their narration included descriptions of their trip from Africa when they were enslaved. Fuliwa, who was "examined on oath similarly to the preceding" testified that "the little girls and boy came from Africa." He described how closely they were arranged on board, and how "his wrists were chained," and that after three months they anchored in Havana. Grabbeau also seconded many aspects of this chain of events, adding that the three of them met in *Jomboko*. From there, along with 400 to 500 people, mostly women and girls, they were crammed into the hold of a ship. The narrator indicated that Grabbeau "was examined by the interpreter, after suitable inquiries by the court." The role of the *Amistad* interpreter again appears extemporaneous. Perhaps at the request of counsel, Covey paraphrased questions or expounded on contextual information in order for the witness to reply to what was asked or even summarized. Following Grabbeau's long interrogation, the court took another recess.

Covey and Sengbe were called to the witness stand next. Counsel for the non-Africans did not hesitate to stall the testimony on the record. They attempted to implicate, first, that Jingua had been a slave owner in Africa. This legal dispute consumed a considerable amount of time in court. Opposing counsels intended to discredit the witness, a common litigation tactic, and one often achieved by finding contradictions and inconsistencies in testimonies. Marshal Wilcox, clerk of the US District Court, declared on this matter. Back in August, Wilcox was the one who enforced the arrest warrant for the Africans with Spanish names, which did not correspond to the Mende names of the defendants given at birth. In court, he recalled the dialogue he had with Sengbe, interpreted by Covey, shortly after Covey and Pratt arrived in New Haven. According to Wilcox, Sengbe's explanation of how he was forced out of Africa alluded to owing a man "two pounds, (holding up his fingers,) and to pay him he had taken two negroes and sold them; that one of them ran away and the man called upon him for one pound . . . and being unable to do so, he was seized and sold to pay the debt." Covey was asked to testify about his recollection of his interpretation between these two interlocutors. Covey assured the court that he had not interpreted this information from Sengbe. Covey's credibility as an interpreter was at stake, not Sengbe's credibility as a witness. The opposing side tried incessantly to close the portal of linguistic access by eliminating the voice of interpreters. They wanted to impeach Covey.

January 9, 1840: Third Day of Trial

The previous day, the court adjourned in the midst of a heated argument heading toward the impeachment of the court interpreter for the Africans. Opposing counsels attempted to controvert Covey's character as a witness, by proving "that James Covey had told a story different from that he had testified in court, under oath."[17] Mr. Baldwin, in an attempt to try to save the credibility of the interpreter, attributed the possible confusion to Covey's deficient bilingualism, because "he is a stranger, speaks the English language imperfectly, and far better than he could when he first came here." On the one hand, in order to be recruited as the *Amistad* interpreter, his English "was good enough"; on the other hand, his proficiency was rather imperfect. The *Amistad* abolitionists found themselves in a bind. Neither they nor the Africans could afford to be without an interpreter, despite any arguments or any means to cinch the linguistic mediator to the proceedings. Baldwin replayed that initial boisterous joy among Covey, Pratt, and the Africans. Probably the marshal was "mistaken, as there was great excitement among the Africans, and the visitors in jail, at the time, owing to Covey, a countryman of the claimants." Covey's repeated testimony negating the utterance of those words and Mr. Baldwin's argument were not enough. To prove the matter, Prof. Gibbs was called to the witness stand again. His testimony "stated that Covey, when first interpreting the statement of Jingua, said nothing about Jingua's having traded in slaves." On its own, Covey's testimony did not suffice. A second witness who had already testified before the court came to the rescue. This controversy exemplifies how precarious it can be to provide a court interpreter for a case whose impact would reverberate beyond the confines of the room. No questions were raised about the original statements by Sengbe, because the goal was to eliminate the court interpreter and the possibility of the Africans' testimonies. A composite of US officials and Spaniards would go to any lengths to win their case. The interpreter, occupying a pivotal role in voicing the Mende stories, became the logical target for discrediting the oral evidence submitted in court. If it was demonstrated that the interpreter had lied under oath, he could be impeached. As a result, all the Africans' testimonies would have been unheard, not placed on the record. After a long judicial debate, the judge questioned Covey directly about his self-awareness of his contradictory statements. Covey replied that he had not interpreted that information. Mr. Baldwin intervened to support his declaration, employing his privilege before the court, and fearful of the dismissal of the long-sought-

[17] *The Emancipator*, January 16, 1839.

found interpreter. The judge concluded. "If he had," the Judge remarked, "the matter, in my mind, would be different."

Col. Pendleton, the jailor, was the last witness to take the stand on this day. He was a white man sworn in to testify on his recollection of Sengbe's story. He declared that Sengbe told him that he "owed a debt, paid two Africans for it [but] one of the Africans got away. Could not pay for him, and he was therefore seized himself."[18] Sengbe could have not "told him" as Jingua did not speak English. As testified, Covey mediated linguistically in this dialogue among both of them. After the upheaval of the second and third trial days, Covey's name and role faded from the court proceedings. Pendleton's testimony failed to sway the trial judge. The litigation plan had worked. Tappan's narration shifted to another interpreting issue in the *Amistad* saga. Despite all pro-slavery litigation maneuvers, Covey was not impeached. His testimony, as a material and expert witness, and that of all Africans was admitted into evidence.

By the fourth and fifth day of the trial, Covey was no longer mentioned. Newspaper articles and letters reproduce how some of the Africans were present during the duration of the trial. Whether Covey interpreted continuously or some parts of the trial using the interpreting technique called chuchotage,[19] the whispering technique, or whether he summarized parts of the proceedings, remained a mystery. Possibly, he remained in open court ready to interpret if necessary, or interested as to the outcome of the case to be able to share a report with the jailed Africans, or just attentive as depicted in the Talladega Murals (refer to Figure 7.3).[20] Hale Woodruff painted three large murals to commemorate the hundred-year anniversary of the *Amistad* story. One of the three portrayed an *Amistad* trial with a distinct man sitting while holding a hat in his hands and wearing a red shirt, the interpreter, watching, observing, but not interpreting. Even without Covey on the record, however, interpreting and translation issues continued to be

[18] *The Emancipator*, October 10, 1839.

[19] "Chuchotage," the whispering technique, distinguishes the interpreter's proximity to the person in need of the interpretation behind or next to the person's ear, without the use of technology.

[20] In 1938, Hale Aspacio Woodruff studied with the Mexican Muralist Diego Rivera in Mexico City. Woodruff was commissioned to produce a three-part panel known as the *Amistad* Murals in commemoration of the centennial of the *Amistad* case. This US African American artist produced three panels: the Revolt, the Court Scene—depicted here—and Back to Africa. These twenty-feet-long murals, considered by some his masterpieces, are housed in the Talladega College, founded as part of the American Missionary Association Ministerial project. In 2013, they travelled to New York University, where Woodruff taught and retired from. James Covey is represented in this mural as the figure sitting at the right of the mural and holding a hat in his hands. In the original color version of this mural, Covey's appears wearing a red-color shirt.

Figure 7.3 "The Court Scene," from the Talladega Murals.

relevant in the course of this case. The *licencias* were admitted as evidence, and Antonio, the cabin boy, was taking the witness stand, and in need of an interpreter.

Antoine, whose name printed in *The Emancipator* took a French morphology, was called to the stand. Lieut. Meade had served as his interpreter during the September 1839 *Amistad* judicial hearing—but not this time around. A financial conflict of interest impeded Meade from acting as interpreter. At the Grand Jury hearings, one was provided for Antonio, but none was present for this trial, even after one of the lawyers made an application to the court to request an interpreter for him. The interrogation commenced without an identified interpreter. At the witness stand, counsel examined Antonio on his version of the events since the revolt on board the *Amistad* up to when "the witness was in the schooner's boat when the Africans were seized on Long Island."[21] He stated how the Spanish-speaking cook communicated to the Africans that "they were going to Príncipe to kill them and eat them," although "in what manner" lacked the specifics. Antonio expressed surprise at the cook's insinuation, since "the Africans were not doing anything." During his testimony, he verified how all of the slaves had recently come from Africa, in a ship called "*La Focora* [*sic*]." The *Amistad* had engaged in enslaving practices for a while. In Cuba, she was known for being part of an enslavement "ring." The cabin boy testified to the unfriendly business of transporting slaves that involved Ferrer, Ruiz, and Montes. Antonio declared that Ruiz "had taken slaves in another vessel."

Antonio, "waiter to the captain of the *Amistad*," appeared in favor of the Spaniards, although his testimony injured their allegations. Mr. Staples cross-examined Antonio after the mid-day recess. Antonio "answered in English, which he understood very imperfectly." Next, he complained about his ability to understand the interpreter, because the interpreter "did not speak Spanish."

[21] *The Emancipator*, October 10, 1839.

Why the complaint was only voiced after hours of interpreting testimonial evidence remains a quandary.[22] Tappan continued explaining that Antonio's first sworn interpreter was "Mr. Ribeiro, a native of Brazil, and who [spoke] the Spanish language imperfectly." Antonio's testimony differed from his own previous testimony in September when Lieut. Meade served as interpreter, yielding to a power imbalance. Now at the January 1840 trial, Antonio "swore that the Africans were put on board the *Amistad* in the evening," contrary to the "four o'clock in the afternoon" of his first testimony. Whether Antonio swore now to an evening hour, or the record reflected a misinterpretation from the Portuguese interpreter—or a misinterpretation from Lieut. Meade—cannot be ascertained. Yet, the court did not take notice of the time difference to question his credibility. The importance of confirming that the Africans boarded at 4:00 p.m. or in the evening did not change the course of the trial. Neither did it revert Antonio as a witness.

The afternoon session began without the assistance of a Spanish or Portuguese interpreter since Mr. Ribeiro had been dismissed. The pro-slavery side avoiding Antonio's testimony neglected to secure a linguistic mediator for his material witness. Even though counsel solicited the court to produce a Spanish interpreter months ago, no one appeared on the day of the trial. When it came to hiring interpreters, nineteenth-century US courts lacked the appropriate protocol, benefitting the pro-enslavement parties. Either way, the application was made for a Spanish, not a Portuguese, interpreter. Although linguistically close to each other, they were not interchangeable. Antonio knew the difference.

On January 9, 1840, *The Daily Herald* reported on this trial day that Antonio's testimony "was given partly through a Spanish interpreter, who happened to be in court, and partly in broken English, and did not vary materially from that heretofore published."[23] Published news about this trial day confirmed that the court had made no provision to supply a suitable interpreter for the witness. The fact that someone "who happened to be in court" served as interpreter in an important trial demonstrates the lack of access given to non-English speakers by the court and parties. If the court followed present legal mandates, postponement of the trial would have been required until an interpreter had been secured. The abolitionists understood the inadequate response of the court and took it upon themselves to locate interpreters for their clients, the only way to ensure the Africans' day in court. Back in November when the interpreter fell ill, they procured the

[22] Was Antonio responding to political pressure or did Tappan misinform the court of the exact time of Antonio's interjection? These continue to be unanswered questions.

[23] *The Daily Herald*, January 9, 1840.

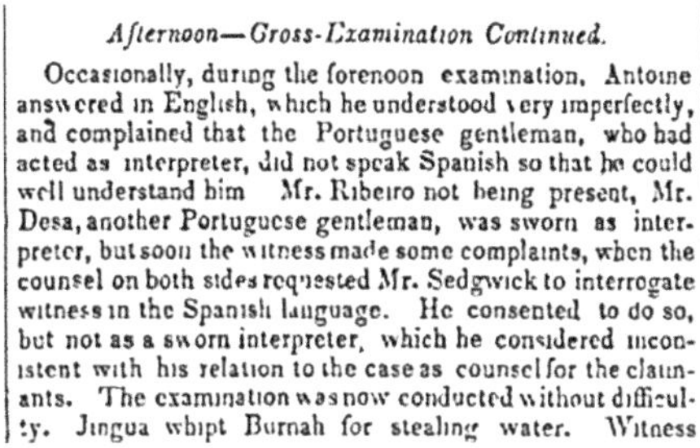

Afternoon—Cross-Examination Continued.

Occasionally, during the forenoon examination, Antoine answered in English, which he understood very imperfectly, and complained that the Portuguese gentleman, who had acted as interpreter, did not speak Spanish so that he could well understand him Mr. Ribeiro not being present, Mr. Desa, another Portuguese gentleman, was sworn as interpreter, but soon the witness made some complaints, when the counsel on both sides requested Mr. Sedgwick to interrogate witness in the Spanish language. He consented to do so, but not as a sworn interpreter, which he considered inconsistent with his relation to the case as counsel for the claimants. The examination was now conducted without difficulty. Jingua whipt Burnah for stealing water. Witness

Figure 7.4 "Afternoon—Cross-examination continued." *The Emancipator*, January 16, 1839.

postponement of the trial, which angered anti-abolitionists as an interpreter opens the doors to contradicting their asseverations.

To make things worse, a second ad hoc interpreter was provided, and Antonio also protested his services: "Mr. Desa, another Portuguese gentleman, was sworn as interpreter, but soon the witness made some complaints." Without official or unofficial Spanish interpreters, the proceedings were halted. Tappan narrated that counsel on both sides "requested Mr. Sedgwick to interrogate witness in the Spanish language" (refer to Figure 7.4). According to the sources consulted, this represented the only time both sides made a stipulation concerning the same issue. Not only did they all agree for Sedgwick—attorney of record for the Africans—to interpret for Antonio, but they also accepted his refusal to be sworn in as interpreter. Sedgwick "consented to do so, but not as a sworn interpreter, which he considered inconsistent with his relation to the case as counsel to the claimants." In contrast to the other African interpreters who took the oath and who were interrogated on the nature of the oath and its religious elements extensively, Sedgwick was exempt from even taking a simple oath. The oath requirement for all interpreters signalled the common practice of interpreters in court procedures. Privilege and cultural capital sided with Sedgwick as a learned professional of European descent, exempting him from taking a required oath.[24]

[24] The discretionary aspect of taking the oath responded to court privileges when evaluating the Christian trustworthiness of the court interpreter. As has been discussed, trust is a relative and subjective concept, which shaped the recruitment process and the relationship of the interpreters to the Africans and to the courts. The Spanish ordinance raises another angle regarding the "trust" factor as it related to the judicial-colonial body. During the January 1840 trial of the *Amistad* case, an interpreter deemed "trustworthy" refused the administration of the oath. He had openly professed his anti-slavery standpoint, without the objection of the court or opposing parties.

A creative solution to an impending problem could not come without inherent difficulties. The language of the court was English. Mr. Sedgwick, a trained lawyer, served as a Spanish–English interpreter who led the witness examination on the defense side. Tappan just noted that now "the examination was conducted without difficulty." Other difficulties must have manifested as a dual role as both interpreter and interrogating counsel would have regarded one of two tasks undone. Antonio continued recounting the *Amistad* journey from Cuba, the ensuing revolt, how Sengbe tied him, and how Sengbe ran a tight ship in charge of the voyage. From Meade to Sedgwick, the pendulum swayed to political opposites. Anti-slavery interests prevailed in the choice of the final interpreter—Sedgwick—for Antonio. In the *Amistad* case, Antonio was the last witness to testify, although not the end for ITS issues—for two remained, including submission of documents.

The Last Day of Trial, and the Last *Amistad* Interpreter, Thomas Sedgwick, III

In the context of the *Amistad* trials, converting Thomas Sedgwick, III, the lawyer to an interpreter made sense. Sedgwick was a polyglot. At the age of twenty-eight, he agreed to represent the *Amistad* Africans as the first lawyer to be recruited for this historical moment. The abolitionists surmised that they needed a team of lawyers to represent the Africans. Janes and others decided to recruit Baldwin, while Sedgwick was responsible for hiring the third lawyer, a neighboring colleague in the same building of the law office he shared with his uncle. His mother began teaching him French by sight translating texts into English at the age of six.[25] At eleven, his parents exposed him to Latin, Spanish, and Drawing.[26] He devoted time and energy developing his linguistic skills in French, German, and Spanish.

From his early years, he showed a proclivity to side with the oppressed, regardless of the consequences. While attending the prestigious Round Hill boarding school,[27] he was expelled "because of trying to liberate a student from the school's dungeon" with other fellow students. He was critical of the Ivy college curriculum in general, and especially of the law school's curriculum. Often, he abandoned formal studies to go back home to study on his own with the assistance of his mother or through mentorship at his uncle's

25 Box 15, Folder 16, Sedgwick Family Papers, Massachusetts Historical Society.
26 Box 15, Folder 16, Sedgwick Family Papers, Massachusetts Historical Society.
27 Box 15, Folder 19, Sedgwick Family Papers, Massachusetts Historical Society.

law firm. As a writer, he often adopted the alias of "Veto" in *The Liberator* to ventilate his anti-slavery views. He also wrote a column in the *NY Evening Post,* in New York City, where eventually, he became the editor. In 1847, eight years before he died, he delivered a speech at Union College in which he denounced "slavery as the opprobrium of the age, the curse and cancer of your country."[28] For Sedgwick, the events of the *Amistad* constituted a conversion experience of profound theological transformation: "I am very glad to have had an opportunity during my short practice at the BAR to advocate interest so important and so interesting as those of these poor Africans."

Opposing counsel submitted as evidence "the schooner's papers relating to this case with a translation of them."[29] During the September proceeding, the litigation team for the Africans submitted these in evidence.[30] At the trial, "the U.S. Attorney" submitted them as well, and Tappan proceeded to list them. *Licencias* submission would prove detrimental to the opposing party. Covey, Pratt, Madden, and Gibbs testified convincingly on the fraudulent nature of these documents. Primarily, the *Amistad* Africans landed in Cuba in the recent past, not qualifying as *Ladinos*. The controversial term, "*licencia*," was translated in three different ways: license, passport, and permit, as discussed in some detail in the translation section. Documents granting passage to the *Amistad* Africans emerged translated as "permits," while those addressed to the Spaniards were translated as "passport" or "licenses." Tappan highlights how "permits" for the African men indicated "forty-nine *Ladinos*," one of the main contentions of counsel of the defendants. These documents damaged the prosecution, Spaniards, and other pro-slavery libellants. On the other hand, they would aid the cause of *Amistad* Africans.

Charles Pratt's deposition, rejected on the first day of trial, was admitted in court with conditions. Baldwin received answers to his inquiries on the rejecting reasons: lack of notification to the New London opposing party of Pratt's deposition. The matter was settled. Baldwin convinced the court that "Pratt's deposition be read as against Ruiz and Montez." The prosecution agreed as long as it did not incriminate the USA. The judge ruled in favor of admitting into evidence the deposition except for the sections referencing Covey, particularly, "of his interpreting the answer to Prof. Gibb's question, &c." At this point, "Mr. Baldwin read it and put it into the judge's hands to mark the passages allowed to be used in evidence." The bracketed areas were sectioned off by Judge Thompson on Pratt's official deposition. The judge

28 MS No. 851; Box 15. Sedgwick Family Papers. Massachusetts Historical Society.
29 MS No. 851; Box 15, Sedgwick Family Papers, Massachusetts Historical Society.
30 The chapter on translation issues expounded on the analysis of these evidentiary documents.

rejected declarations considered as "hearsay," *testimonio de tercera o de oido*. These hearsay statements involved Pratt's observations on James Covey's interpretation between the Africans and Prof. Gibbs. Other sectioned-off areas involved the Africans' recollection of seeing Pedro Blanco, the Spanish enslaver in *Jomboko*, Africa, who travelled back and forth from Cuba from his inlet home by the Gallina River. More than hearsay, Pratt's declarations supported the anti-slavery claims of the abolitionists on behalf of their clients. Tappan, the narrator, secured a copy, since the published article contained sections not admitted into evidence, relating the knowledge of the Africans of Pedro Blanco and *Jomboko*. This last *Amistad* trial established a close connection between hearsay[31] and the interpreting activity, both sharing the quality of involving "mediated testimony."[32] Hearsay exclusions in this case included contentious information further questioning the evidence of the pro-slavery side. Interpreting, as a linguistically mediated communication, was the focus of open court debates by the prosecution in hopes that the interpreter would be impeached and the Africans' voices would be silenced. At the end, the remainder of the deposition was read into the record.

Tappan concluded his narration of the third day witnessing that "the court room has been crowded . . . many of the distinguished citizens attending, officers of college, &c. several of the Africans are in court when it is in session." The *Amistad* case attracted community leaders, people of means, and the unnamed who were moved by the human issues at stake. Regarding the possible outcome of the trial, public opinion expressed "that the cause stands well for the Africans." The fourth and fifth days of trial involved mostly closing arguments from all parties, the prosecution, the libellants, and the defense. Two attorneys per side argued their case, leaving for last the counsel for the *Amistad* Africans—Baldwin with Sedgwick or Staples—since "no precedent exist[ed] for such a novel case." After five trial days, Tuesday to Saturday, the verdict in favor of the *Amistad* Africans containing eight fundamental points was pronounced on Monday, January 13, 1840, and published on *The Emancipator* (refer to Figure 7.5).

[31] Hearsay exclusions in cases involving Black litigants were established in the Court's decision in the *Queen v. Hepburn* case, where mother and daughter, Mina Queen and Louisa Queen, respectively, argued that their great grandmother, Mary Queen, was a freed woman from Ecuador who came to the USA as an indentured servant through England. She claimed this right as other relatives in her filed suits. The court, however, found inadmissible the hearsay testimony of witnesses generationally removed from the statement. This case, according to Sklansky, closed the door for enslaved people to rely upon hearsay as evidence to gain their freedom, impacting hearsay ruling up to today (Sklansky, *The Neglected Origins of the Hearsay Rule in American Slavery*, 424).

[32] Personal communication with William G. Thomas, III. August 24, 2023.

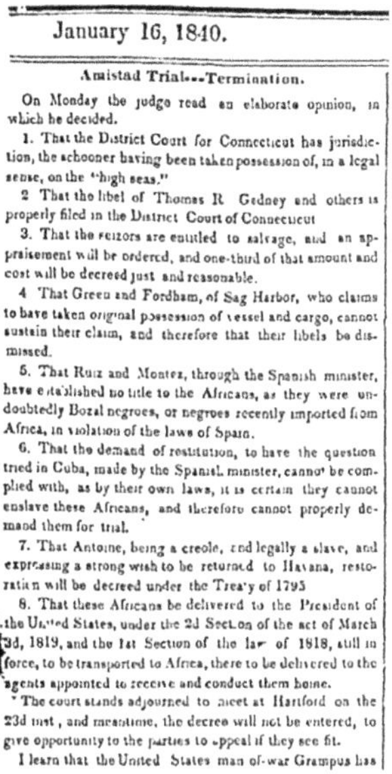

January 16, 1840.

Amistad Trial---Termination.

On Monday the judge read an elaborate opinion, in which he decided.

1. That the District Court for Connecticut has jurisdiction, the schooner having been taken possession of, in a legal sense, on the "high seas."

2 That the libel of Thomas R Gedney and others is properly filed in the District Court of Connecticut

3. That the seizors are entitled to salvage, and an appraisement will be ordered, and one-third of that amount and cost will be decreed just and reasonable.

4 That Green and Fordham, of Sag Harbor, who claims to have taken original possession of vessel and cargo, cannot sustain their claim, and therefore that their libels be dismissed.

5. That Ruiz and Montez, through the Spanish minister, have established no title to the Africans, as they were undoubtedly Bozal negroes, or negroes recently imported from Africa, in violation of the laws of Spain.

6. That the demand of restitution, to have the question tried in Cuba, made by the Spanish minister, cannot be complied with, as by their own laws, it is certain they cannot enslave these Africans, and therefore cannot properly demand them for trial.

7. That Antoine, being a creole, and legally a slave, and expressing a strong wish to be returned to Havana, restoration will be decreed under the Treaty of 1795

8. That these Africans be delivered to the President of the United States, under the 2d Section of the act of March 3d, 1819, and the 1st Section of the law of 1818, still in force, to be transported to Africa, there to be delivered to the agents appointed to receive and conduct them home.

The court stands adjourned to meet at Hartford on the 23d inst, and meantime, the decree will not be entered, to give opportunity to the parties to appeal if they see fit.

I learn that the United States man of-war Grampus has

Figure 7.5 "*Amistad* Trial Termination." *The Emancipator*, January 16, 1840.

Final verdict: the judge decided that Ruiz and Montes, who failed to testify in court, neglected to establish their "title to the Africans." In his verdict, the judge alluded to the fact that the Africans were "*Bozales*" and not "*Ladinos*." The litigation strategy proved successful. James Covey's gruelling cross-examination on the witness stand confirmed the Africans' testimony and those of the experts. Finally, point eight ordered that "the Africans be delivered to the President of the USA . . . to be transported to Africa."[33]

The abolitionists had won the case, and the Africans their freedom. Antonio was deemed to be a "legal slave" and could return to Havana in response to his original wishes. It was Covey's turn to interpret the news to the Africans who were in the jail. The *Journal of Commerce* published an article, republished in *The Emancipator*, describing the heartfelt response from Sengbe when he heard the interpreted verdict. Rev. H. G. Ludlow reported: "our interpreter communicated the decision to him. He instantly prostrated himself at my feet at full length, clapping his hands for gladness of heart."[34]

[33] *The Emancipator*, January 16, 1840.

[34] *The Emancipator*, January 16, 1840.

However, the joy speedily dissipated for them and their liberation postponed de novo. The pro-slavery side represented by the prosecution went on appeal to the Supreme Court. On March 1841, a year after the original verdict, the higher court upheld the decision of the lower court. The *Amistad* Africans won their freedom and this case.

Conclusion

On May 17, 1886, Simeon E. Baldwin, son of the *Amistad* case attorney of record, Roger Baldwin, Esq., read his paper entitled "The Captives of the *Amistad*" to the New Haven Colony Historical Society. Forty-seven years after the case had been filed in state and federal courts, Baldwin's son reminisced about the importance of finding an interpreter to act on behalf of the Africans. In this forty-page-long speech, he recalled the events and impact of what he called "the most famous case ever tried in Connecticut . . . none ever awakened a wider interest or a deeper feeling . . . the first fluid-posts that pointed the way to the yet unopened grave of slavery in the United States."[1] Simeon E. Baldwin, half a century removed from the immediacy of the *Amistad*, detailed how the abolitionists opted for a public appeal to satisfy the urgent linguistic need "to find an interpreter through whom their story could be fully learned." Captured miles from their multilingual homelands, the *Amistad* Africans mastered many languages that made, and make, the African continent, except Spanish and English. From the other shore, none of the Christian abolitionists spoke their African vernaculars. To make matters worse, the US judicial system was devoid of an administrative culture or willingness to make room for other languages, cultures, and ethnicities, making English a ruling language.

At the onset of this book, I aimed to provide a method as a call to researchers to bring to the surface the interpreters and translators they may encounter in the archival materials. I coined this approach an Interpreting and Translation Filter (ITF) in hopes that this book, *Interpreting the* Amistad*: How Interpreters and Translators Make and Shape History*, features as a case study of how ITF may be applied, explored, and exported to research and academic arenas outside of the interpreting and translation fields. This proposal attempts to demonstrate how interpreters, translators, and the issues affecting their interpreting and translation services, or lack thereof, shaped and made macro and micro histories. Sampling this ITF method may avail us of narratives and nuances that expand and enrich our understanding of histories in general. This kind of application yields an augmented interdisciplinary storyline of events involving interpreting and translation issues. Probing primary or secondary sources using this filter will advance a

[1] Baldwin, *The Captives of the Amistad*, 1.

dialogue between these interlocutors and their activities, as well as other key elements that affected who they were, what they did, and their impact. Some of those inextricable variables are race, ethnicity, coloniality, and imperial actions, mirrored through transatlantic slave narratives, by legal, Latin American, Caribbean, Africana, and US histories. The following summary strives to respond specifically to some of the guiding ITF-posed queries and curiosities.

Applying an ITF to archival materials unearthed important components of the *Amistad* story. Because of it, the end result of finding a court interpreter uncovered an innovative central legal strategy to win a case, in line with a Critical Race Theory approach. The process tripled the names of the *Amistad* interpreters, now to be remembered: Antonio Ferrer, Thomas Meade, John Ferry, Bowle, Grabbeau, George Day, James Covey, Charles Pratt, Thomas Gallaudet, John Jay Hyde, Mr. Ribeiro, Mr. Desa, and Theodore Sedgwick. The important contributions of the Sign Language community, another minoritized sector, were brought to the limelight. ITF afforded the stories of agency and leadership, especially of the African-born interpreters, to rise to the surface, particularly that of Covey, Ferry, and Pratt. By applying this IT filter, we learned how the captured Africans located in prison cells had the final say on their preferred selection of their ideal interpreter and how affectivity and corporal language communicated truth, consent, and trust. Without the passion and perseverance of the *Amistad* legal team and the committee to furnish a linguistic mediator, this story would have appeared dull. Having an interpreter did not guarantee winning the case. But not having one guaranteed the Africans losing their lives. The accelerated pace of identifying a trustworthy interpreter and of sending a dozen candidates through a trusted network from Boston to Washington, D.C., occupied a prominent role. Ends and means were justified. Identifying an interpreter served a double cause: to obtain the liberation of all Africans aboard the *Amistad* and, in doing so, to press on the urgency of ending the practices of enslavement. The distinct recruitment strategies and precise job description of the *Amistad* interpreters were designed to consider the racialized, cultural, and linguistic prejudices, and the imperial background of the US and the Spanish empires. Because the abolitionists had a will, they made a way.

John Quincy Adams, a renowned US historical and political figure, flourished as an experienced translator, a new insight into his biographical data. As a key advocate in Congress on behalf of the *Amistad* Africans, he envisioned a larger linguistic strategy toward a greater plan to see the demise of an enslaving society. The active role of the US DOS office in translating the evidentiary *licencias* and diplomatic letters and in sending dragomans in the early years of the US-imperial republic became apparent. The collusion of the three branches of the US government in the translation and editorial matters and the outraged response of the *Amistad* friends did not come as a surprise. Translators were pivotal. The backstage translators—William Jay and William Hodgson—who reviewed the Spanish *licencias*, argued against the politically manipulated translations. Additionally, the archival material brought to the forefront Robert Greenhow, as the first *Amistad* translator of the *licencias*. Hodgson and Greenhow worked for the US DOS, where Adams had served as DOS secretary, while Jay was an abolitionist and a lawyer. Because Spanish to English translators abounded during this period, the *Amistad* Committee did not place an ad to solicit their services, confident that this need would be satisfied in-house. Through this research I uncovered the widespread practice of the translating culture of the nineteenth-century US-educated class, locus of my investigation endeavors in my future. When judicial files appear insufficient to unearth the interpreting and translation elements of this legal case, the handwritten letters of many, including the interpreters and translators, the *Amistad* African allies, their relatives and friends, newspapers, newsletters, and related pamphlets filled the historical gaps. The detailed history of the interpreting and translation matters allowed for the counter-stories of the *Amistad* legal case, particularly those of the African defendants, to materialize, the crux of the litigation strategy. Analyzing the *Amistad* story, through the magnifying glass of an interpreting and translation filter, increases the corpus of interpreting and translation histories.

Adams's involvement exemplified how using your social, cultural, and political privileges may serve a cause—a model to replicate. For him, it took convincing. His letters confessed his pained apprehension of the *Amistad* legal team winning this case on behalf of the Africans. But he persevered, creatively dismissing an active gag rule in Congress against any discussion related to anti-slavery petitions which passed. Coincidently, in January 1840, Adams, a lawyer as well, mastered a way to bring to the floor anti-slavery matters through the *Amistad* translation issues that turned up the public volume on this *Amistad* controversy. On March 1841, before the Supreme Court, Adams and Baldwin won the appeal on behalf of the *Amistad* Africans. And when the judge issued his decision, sending Antonio back to Cuba as the "lawful property" of the widow of the late Captain Ferrer, the abolitionists, once again, mobilized their network effectively to send Antonio north via the Underground Railroad. In April 1841, a month after the verdict, Antonio, the first African interpreter in this saga, arrived safely in Montreal, Canada, liberated.[2]

2 AMA Archives FI 4983. The *Amistad* Research Center, New Orleans, Louisiana, USA.

Finding Covey marked a before-and-after, almost a grand finale, in a frantic forty-day search for a linguistic mediator who could make the difference between life and death. Translation and interpretation made the *Amistad* story possible despite the many factors that hindered effective linguistic mediation. The US judicial systems were (and are) inclined to discriminate linguistically against non-English defendants and claimants in both the nineteenth and twenty-first centuries.[3] Witness testimonies from Ferry, Madden, Bacon, Gibbs, and Janes may have sufficed to verify the story of the ethnic origins of the *Amistad* Africans. Sworn testimonies by Hansen, Ferry, and Pratt may have been plenty. But in reality, they were not enough to defend the *Amistad* captives. The *Amistad* abolitionists could not afford the risk of losing this case. They knew not to rely on the disinterested court to provide these linguistic services for their clients. In affirming the linguistic rights of their clients, they stood for freedom, racialized equality, and chipped away at the institution of slavery. It was a strategy that created an effective justice-seeking cocktail. And yet, their honorable ambitions faced dichotomies. It got messy. In this process of liberation, the contradictions in this story surfaced with their evangelization and racist ways of treating the prisoners and restricting Covey's return to Africa. The abolitionists' binary frameworks, unchecked privileges, and unchecked internalized imperial leanings influenced their philosophies, commitments, and actions. But giving up this fight for equality was not an option either. Despite the differences in the ideological spectrum of the abolitionist movement, they closed rank with one aim in sight: to eradicate the institution of slavery and free the *Amistad* captives: a strategy to be embraced by those on the equity and human-rights side of the social equation. It never is.

The shaping and making of the *Amistad* story through the search, availability, and renditions of the interpreters and translators points toward further discussion on a number of issues. For starters, it challenges the preservation of neutrality, objectivity, and impartiality as professional ideals for these linguistic mediators. These findings suggest that this insistence be put to rest. Actions and decisions motivated by ideological stances guided all of the surrounding players in the anti-slavery and pro-slavery continuum. The abolitionists who strategized to win the case in favor of the *Amistad* Africans lined up their resources toward this end and to eventually bring down the institution of slavery. The actions of the *Amistad* Spaniards supported the

[3] Brian Ross and Angela M. Hill, "Tug-of-Love: Immigrant Mom Loses Effort to Regain Son Given to US Parents," https://abcnews.go.com/Blotter/immigrant-mom-loses-effort-regain-son-us-parents/story?id=16803067. In 2012, a Guatemalan mom in Missouri courts fought to keep the maternity rights of her son. Although she appeared in court with her lawyer, no Spanish–English court interpreter was provided by the court or by her counsel.

colonizing and enslaving ideology of the Spanish Crown, which paired up with the US Executive and parts of the Legislative branch, as well as a racialized court system, far removed from objective and neutral positions. As has been shown, this ideological battle required interpreters, translators, and editors who would respond faithfully to the side they believed in. Constant examination of the ideological positions of individuals, professionals, institutions, and systems seems imperative for justice to prevail. In situations of this heightened conflict, or in the context of the day-to-day in a community interpreting encounter, it bears to question who benefits from attempting to remain impartial and objective in the face of subjective decisions, whose agency is being suppressed, and whose power is being secured. These queries stemming from the *Amistad* story call for greater awareness, critical analysis, transparency, and decision-making power by all participating in linguistic-mediated contexts and their researchers.

This story reinforces the connection of language, power, agency, and racialization from the individual to the collective to the systemic. The complex and contradictory journey, from inland to the coast, became the stage for multiple enslavement and resistance dialogues in both African and European languages that beckons further exploration. Although the archival materials lack documentation of the multilingual activities that took place on the enslaving ships, above or under board, the circumstances forced the captured to interpret for each other constantly as they attempted to survive the unsurvivable in the bellies of ships or prison cells. From Europe, to Africa, through the Atlantic Crossing, and in the Americas, their interpreting skills helped them live and thrive and develop a sense of identity. This research unfolds the multilingual and multi-interpreting realities at the various junctures in the enslaving and liberation journey. This ITF case study urges similar research, because language mediation shaped and made history.

Epilogue

Interpreting beyond January 1840[1]

And it so happened that while in the reverse-Atlantic Crossing from the Americas to Africa, to Spain, and then Portugal, I edited one of the final versions of this manuscript. Enjoying all the comforts of a state room with a balcony, I attempted to envision the transatlantic journey of the Africans and all those aboard. Mesmerized by the beauty and mysteries of the Atlantic deep-blue waters, listening to the divergent ancestral voices in the crashing of the waves, and inspired by the shining moonlight on the ocean, I tried reimagining the knowns and unknowns of their lengthy inhuman voyages, as well as the lives of those ending abruptly in the Atlantic by the horrifying actions of the enslavers or as a cry to stop the brutal horror. I contemplated on the route that conjured the beginning of the story of the fifty-three *Amistad* Africans and the finale of the thirty-five that made it in the reverse-Atlantic crossing back home. James Covey accompanied them, but this came with a prior struggle.

After the January 1840 trial, Covey vacillated among various options: staying alongside the *Amistad* Africans, leaving to go back to Africa, or joining the *Buzzard* brig to work again as a sailor. Letters written by Covey to Lewis Tappan recall his plea to return home, his contradictory feelings in leaving the *Amistad* children and the rest of them, and his passionate arguments to be allowed to leave. In the wake of the trial, Covey's financial situation seemed dire. Some of his expenses were being paid, but not enough to sustain his livelihood. His letter reflected his discontent. In June 1840, Covey wrote: "Mr. Tappan, You say when I was to go home I must write to you. I stay more long enough. I want to go home. I can get no money so much as I want."[2] During this time, he lived with Amos Townsend[3] in Westville, a

[1] Interpreting issues continued after winning the Supreme Court appeal; in contrast, the translation issues faded from the story.

[2] AMA Archives FI 4736. The *Amistad* Research Center, New Orleans, Louisiana, USA. Covey's letters also revealed the level of English competency he had acquired for his role as interpreter to the court. More on this will be expounded in future writings. So far, the archives are missing the respond of Covey's letters.

[3] AMA Archives FI 4659, The *Amistad* Research Center, New Orleans, Louisiana, USA. A four-page document listed expenses paid to Townsend for expenses incurred for Covey, from October 1839 to October 22, 1841, for "passages, boots, board, washing, clothing, cash."

few miles north of New Haven, Connecticut. Covey lived in proximity to the *Amistad* prisoners transferred from New Haven to Westville while awaiting the appeal. His letters expressed his deep love and care for the *Amistad* Africans, his emotional strife of abandoning the orphaned children, and his frustration with Tappan for not allowing him to leave. Covey lived in a state of emancipation, not liberation, during the *Amistad* trials. In the midst of another racialized contradiction of this anti-slavery movement, Covey's heart ached to return home.

In addition to the issues of power, racialization, and privilege keeping Covey on the other side of the Atlantic, the *Amistad* abolitionists stuttered on whether or not his interpreting skills would be needed in the upcoming judicial proceedings between the January 1840 trial and the March 1841 appeal. Baldwin, counsel for the Africans, opined that most likely his services would be necessary for the hearing at the Circuit Court in September of 1840. In case Covey were to return to the African continent, English-linguistic immersion techniques trained some of the *Amistad* Africans who could now serve as interpreters. Covey also acted as an interpreter trainer. After a visit to the Africans in the Westville prison, Townsend reported "that they can understand a great deal without the intervention of an Interpreter and moreover that some two or three of them informed that the others, can act as Interpreters to their fellow."[4] By October of 1840, Kinna and Kale[5] were being trained as possible interpreters in case they would be needed for the Africans. Interpreting training was ongoing. In April of 1841, at an anti-slavery meeting Kinna mediated linguistically between Cinque, one of the speakers of the fundraising event, and the enthralled audience: "and in a most eloquent manner [Cinque] spoke for some 15 minutes and in this manner too while waiting for Kinna to interpret."[6]

Throughout this period, James Kaweli Covey stayed and waited, against his will. His specific role was determined in a meeting of the Mendean Committee which evolved from the *Amistad* Committee. They met in New York City on August 24, 1841, to discuss the return of the liberated Mendeans to Africa. The four-point resolution, including one dedicated to the future of James Covey, read: "That a competent person be employed to go immediately to Sierra Leone, accompanied by two of the Mendeans, and James Covey, a native of Mende, who has acted as interpreter, to make inquiries there, and, if necessary, to visit Mende". Initially, his role was to accompany the first group to Sierra Leone to assess the safety of the Africans on their return. African

4 AMA Archives FI 4738. The *Amistad* Research Center, New Orleans, Louisiana, USA.
5 *The American and Foreign Anti-Slavery Reporter*, August 24, 1841 (also see Figure E.1).
6 AMA Archives FI 4988A. The *Amistad* Research Center, New Orleans, Louisiana, USA.

Figure E.1 "Little Kale." Sketches of the Amistad Captives. General Collection. Beinecke Rare Book and Manuscript Library. Yale University.

coastal activities represented a threat for liberated Africans who could be easily recaptured and re-enslaved. The Committee needed to surmise the state of affairs in Sierra Leone in order to analyze the likelihood of the Mende Mission's success.[7] It was left to the interpreter to garner information from locals. Who better than Covey—trustworthy, trained, familiarized with Christianity, friends to the Africans and *Amistad* abolitionists, bilingual, bicultural, and now bicoastal. But plans changed. On November 25, 1841, having raised close to USD $2,000 to charter the *Gentleman* brig, only thirty-five of the original fifty-three *Amistad* Africans escorted by missionaries returned to Sierra Leone. Covey returned with all of them, one last time, to stay there.

[7] Within the complexity of their missionary-colonizing activities, the AMA archives represent a sizable portion of the primary sources in this research. This departure marked the beginning of the Congregationalist Christian mission in Africa and the Mende Mission, which in turn, in 1846, became the American Missionary Association (AMA).

Bibliography

Books and Journals

Álvarez, Torres, Osvaldo Manuel, Luis Pérez Orozco, Melissa Lang Morales, and Daisy Pérez Vera. "La conspiración De La Escalera: Una visión histórico-jurídica." *Justicia y Derecho* 10 (enero-diciembre 2022): 8–23.

Baigorri-Jalón. *Languages in the Crossfire: Interpreters in the Spanish Civil War.* New York: Routledge, 2023

Baigorri-Jalón. *Interpreters at the United Nations: A History.* Salamanca, Spain: University of Salamanca. 2004.

Barber, John W. *A History of the Amistad Captives: Being a Circumstantial Account of the Capture of the Spanish Schooner Amistad, by the Africans on Board; their Voyage, and Capture Near Long Island, New York; with Biographical Sketches of Each of the Surviving Africans also, an Account of The Trials.* New Haven, CT: E.L. & J. W. Barber, 1840.

Blight, David W. *Frederick Douglass: Prophet of Freedom*. New York: Simon & Schuster, 2018. ProQuest Ebook Central.

Brewer-García, Larissa. *Beyond Babel: Translations of Blackness in Colonial Perú and New Granada.* Cambridge: University of Chicago Press, 2021.

Cable, Mary. *Black Odyssey: The Case of The Slave Ship Amistad.* New York: The Viking Press, 1971.

Carr, Edward Hallett. *What is History?* New York: Random House, 1961.

Castellanos, Jorge e Isabel Castellanos. *Cultural Afrocubana 1: El negro en Cuba (1492–1844).* Miami: Ediciones Universal, 1988.

Cepeda, Jesús and Dimas Sánchez. *Ritmos Afro Puertorriqueños.* Fundación Rafael Cepeda, 2022.

Coronado, Raúl. *A World not to Come: A History of Latino Writing and Print Culture.* Cambridge, MA: Harvard University Press, 2013.

Delbanco, Andrew. *The Abolitionists Imagination.* Cambridge, MA: Harvard University Press, 2012.

Delgado, Richard and Jean Stefancic. *Critical Race Theory: An Introduction*. New York: New York University, 2017.

Ducoudray Holstein, H. L. V. *Memoirs of Simon Bolivar, President Liberator of the Republic of Colombia, and of His Principal Generals: Secret History of the Revolution and the Events Which Preceded It from 1807 to the Present Time: With an Introduction Containing an Account of the Statistics and the Present Situation of Said Republic, Education, Character, Manners and Customs of the Inhabitants.* Boston: S.G. Goodrich & Co., 1830.

Fabre, Geneviève. "The Slave Ship Dance." In *Black Imagination and the Middle Passage*. Edited by Maria Diedrich, Henry Louis Gates, Jr., and Carl Pedersen, 33–40. London: Oxford University Press, 1999.

Fernández Sánchez, María Manuela. "History and Historiography." In *Researching Translation and Interpreting*. Edited by Claudia V. Angelelli and Brian James Baer, 97–107. London: Routledge, 2012.

Ferrer, Ada. "Cuban Slavery and Atlantic Anti-Slavery." In *Slavery & Antislavery in Spain's Atlantic Empire*. Edited by Josep M. Fradera and Christopher Schmidt-Nowara, 134–58. New York: Berghahn Books, 2013.

García Martínez, Orlando and Michael Zeuske. *La sublevación esclava en la goleta Amistad: Ramón Ferrer y las redes de contrabando en el mundo atlántico*. La Habana, Cuba: Ediciones Unión, 2012.

Garner, Bryan A., ed. *Black's Law Dictionary*, 8th ed. St. Paul, MN: Thomson West, 2004.

Giambruno, Cynthia. "The Role of the Interpreter in the Governance of Sixteenth-and Seventeenth-Century Spanish Colonies in the 'New World.'" In *Crossing Borders in Community Interpreting: definitions and dilemmas*. Edited by Carmen Valero-Garcés and Anne Martin, 27–49. Philadelphia: John Benjamins Publishing Company, 2008.

González, Roseann Dueñas, Victoria F. Vásquez, and Holly Mikkelson. *Fundamentals of Court Interpretation: Theory, Policy and Practice*, 2nd ed. Durham, NC: Carolina Academic Press, 2012.

Gravely, William. *Gilbert Haven Methodist Abolitionist: A Study in Race, Religion, and Reform, 1850–1880*. Nashville: Abingdon Press, 1973.

Gresko, Jessica A. "Coming to the Aid of the *Amistad* Africans." In *African American Connecticut Explored*. Edited by Elizabeth M. Normen, with Stacey K. Close, Kathering J. Harris, and W. M. Frank Mitchell, 126–36. Middletown: Wesleyan University Press, 2014.

Grupo Alfaqueque. *Los límites de Babel: Ensayos sobre la comunicación entre lenguas y culturas*. Madrid, Spain: Iberoamericana, 2010.

Hanley, Julian R. and Wayne W. Schmidt. *Legal Aspects of Criminal Evidence*, 3rd ed. Berkeley, CA: McCutchan Publishing, 1984.

Inghilleri, Moira. "Translation and Violence." In *The Routledge Handbook of Translation and Politics*. Edited by Fruela Fernández and Jonathan Evans, 147–61. London; New York: Routledge, 2018.

Johnson, Clifton H. "The *Amistad* Case and the Consequences in U.S. History." *Journal of the New Haven Colony Historical Society* 36, no. 2 (Spring 1990): 3–22.

Jones, Howard. *Mutiny on the Amistad*. New York: Oxford University Press, 1987.

Jurmain, Suzanne. *Freedom's Sons: The True Story of the Amistad Mutiny*. New York: Lothrop, Lee & Shepard Books, 1998.

Kromer, Helen. *Amistad: The Slave Uprising Aboard the Spanish Schooner*. Cleveland, OH: The Pilgrim Press, 1997.

Lawrance, Benjamin N. Amistad *Orphans: An Atlantic Story of Children*. New Haven, CT: Yale University Press, 2015.

Lawrance, Benjamin N. "*La Amistad*'s 'Interpreter' Reinterpreted: James 'Kaweli' Covey's Distressed Atlantic Childhood and the Production of Knowledge about Nineteenth-Century Sierra Leone." In *Slavery Abolition and the Transition to Colonialism in Sierra Leone*. Edited by Suzanne Schwarz and Paul Lovejoy, 217–55. Trenton: Africa World Press, 2014.

Lay, Benjamin. *All Slavekeepers that Keep the Innocent in Bondage, Apostates.* Philadelphia: Printed for the author, 1737 [i.e. 1738] Pdf. https://www.loc.gov/item/66038906/.

Lefevere, André. *Translation/History/Culture: A Sourcebook*. London: Routledge, 2002.

Mayoral Asensio, Roberto. "¿Existe la teoría de la traducción?" *Apuntes* 10, no. 4 (Otoño 2002): 12–13.

Mikkelson, Holly. "Evolving Views of the Court Interpreter´s Role: Between Scylla and Charybdis." In *Crossing Borders in Community Interpreting: Definitions and Dilemmas*. Edited by A. Martin and C. Valero Garcés, 73–89. Amsterdam: John Benjamins, 2008.

Minguet, Charles. *Bolívar y el mundo de los libertadores*. México: Universidad Nacional Autónoma de México, 1993.

Osagie, Iyunolu Folayan. *The Amistad Revolt: Memory, Slavery, and the Politics of Identity in the United States and Sierra Leone*. Athens, GA: University of Georgia Press, 2000.

Pichardo, Esteban. *Diccionario provincial de voces cubanas*. Matanzas, Cuba: Imprenta de la Real Marina, 1836.

Pond, Enoch. *Slavery and the Bible*. Boston, MA: American Tract Society, 1850.

Price, J. Martin. *Translation and Epistemicide: Racialization of Languages in the Americas*. Crownhill: University of Arizona Press, 2023.

Pym, Anthony. *Methods in Translation History*. London: St. Jerome Publishing, 1998.

Quarles, Benjamin. *Black Abolitionists*. New York: Oxford University Press, 1969.

Rediker, Marcus. *The Amistad Rebellion*. New York: Viking, Penguin Group, 2012.

Rediker, Marcus. *Outlaws of the Atlantic*. Boston,MA: Beacon Press, 2014.

Rediker, Marcus. *The Slave Ship: A Human History*. London:John Murray, 2007.

Rodrigo y Alharilla, Martín. "Spanish Merchants and the Slave Trade: From Legality to Illegality, 1814–1870." In *Slavery and Antislavery in Spain's Atlantic Empire*. Edited by Josep Fradera and Christopher Schmidt-Nowara. New York: Berghahn Books, 2013, 176–99.

Ruiz Rosendo, L. and C. Persaud. "Interpreting in Conflict Zones Throughout History." *Lingüística Antverpiensia*, New Series: Themes in Translation Studies 15 (2016): 1 35.

Saldanha, Gabriela and Sharon O'Brien. *Research Methodologies in Translation Studies*. London: Routledge, 2014.

Sarmiento Pérez, Marcos. "Interpreting for the Inquisition." In *New Insights in the History of Interpreting*. Edited by K. Takeda and J. Baigorri-Jalón, 47–73. Amsterdam: John Benjamins, 2016.

Schmidt-Nowara, Christopher. "Wilberforce Spanished." In *Slavery and Antislavery in Spain's Atlantic Empire*. Edited by Josep M. Fradera ānd Christopher Schmidt-Nowara, 158–75. New York: Berghahn, 2013.

Setton, Robin and Erich Prunč. "Ethics." In *Routledge Encyclopedia of Interpreting Studies*. Edited by Franz Pöchhacker, 144–47. Abingdon, Oxon: Routledge, 2015.

Silva, Kim A. "Signs of Freedom: Deaf Connections in the *Amistad* Story." In *Telling Deaf Lives: Agents of Change*. Edited by Kristin Snoddon, 136–47. Washington, DC: Gallaudet University Press, 2014.

Sinha, Manisha. *The Slave's Cause: A History of Abolition*. New Haven, CT: Yale University Press, 2016.

Smith, Linda Tuhiwai. *Decolonizing Methodologies*. London: Zed Books Ltd., 1999.

Sterns, Emma Gelders. *The Long Black Schooner*. New York: Aladdin Books, 1953.

Stone, J. L. *Slavery and the Bible: Slavery as Seen in Its Punishment*. San Francisco, CA: B.P. Street, 1868.

Stuart, Graham H. *The Department of State: A History of His Organization, Procedure and Personnel*. New York: MacMillan Co., 1949.

Takeda, Kayoko. *New Insights in the History of Interpreting*. Amsterdam: John Benjamin Publishing Company, 2016.

Tomich, Dale W. *Through the Prism of Slavery: Labor, Capital, and World Economy*. New York: Rowman & Littlefield, 2004.

Tryuk, Malgorzata. *On Ethics and Interpreters*. Frankfurt am Main: Peter Lang, 2015.

Valdes, Francisco, Jerome McCristal Culp, and Angela P. Harris, eds. *Crossroads, Directions, and a New Critical Race Theory*. Philadelphia: Temple University Press, 2002.

Webber, Christopher L. *American to the Backbone: The Life of James W. C. Pennington, the Fugitive Slave Who Became One of the First Black Abolitionists*. New York: Pegasus Books, 2011.

Zaragoza De León, Jeanette. "From this Side of the Horizon: Feminist Biblical Hermeneutics." MA Thesis. University of Puerto Rico. A translation of "Capítulo 16: Análisis feminista." In *Para que comprendiesen las Escrituras: Introducción a los Métodos Exegéticos*, Edited by Ediberto López-Rodríguez. 2011.

Zaragoza De León, Jeanette. "Los abolicionistas cristianos contratan a un intérprete judicial para los Mende-africanos en el caso *Amistad* para desafiar la institución de la esclavitud en los EE UU del siglo XIX." *Revista Iberoamericana de Lingüística*, no. 12 (2017): 67–82.

Zaragoza De León, Jeanette. "The Search for a Mende-Court Interpreter in the *Amistad* Case in Order to Challenge the Institution of Slavery." (TFM). November 17, 2015.

Zeinert, Karen. *The Amistad Slave Revolt and American Abolition.* North Haven, CT: The Shoe String Press, 1997.
Zeuske, Michael. *Amistad: A Hidden Network of Slavers and Merchants.* Princeton: Markus Wiener Publishers, 2015.
Zeuske, Michael and Orlando García Martínez. "*La Amistad*: Ramón Ferrer in Cuba and the Transatlantic Dimensions of Slaving and Contraband Trade." In *Slavery and Antislavery in Spain's Atlantic Empire.* Edited by Josep M. Fradera and Christopher Schmidt-Nowara, 200–28. New York: Berghahn Books, 2013.

Dissertations

Alcalde, John. "Babel Fish: Court interpreters in America (1790–1921)." PhD diss., Northern Illinois University, 2022.

Documentaries

Buba, Tony, dir. *Ghosts of the Amistad: In the Footsteps of the Rebels.* Produced and narrated by Marcus Rediker. Filmmakers Library; Alexander Street Press, 2014.

Electronic Sources

ABC News. "Tug-of-Love: Immigrant Mom Loses Effort to Regain Son Given to US Parents." July 18, 2012, 11:14 AM. https://abcnews.go.com/Blotter/immigrant-mom-loses-effort-regain-son-us-parents/story?id=16803067.
Anderson, Richard. "Abolition's Adolescence: Apprenticeship as 'Liberation' in Sierra Leone, 1808–1848." *The English Historical Review* 137, no. 586 (June 2022): 763–93, https://doi.org/10.1093/ehr/ceac117.
Archivo Histórico Provincial de Cádiz. "Cádiz, un puerto de paso: Pasaportes del siglo XIX." *El documento destacado* (noviembre de 2015): 3–17. http://www.juntadeandalucia.es/cultura/archivos_html/sites/default/contenidos/archivos/ahpcadiz/documentos/DM1115.pdf.
Baigorri Jalón, Jesús y Concepción Otero Moreno (Grupo Alfaqueque). "Understanding the Other: News from the Past and the Present." In *Intercultural Communication in Action.* Edited by Francis Jarmar, 165–98. Cabin John, MD: Wildside Press, 2012. http://campus.usal.es/~alfaqueque/publicaciones/alfaqueque/Encountering%20the%20Other.pdf.
Brickhouse, Anna. *The Unsettlement of America: Translation, Interpretation, and the Story of Don Luis de Velasco, 1560–1945.* New York: Oxford University Press, 2014. https://doi.org/10.1093/acprof:oso/9780199729722.001.0001.

Burns, K. "Unfixing Race." In *Histories of Race and Racism: The Andes and Mesoamerica from Colonial Times to the Present*. Edited by L. Gotkowitz, 57–71. Duke University Press. https://doi.org/10.2307/j.ctv11hpnf1.5.

Cáceres-Würsig, Ingrid. "Breve historia de la secretaría de interpretación de lenguas." *Meta: Journal des traducteurs* 49, no. 3 (September 2004): 609–28. https://id.erudit.org/iderudit/009381ar, https://doi.org/10.7202/009381ar.

Coffey, John. "The Abolition of the Slave Trade: Christian Conscience and Political Action." *Cambridge Papers* 15, no. 2 (June 2006): 1–6. https://www.jubilee-centre.org/cambridge_papers.

Commonwealth of Massachusetts. The Committee for the Administration of Interpreters for the Trial Court. "The Code of Professional Conduct for Court Interpreters of the Trial Court." In *Standards & Procedures of the Office of Court Interpreter Services*. 2009. https://www.mass.gov/doc/code-of-professional-conduct-for-court-interpreters-of-the-trial-court/download.

Cuesta, Leonel-Antonio de la. "Intérpretes y traductores en el descubrimiento y conquista del nuevo mundo." *Livius* 1 (1992): 25–34. https://buleria.unileon.es/bitstream/handle/10612/6323/Int%C3%A9rpretes%20y%20traductores%20en%20el%20descubrimiento.pdf?sequence=1 (accessed July 20, 2023).

Fold3 by Ancestry. "US *Amistad*." *Black History*. https://www.fold3.com/collection/african-american.

Gifis, Steven H. *Dictionary of Legal Terms: Definitions and Explanations for Non-Lawyers,* 5th ed. Hauppauge, NY: Barron's Educational Series, 2016. https://search.credoreference.com.

Graden, Dale T. "Interpreters, Translators, and the Spoken Word in the Nineteenth-Century Transatlantic Slave Trade to Brazil and Cuba." *Ethnohistory* 58, no. 3 (Summer 2011). doi:10.1215/00141801-1263839. Copyright 2011 by American Society for Ethnohistory.

Hargis, Thomas F. "The Law's Delay Author(s)." *The North American Review* 140, no. 341 (April 1885): 309–15. http://www.jstor.org/stable/25118474.

Johnson, Charles J. "William Brown Hodgson 1801–1871." https://www.georgiaencyclopedia.org/articles/history-archaeology/william-brown-hodgson-1801-1871/ (accessed March 15, 2023).

Judicial Council of California. Administrative Office of the Courts. Executive Office Programs Division. Court Interpreters Program. *Professional Standards and Ethics for California Court Interpreters,* 4th ed. San Francisco: The Council, 2008. http://www.soniamelnikova.com/CodeOfEthics.pdf.

Kalina, Sylvia. "Ethical Challenges in Different Interpreting Settings." In MONTI Special Issue 2 *Insights In Interpreting. Status And Developments/ Reflexiones Sobre La Interpretación. Presente Y Futuro*. Edited by Catalina Iliescu Gheorghiu and Juan Miguel Ortega Herráez. 2015. https://rua.ua.es/dspace/bitstream/10045/52569/1/MonTI_2015_Special_Issue.pdf.

Lawrance, Benjamin N., Lynn Osborn, and L. Roberts. *Intermediaries, Interpreters, and Clerks: African Employees in the Making of Colonial Africa*. Madison: University of Wisconsin Press, 2015. Project MUSE. https://muse.jhu.edu/.

Linder, Douglas O. "The *Amistad* Case." 2007. https://ssrn.com/abstract=1021314 or http://dx.doi.org/10.2139/ssrn.1021314.

Linder, Douglas O. "*Amistad* Trials (1839–1840)." *Famous Trials*. https://www.famous-trials.com/amistad.

National Association of the Deaf. "Community and Culture – Frequently Asked Questions." 2023. https://www.nad.org/resources/american-sign-language/community-and-culture-frequently-asked-questions/.

"New England Anti-Slavery Society." *The Abolitionist: Or Record of the New England Anti-Slavery Society* (1833–1833) 1, no. 1 (1833): 2. https://www.proquest.com/historical-periodicals/new-england-anti-slavery-society/docview/124720253/se-2.

New Jersey Supreme Court. "Code of Professional Conduct for Interpreters, Transliterators, and Translators." Rev. 2016. https://www.njcourts.gov/sites/default/files/public/language-services/codeconduct.pdf.

Powell, Richard J. "How Cinque was Painted." *The Washington Post*, December 28, 1997. https://www.washingtonpost.com/archive/lifestyle/style/1997/12/28/how-cinque-was-painted/64bcb5bd-bae9-4db4-9be8-52352c21a829/?utm_term=.c9b94ff237e2.

Real Academia Española. *Diccionario Histórico de la Lengua Española*. Academia Usual. 1817. https://apps2.rae.es/ntllet/SrvltGUILoginNtlletPub.

Rocha, Gabriel de Avilez. "Maroons in the Montes: Toward a Political Ecology of Marronage in the Sixteenth-Century Caribbean." In *Early Modern Black Diaspora Studies*. Edited by C. L. Smith et al. 2018. https://doi.org/10.1007/978-3-319-76786-4_2.

Rosefield, Hannah. "A Brief History of Oaths and Books." *The New Yorker*, June 20, 2014. https://www.newyorker.com/books/page-turner/a-brief-history-of-oaths-and-books.

Rundle, Christopher. "Translation as an Approach to History." *Translation Studies* 5, no. 2 (2012): 232–40. doi:10.1080/14781700.2012.663615.

Schulist, Sarah. "Another Slice of Linguistic Racism." *Ancestry As* (blog), June 16, 2017. https://anthropologyas.wordpress.com/2017/06/26/another-slice-of-linguistic-racism/.

Schweda-Nicholson, Nancy. "Court Interpreter Training: A Growing Need." *ERIC* (May 1985): 1–53. ED272024. http://files.eric.ed.gov/fulltext/ED272024.pdf.

Sklansky, David. *The Neglected Origins of the Hearsay Rule in American Slavery: Recovering Queen v. Hepburn*. 2022 Supreme Court Review 413, September 12, 2022. SSRN: https://ssrn.com/abstract=4207141 or http://dx.doi.org/10.2139/ssrn.4207141.

Slavery and Anti-Slavery Transnational Archive: http://search.library.yale.edu/catalog/12976167.

Vicente L. Rafael. "Linguistic Currencies: The Translative Power of English in Southeast Asia and the United States." *The Translator* 25, no. 2 (2019): 142–58, doi:10.1080/13556509.2019.1654061.

Vinatea, María Julia de. "Las Aboliciones de la Esclavitud en Iberoamérica: El Caso Peruano (1812-1854)." *Revista Historia de la Educación*

Latinoamericana 16, no. 23 (2014): 187–204. https://doi.org/10.19053/01227238.3069.
Welch, Kimberly M. *Black Litigants in the Antebellum American South.* 2020. Project Muse. muse.jhu.edu/book/57346.
Zeuske, Michael. "Rethinking the Case of the Schooner *Amistad*: Contraband and Complicity after 1808/1820." *Slavery & Abolition* 35, no.1 (2014): 156–64. https://doi.org/10.1080/0144039X.2013.798173.

Archival Sources

American Missionary Association (AMA) Archives. Amistad Research Center, New Orleans, LA, USA.

AMA Archives FI 4612.
Janes to Leavitt. August 30, 1839. AMA FI 4593.
Janes to Leavitt. August 31, 1839. AMA FI 4594.
Janes to Leavitt. September 2, 1839. AMA FI 4594.
Janes to L. Tappan. September 6, 1839. AMA FI 4599.
Burguess to Baldwin. September 6, 1839. AMA Archives FI 4601.
Townsend to Leavitt/Jocelyn. September 6, 1839. AMA Archives FI 4602.
Hon. John Pickering to L. Tappan. September 10, 1839. AMA Archives FI 4606.
D. Burguess to Rev. Joshua Leavitt. September 10, 1839. AMA Archives FI 4607.
Pickering to Friend. September 12, 1839. AMA Archives FI 4611.
Parish to Leavitt. September 12, 1839. AMA Archives FI 4613.
A friend of the Blacks to Tappan. September 12, 1839. AMA Archives FI 4612.
Harris to Leavitt. September 13, 1839. AMA Archives FI 4616.
Knight to Col. Rooms. September 14, 1839. AMA Archives FI 4620.
Warrimer to Tappan. September 14, 1839. AMA Archives FI 4622.
Parish to Tappan. September 15, 1839. AMA Archives FI 4624.
Coffin to Tappan. September 16, 1839. AMA Archives FI 4626.
Pickering to Gibbs. September 16, 1839. AMA Archives FI 4625.
Parish to Tappan. September 20, 1839. AMA Archives FI 4634.
Loring to Tappan September 20, 1839. AMA Archives FI 4631.
Townsend to Leavitt. October 3, 1839. AMA Archives FI 4659.
Townsend to Tappan. October 5, 1839. AMA Archives FI 4660.
Memorandum from Prof. Gibbs. September 28, 1841. AMA FI 4592B.
Pickering to Gibbs AMA September 16, 1839. Archives FI 4625.
Jocelyn to Tappan. September 16, 1839. AMA Archives FI 4628.
Townsend to Leavitt AMA Archives FI 4638 A. Envelope.
Day to Tappan. October 19, 1839. AMA Archives FI 4648.
Day to Tappan. October 23, 1839. AMA Archives FI 4650.
Parish to Tappan. November 5, 1839. AMA Archives FI 4671.
Dougall to Leavitt. April 26, 1841. AMA Archives FI 4983.

Biblioteca José Martí, La Habana, Cuba

Diario de La Habana, martes, 1ero de enero de 1839.
La Aurora: boletín oficial y diario de gobierno de Matanzas, 17, 18 y 22 de noviembre de 1839.
Pichardo, Esteban. *Diccionario Provincial de Voces Cubanas.* Matanzas, Cuba: Imprenta de la Real Marina, 1836.

El Archivo Nacional de La Habana, Cuba

Fondo Gobierno Superior Civil. Legajo 1272, no. 49909.
Fondo Asuntos Políticos. Legajo 41, no. 16.

Collection of the Massachusetts Historical Society

Adams Family Papers: An Electronic Archive

John Quincy Adams Digital Diary. http://www.masshist.org/digitaladams
June 11, 1839, v. 41.
September 23, 1839, v. 42.
October 27, 1840, v. 41.
April 4, 1840, v. 42.
December 9, 1840, v. 41.
December 10, 1840, v. 41.
December 11, 1840, v. 41.
December 12, 1840, v. 41.
December 21, 1840, v. 41.
December 31, 1840, v. 41.
January 8, 1841, v. 41.
January 14, 1841, v. 41.
March 14, 1841, v. 41.
April 8, 1841, v. 41.
September 5, 1841, v. 41.
October 5, 1841, v. 41.
Reel 517, Record 31180.

Sedgwick Family Papers

"In Memory of Theodore Sedgwick." MS No. 851: Box 15; Folder 16; and Folder 19.

The Liberator, 1839 to 1841

National Archives in Boston, Waltham, MA, USA.

The *Amistad* Case Court Files (including www.fold3.com for prints).

U.S v. Cinque and the Africans (September 1839 Term).
U.S. v. Fagnannah, et al. (September 1839 Term).
In the Matter of the Habeus Corpus of the Three African Girls (September 1839 Term).
Pedro Montes and José Ruiz v. Merchandise, etc. (January 1840).
United States. District Court (Connecticut). Thomas R. Gedney v. Schooner *Amistad*. [September 1839 Term]. Record Group 021.
Thomas A. Gedney, et al. v Schooner *Amistad*, etc. (September 1840 Term).
Thomas A. Gedney, et al. v Schooner *Amistad*, etc. (April 1841 Term).
Thomas A. Gedney, et al. v Schooner *Amistad*, etc. (April 1845 Term).

New Haven Museum, Whitney Library

The Daily Herald. September 16, 1839.
The Daily Herald. November 21, 1839.
The Daily Herald. January 9, 1840.
The Daily Herald. January 11, 1840.
The Daily Herald. January 8, 1840.

The Schomburg Center for Research in Black Culture, Archives and Rare Books Division, The New York Public Library

Noticioso de Ambos Mundos. 31 de agosto de 1839.
Noticioso de Ambos Mundos. 7 de septiembre de 1839.
Noticioso de Ambos Mundos. 28 de septiembre de 1839.
Noticioso de Ambos Mundos. 23 de noviembre de 1839.
Noticioso de Ambos Mundos. 4 de abril de 1840.
The Colored American. September 14, 1839.
The Colored American. September 28, 1839.
The Emancipator. September 5, 1839.
The Emancipator. September 12, 1839.
The Emancipator. September 22, 1839.
The Emancipator. September 26, 1839.
The Emancipator. October 10, 1839.
The Emancipator. November 23, 1839.
The Emancipator. January 9, 1839.
The Emancipator. January 16, 1839.

Yale University

Yale University Library. Manuscript and Archives

Baldwin Family Papers (MS 55).
Staples to Baldwin. September 4, 1839.
Loring to Baldwin. September 19, 1839.
Tappan to Baldwin. October 4, 1839.
Tappan to Baldwin. October 12, 1839.
Tappan to Baldwin. November 11, 1839.
Baldwin to Sherman. February 16, 1858.
"Deposition" by James Covey. October 4, 1839.
"Letter by Elizabeth Baldwin." January 8, 1841.

Yale Law School. Rare Book Room, Lillian Goldman Law Library

Baldwin, Simeon E. "The Captives of the *Amistad*: A Paper Read Before the New Haven Colony Historical Society." May 17, 1886.

"Documents Relating to the Africans Taken in the *Amistad*." (1840). *American Trials*. 16. http://digitalcommons.law.yale.edu/amtrials/16.

U.S. Circuit Court (Connecticut). Thomas R. Gedney, Smith Thompson, and Andrew T. Judson. *The African Captives: Trial of the Prisoners of the Amistad on the Writ of Habeas Corpus, Before the Circuit Court of the United States, for the District of Connecticut, at Hartford*. New York, 1839.

U.S. Congress. House of Representatives. *Amistad* Case. 26th Congress, 1st Session, 1840. H. Doc. 185.

U.S. Department of State. *Africans Taken in the Amistad: Congressional Document: Containing, the Correspondence, &c.: In Relation to the Captured Africans*. [Reprint of the House of Representatives Document no. 185, 26th Congress, 1st sess]. New York: Anti-Slavery Depository, 1840.

The United States, Appellants vs. The Libellant and Claimants of the Schooner Amistad. "No. 42" (March 1841?).

Beinecke Rare Book and Manuscripts Library, Yale University

Townsend, William H. (ca. 1839–1840). "Margu." Sketches of the *Amistad* Captives. General Collection. Beinecke Rare Book and Manuscript Library. Yale University.

Townsend, William H. (ca. 1839–1840). "Little Kale." Sketches of the *Amistad* Captives. General Collection. Beinecke Rare Book and Manuscript Library. Yale University.

Newspapers

The American and Foreign Anti-Slavery Reporter. December 1, 1840.
The American and Foreign Anti-Slavery Reporter. October 1, 1840.
The American and Foreign Anti-Slavery Reporter. August 24, 1841.
The Liberator. December 18, 1840.
New York Herald, published as Morning Herald. September 29, 1839.
New York Herald, published as Morning Herald. November 22, 1839.
New York Herald, published as Morning Herald. February 22, 1840.
New York Sun. August 31, 1839.
Zion's Watchman. November 30, 1839.

Paintings (used with permission)

Jocelyn, Nathaniel. Portrait of "Cinque." New Haven Museum. New Haven, CT, USA.

Woodruff, Hale Aspacio. "The Court Scene." From the "The *Amistad* Murals." "From the Hale Woodruff Collections at Talladega College, 627 W. Battle Street, Talladega, Alabama 35160.

Personal Communication/Interviews

Captain Bill Pickney, RIP. January 8, 2017.
Erika Melek. April 20, 2023.
Howard Jones, RIP. Circa, March 2012.
Miguel A. de la Carrera. April 21, 2024.
Samuel Pieh, Zoom interview. February 8, 2023.
William G. Thomas, III. August 24, 2023.

Index

www.ingramcontent.com/pod-product-compliance
Ingram Content Group UK Ltd.
Pitfield, Milton Keynes, MK11 3LW, UK
UKHW020206290926
15470UKWH00001B/23